Aṅguttara Nikāya Anthology

An anthology of discourses
from
the Aṅguttara Nikāya

Selected and translated from the Pāli
by
Nyanaponika Thera
and
Bhikkhu Bodhi

Buddhist Publication Society
Kandy • Sri Lanka

Buddhist Publication Society
P.O. Box 61
54 Sangharaja Mawatha
Kandy, Sri Lanka
http://www.bps.lk

Earlier published as Wheel Publications 155–158; 208–211; 238–240

For this edition, the revised translations by Venerable Bodhi as given in the *Numerical Discourses of the Buddha* have been used with his kind permission.

ISBN-13 : 978-955-24-0297-5

National Library of Sri Lanka — Cataloguing-in-Publication data:

Thripitaka. Sutra pitaka. Aṅguttara nikāya
Aṅguttara Nikāya Anthology : An anthology of discourses from the Aṅguttara nikāya / Nyanaponika himi and Bhikkhu Bodhi - Kandy : Buddhist Publication Society, 2007. - p.260; 22cm

ISBN : 978-955-24-0297-5 Price :
i. 294.3832 DDC 22 ii. Title
iii. Nyanaponika Himi iv. Bodhi, Bhikkhu

Typeset at BPS

Printed in Sri Lanka by
Creative Printers & Designers,
Bahirawakanda, Kandy.

Key to Abbreviations

A-a	Aṅguttara Aṭṭhakathā
A-ṭ	Aṅguttara-ṭīkā
AN	Aṅguttara Nikāya
Be	Burmese script edition (of AN)
BPS	Buddhist Publication Society (Kandy, Sri Lanka)
Comy	Commentary
Dhp	Dhammapada (by verse)
DN	Dīgha Nikāya (by sutta)
Ee	European (PTS) edition (of AN)
It	Itivuttaka (by sutta)
MN	Majjhima Nikāya (by sutta)
Paṭis	Paṭisambhidāmagga (by volume, page)
PTS	Pāli Text Society (Oxford, UK)
Pug	Puggalapaññatti (by page)
Skt	Sanskrit
Sn	Suttanipāta (by verse)
SN	Saṃyutta Nikāya (by chapter and sutta)
Th	Theragāthā (by verse)
Ud	Udāna (by chapter and sutta)
Vibh	Vibhaṅga (by page)
Vin	Vinaya (by volume, page)
Vism	*Visuddhimagga*

References to volume and page are to PTS editions. References to Vism are to chapter and paragraph in the English translation, *The Path of Purification,* by Ñāṇamoli Bhikkhu, BPS, 1999. Page references to Vibh are followed by the paragraph number in the PTS English translation, *The Book of Analysis,* by Ashin Thittila, 1969.

Table of Contents

Namo tassa Bhagavato Arahato Sammā-sambuddhassa

Homage to the Blessed One, the Arahant, the Fully Enlightened One

Aṅguttara Nikāya

I. The Chapter of the Ones

1. The Mind-I

No other thing do I know, O monks, that is so intractable as an undeveloped mind.[1] An undeveloped mind is truly intractable.

No other thing do I know, O monks, that is so tractable as a developed mind. A developed mind is truly tractable.

No other thing do I know, O monks, that brings so much suffering as an undeveloped and uncultivated mind. An undeveloped and uncultivated mind truly brings suffering.

No other thing do I know, O monks, that brings so much happiness as a developed and cultivated mind. A developed and cultivated mind truly brings happiness.

(1:3.1–10; selected)

No other thing do I know, O monks, that brings so much harm as a mind that is untamed, unguarded, unprotected and uncontrolled. Such a mind truly brings much harm.

No other thing do I know, O monks, that brings so much benefit as a mind that is tamed, guarded, protected and controlled. Such a mind truly brings great benefit.

(1:4.1–10; selected)

2. The Mind-II

No other thing do I know, O monks, that changes so quickly as the mind. It is not easy to give a simile for how quickly the mind changes.[2]

(1:5.8)

This mind, O monks, is luminous, but it is defiled by adventitious defilements.[3] The uninstructed worldling does not understand this as it really is; therefore for him there is no mental development.

This mind, O monks, is luminous, and it is freed from adventitious defilements. The instructed noble disciple understands this as it really is; therefore for him there is mental development.

(1:6.1–2)

3. Loving-kindness

Monks, if for just the time of a finger-snap a monk produces a thought of loving-kindness, develops it, gives attention to it, such a one is rightly called a monk. Not in vain does he meditate. He acts in accordance with the Master's teaching, he follows his advice, and eats deservingly the country's alms-food.[4] How much more so if he cultivates it!

(1:6.3–5)

4. Mind Is the Forerunner

Monks, whatsoever states are unwholesome, partake of the unwholesome, pertain to the unwholesome—all these have the mind as their forerunner.[5] Mind arises as the first of them, followed by the unwholesome states.

Monks, whatsoever states are wholesome, partake of the wholesome, pertain to the wholesome—all these have mind as their forerunner. Mind arises as the first of them, followed by the wholesome states.

No other thing do I know, O monks, which is so responsible for causing unarisen unwholesome states to arise and arisen wholesome states to wane as negligence.[6] In one who is negligent, unarisen unwholesome states will arise and arisen wholesome states will wane.

No other thing do I know, O monks, which is so responsible for causing unarisen wholesome states to arise and arisen unwholesome states to wane as diligence. In one who is diligent, wholesome states not yet arisen will arise and unwholesome states that have arisen will wane.

(1:6.6–9)

5. THE HIGHEST GAIN

Insignificant, O monks, is the loss of relatives, wealth and fame; the loss of wisdom is the greatest loss.

Insignificant, O monks, is the increase of relatives, wealth and fame; the increase of wisdom is the highest gain.

Therefore, O monks, you should train yourselves thus: "We will grow in the increase of wisdom." Thus, O monks, should you train yourselves.

(1:8.6–10)

6. ONE PERSON

Monks, there is one person whose arising in the world is for the welfare of the multitude, for the happiness of the multitude, who comes out of compassion for the world, for the good, welfare and happiness of devas and humans. Who is that one person? It is the Tathāgata, the Arahant, the Fully Enlightened One. This is that one person.[7]

Monks, there is one person arising in the world who is unique, without a peer, without counterpart, incomparable, unequalled, matchless, unrivalled, the best of humans. Who is that one person? It is the Tathāgata, the Arahant, the Fully Enlightened One. This is that one person.

Monks, the manifestation of one person is the manifestation of great vision, of great light, of great radiance; it is the manifestation of the six things unsurpassed; the realization of the four analytical knowledges; the penetration of the various elements, of the diversity of elements; it is the realization of the fruit of knowledge and liberation; the realization of the fruits of stream-entry, once-returning, non-returning, and arahantship.[8] Who is that one person? It is the Tathāgata, the Arahant, the Fully Enlightened One. This is that one person.

(1:13.1, 5, 6)

7. IMPOSSIBLE

It is impossible, O monks, and it cannot be that a person possessed of right view should regard any formation as permanent.[9] But it is possible for an uninstructed worldling to regard a formation as permanent.

It is impossible, O monks, and it cannot be that a person possessed of right view should regard any formation as a source of happiness. But it is possible for an uninstructed worldling to regard a formation as a source of happiness.

It is impossible, O monks, and it cannot be that a person possessed of right view should regard anything as a self.[10] But it is possible for an uninstructed worldling to regard something as a self.

(1:15.1–3)

8. MINDFULNESS DIRECTED TO THE BODY

I.

Even as one who encompasses with his mind the mighty ocean includes thereby all the rivulets that run into the ocean; just so, O monks, whoever develops and cultivates mindfulness directed to the body includes thereby all the wholesome states that partake of supreme knowledge.[11]

One thing, O monks, if developed and cultivated, leads to a strong sense of urgency; to great benefit; to great security from bondage; to mindfulness and clear comprehension; to the attainment of vision and knowledge; to a pleasant dwelling in this very life; to the realization of the fruit of knowledge and liberation. What is that one thing? It is mindfulness directed to the body....

If one thing, O monks, is developed and cultivated, the body is calmed, the mind is calmed, discursive thoughts are quietened, and all wholesome states that partake of supreme knowledge reach fullness of development. What is that one thing? It is mindfulness directed to the body....

If one thing, O monks, is developed and cultivated, ignorance is abandoned, supreme knowledge arises, delusion of self is given up, the underlying tendencies are eliminated, and the fetters are discarded.[12] What is that one thing? It is mindfulness directed to the body.

II.

They do not partake of the Deathless who do not partake of mindfulness directed to the body. They partake of the Deathless who partake of mindfulness directed to the body.

The Deathless is lost to those who have lost mindfulness directed to the body. Not lost is the Deathless to those who have not lost mindfulness directed to the body.

They will fail to reach the Deathless who fail in mindfulness directed to the body. They gain the Deathless who gain mindfulness directed to the body.

They neglect the quest for the Deathless who neglect mindfulness directed to the body. They do not neglect the quest for the Deathless who do not neglect mindfulness directed to the body.

They forget the Deathless who forget mindfulness directed to the body. They do not forget the Deathless who do not forget mindfulness directed to the body.

They are undeveloped in the quest for the Deathless who are undeveloped in mindfulness directed to the body. They are developed in the quest for the Deathless who are developed in mindfulness directed to the body.

They have not comprehended the Deathless who have not comprehended mindfulness directed to the body. They have comprehended the Deathless who have comprehended mindfulness directed to the body.

They have not realized the Deathless who have not realized mindfulness directed to the body. They have realized the Deathless who have realized mindfulness directed to the body.

(1:21; selected)

II. The Chapter of the Twos

9. Unremitting Effort

Two things, O monks, I came to know well: not to be content with good states of mind so far achieved, and to be unremitting in the struggle for the goal.[1] Unremittingly, indeed, did I struggle, and I resolved: "Let only my skin, sinews and bones remain; let the flesh and blood in my body dry up; yet there shall be no ceasing of energy till I have attained whatever can be won by manly strength, manly energy, manly effort!"

Through diligence have I won enlightenment, through diligence have I won the unsurpassed security from bondage.

If you too, O monks, will struggle unremittingly and resolve: "Let only my skin, sinews and bones remain; let the flesh and blood in my body dry up; yet there shall be no ceasing of energy till I have attained whatever can be won by manly strength, manly energy, manly effort!"—then you too will soon realize through your own direct knowledge, in this very life, that unsurpassed goal of the holy life for which sons of good family rightly go forth from home into homelessness, and entering into it you will dwell in it.

Therefore, O monks, you should train yourselves thus: "Unremittingly shall I struggle and resolve: 'Let only my skin, sinews and bones remain; let the flesh and blood in my body dry up; yet there shall be no ceasing of energy till I have attained whatever can be won by manly strength, manly energy, manly effort!'" Thus should you train yourselves.

(2:1.5)

10. Abandon Evil

Abandon evil, O monks! One can abandon evil, monks. If it were impossible to abandon evil, I would not ask you to do so. But as it can be done, therefore I say, "Abandon evil!"

If this abandoning of evil would bring harm and suffering, I would not ask you to abandon it. But as the abandoning of evil brings well-being and happiness, therefore I say, "Abandon evil!"

Cultivate the good, O monks! One can cultivate the good, monks. If it were impossible to cultivate the good, I would not ask you to do so. But as it can be done, therefore I say, "Cultivate the good!"

If this cultivation of the good would bring harm and suffering, I would not ask you to cultivate it. But as the cultivation of the good brings well-being and happiness, therefore I say, "Cultivate the good!"[2]

(2:2.9)

11. TRANQUILLITY AND INSIGHT

Two things, O monks, partake of supreme knowledge.[3] What two? Tranquillity and insight.[4]

If tranquillity is developed, what benefit does it bring? The mind becomes developed. And what is the benefit of a developed mind? All lust is abandoned.[5]

If insight is developed, what benefit does it bring? Wisdom becomes developed. And what is the benefit of developed wisdom? All ignorance is abandoned.[6]

A mind defiled by lust is not freed; and wisdom defiled by ignorance cannot develop. Thus, monks, through the fading away of lust there is liberation of mind; and through the fading away of ignorance there is liberation by wisdom.[7]

(2:2.10)

12. REPAYING ONE'S PARENTS

I declare, O monks, that there are two persons one can never repay. What two? One's mother and father. Even if one should carry about one's mother on one shoulder and one's father on the other, and while doing so should live a hundred years, reach the age of a hundred years; and if one should attend to them by anointing them with salves, by massaging, bathing and rubbing their limbs, and they should even void their excrements there—even by that would one not do enough for one's parents, one would not repay them. Even if one were to establish one's parents as the supreme lords and rulers over this earth so rich in the seven treasures, one would not do enough for them, one would not repay them. What is the reason for this? Parents do much for their children: they bring them up, feed them, and guide them through this world.

But, O monks, one who encourages his unbelieving parents, settles and establishes them in faith; who encourages his immoral parents, settles and establishes them in virtue; who encourages his stingy parents, settles and establishes them in generosity; who encourages his ignorant parents, settles and establishes them in wisdom—such a one, O monks, does enough for his parents: he repays them and more than repays them for what they have done.

(2:4.2)

13. Two Kinds of Happiness

There are two kinds of happiness, O monks. The happiness of the home life and the happiness of monkhood. But the happiness of monkhood is the higher of the two.

The happiness of the senses and the happiness of renunciation. But the happiness of renunciation is the higher of the two.

Tainted happiness and taintless happiness.[8] But taintless happiness is the higher of the two.

Carnal and non-carnal happiness—the non-carnal is the higher. Noble and ignoble happiness—the noble is the higher. Bodily and mental happiness—the mental is the higher.

(2:7; selected)

III. The Chapter of the Threes

14. The Fool and the Wise Person

His action marks the fool, his action marks the wise person, O monks. Wisdom shines forth in behaviour.

By three things the fool can be known: by bad conduct of body, speech, and mind.

By three things the wise person can be known: by good conduct of body, speech, and mind.

(3:2)

15. Dhamma, the Co-Regent

The Blessed One said: "Monks, even a world ruler, a just and righteous king, does not govern his realm without a co-regent."[1]

When he had spoken, a certain monk addressed the Blessed One thus: "But who, Lord, is the co-regent of the world ruler, the just and righteous king?"

"It is the Dhamma, the law of righteousness, O monk," replied the Blessed One.[2]

"In this case, the world ruler, the just and righteous king, relying on the law of righteousness (Dhamma), honouring it, regarding it highly and respecting it, with the law of righteousness as his standard, banner and sovereign, provides lawful protection, shelter and safety for his own dependants. He provides lawful protection, shelter, and safety for the warrior-nobles attending on him; for his army, for the brahmins and householders, for the inhabitants of town and countryside, for ascetics and brahmins, for the beasts and birds.

"A world ruler, a just and righteous king, who thus provides lawful protection, shelter, and safety for all, is the one who rules by righteousness only. And that rule cannot be overthrown by any hostile creature in human form.

"Even so, O monk, the Tathāgata, the Arahant, the Fully Enlightened One, the just and righteous King of the Dhamma, relying on the Dhamma, honouring the Dhamma, regarding it highly and respecting it, with the Dhamma as his standard, banner and sovereign, provides lawful protection, shelter and safety in regard to action by body, speech, and mind. (He teaches thus): 'Such bodily action should be undertaken and such should not be undertaken. Such verbal action should be undertaken and such should not be undertaken. Such mental action should be undertaken and such should not be undertaken.'

"The Tathāgata, the Arahant, the Fully Enlightened One, the just and righteous King of the Dhamma, who thus provides lawful protection, shelter and safety in regard to action by body, speech, and mind, is the one who turns the incomparable Wheel of the Dhamma in accordance with the Dhamma only. And that Wheel of the Dhamma cannot be turned back by any ascetic or brahmin, by any deva or Māra or Brahmā or by anyone in the world."[3]

(3:14)

16. CAUSE FOR SHAME

"If, monks, wandering ascetics of other beliefs should ask you: 'Is it, friend, for the sake of rebirth in a heavenly world that you live the holy life under the ascetic Gotama?'—would you not feel repelled, ashamed, and humiliated?"

"Certainly, Lord."

"So then, monks, you say you feel hurt, ashamed and repelled by the idea of divine longevity, divine beauty, divine bliss, divine glory, and divine sovereignty. How much more then should you feel repelled, ashamed and humiliated by bad conduct of body, speech, and mind!"

(3:18)

17. Three Types of Patients

There are, O monks, three types of patients found in the world. What three?

There is one patient: whether or not he obtains proper nourishment, proper medicine, and adequate nursing, he will not recover from his illness.

There is another patient: whether or not he obtains all these things, he will recover from his illness.

There is still another patient who will recover from his illness only if he receives proper nourishment, proper medicine, and adequate nursing, but not if he lacks these. For him, O monks, a special diet, curative medicine, and good nursing are prescribed. But apart from him, also the other two types of patients should be attended to.[4]

These three types of patients are found in the world.

Similarly, monks, there are three other types of persons comparable to those three patients.

There is one type of person: whether or not he has the chance of seeing the Tathāgata and of listening to the Dhamma and Discipline proclaimed by him, he will not enter the path of assurance and will not reach perfection in wholesome states.[5]

There is another person: whether or not he has the chance of seeing the Tathāgata and of listening to the Dhamma and Discipline proclaimed by him, he will in any case enter upon the path of assurance and will reach perfection in wholesome states.

Again, there is one person who will enter upon the path of assurance and will reach perfection in wholesome states only if he has the chance of seeing the Tathāgata and of listening to the Dhamma and Discipline proclaimed by him, but not if he lacks this opportunity. It is for this person, O monks, that instruction in the Dhamma has been prescribed. But apart from him, the two others should also be instructed in the Dhamma.[6]

These are the three types of persons found in the world who are comparable to the three patients.

(3:22)

18. THREE MENTALITIES

There are, O monks, three types of persons found in the world. What three? There is one with a mind like an open sore; one with a mind like lightning; one with a mind like a diamond.

Of what nature, monks, is the person with a mind like an open sore? He is one who is irascible and irritable. If he is criticized even slightly he loses his temper and becomes angry and upset; he is stubborn and displays anger, hatred, and resentment. Just as, for instance, a festering sore, if struck by a stick or a sherd, will discharge matter all the more, even so is the person who is irascible ... and displays anger, hatred and resentment. Such a person is said to have a mind like an open sore.

And of what nature is the person with a mind like lightning? He is one who understands as it really is, "This is suffering"; he understands as it really is, "This is the origin of suffering"; he understands as it really is, "This is the cessation of suffering"; he understands as it really is, "This is the path leading to the cessation of suffering." Just as a man with good sight can see objects in the darkness of night by a flash of lightning, even so a person understands these Four Noble Truths as they really are. Such a person is said to have a mind like lightning.

And of what nature is a person with a mind like a diamond? He is one who, by the destruction of the taints, in this very life enters and dwells in the taintless liberation of mind, liberation by wisdom, having realized it for himself by direct knowledge. Just as there is nothing that a diamond cannot cut, be it gem or rock, even so a certain person, by the destruction of the taints, in this very life enters and dwells in the taintless liberation of mind, liberation by wisdom, having realized it for himself by direct knowledge. Such a person is said to have a mind like a diamond.[7]

These three types of persons are found in the world.

(3:25)

19. FREE OF "I"-MAKING

On one occasion the Venerable Sāriputta approached the Blessed One, paid homage to him and sat down to one side.[8] The Blessed One then said to him:

"Sāriputta, whether I teach the Dhamma in brief, or whether I teach it in detail, or whether I teach it both in brief and in detail, those who understand are hard to find."

"Now, O Blessed One, is the time for it! Now, Sublime One, is the time for the Blessed One to teach the Dhamma in brief, to teach it in detail, and to teach it both in brief and in detail. There will be those who will understand the Dhamma."

"Well then, Sāriputta, thus should one train oneself: 'We shall not entertain any I-making, mine-making or underlying tendency to conceit either in regard to this conscious body or in regard to all external objects;[9] and we shall enter and dwell in the liberation of mind, liberation by wisdom, so that we are no longer subject to I-making, mine-making and the underlying tendency to conceit.' That is how one should train oneself.

"When, Sāriputta, a monk has no more I-making, mine-making and underlying tendency to conceit either in regard to this conscious body or in regard to external objects, and when he thus enters and dwells in the liberation of mind, liberation by wisdom, he is then called a monk who has cut off craving and removed the fetters, one who, by fully breaking through conceit, has made an end of suffering.

"About this, Sāriputta, I have spoken in 'The Questions of Udaya' in 'The Way to the Far Shore':[10]

"The abandoning of sensual desires
Along with the bitter touch of grief;
The dispelling of sloth, mental dullness,
The warding off of anxious worry;
Purified mindfulness and equipoise
Preceded by thinking on the Dhamma:
This, I declare, is release by knowledge,
The breaking apart of ignorance."[11]

(3:32)

20. Causes of Action

There are, O monks, three causes for the origination of action. What three? Greed, hatred, and delusion.[12]

An action done in greed, born of greed, caused by greed, arisen from greed, will ripen wherever the individual is reborn; and wherever the action ripens, there the individual experiences the fruit of that action, be it in this life, or in the next life, or in subsequent future lives.[13]

An action done in hatred, born of hatred, caused by hatred, arisen from hatred, will ripen wherever the individual is reborn; and wherever the action ripens, there the individual experiences the fruit of that action, be it in this life, or in the next life, or in subsequent future lives.

An action done in delusion, born of delusion, caused by delusion, arisen from delusion, will ripen wherever the individual is reborn; and wherever the action ripens, there the individual experiences the fruit of that action, be it in this life, or in the next life, or in subsequent future lives.

It is, monks, as with seeds that are undamaged, not rotten, unspoiled by wind and sun, capable of sprouting and well embedded in a good field, sown in well-prepared soil: if there is plenty of rain, these seeds will grow, shoot up, and develop abundantly.

Similarly, monks, whatever action is done out of greed, hatred or delusion ... will ripen wherever the individual is reborn; and wherever the action ripens, there the individual experiences the fruit, be it in this life, or in the next life, or in subsequent future lives.

These, monks, are three causes for the origination of action.

There are, O monks, three other causes for the origination of action. What three? Non-greed, non-hatred, and non-delusion.

If an action is done in non-greed, born of non-greed, caused by non-greed, arisen from non-greed. ... If an action is done in non-hatred. ... If an action is done in non-delusion, born of non-delusion, caused by non-delusion, arisen from non-delusion, once greed, hatred, and delusion have vanished that action is thus abandoned, cut off at the root, made barren like a palm-tree stump, obliterated so that it is no more subject to arise in the future.[14]

It is, monks, as with seeds that are undamaged, not rotten, unspoiled by wind and sun, capable of sprouting and well embedded: if a man were to burn them in fire and reduce them to ashes, then winnow the ashes in a strong wind or let them be carried away by a swiftly flowing stream, then those seeds would have been radically destroyed, fully eliminated, made unable to sprout, and would not be liable to arise in the future.[15]

Similarly it is, monks, with actions done in non-greed, non-hatred, and non-delusion. Once greed, hatred, and delusion have vanished, these actions are thus abandoned, cut off at the root, made barren like palm-tree stumps, obliterated so that they are no more subject to arise in the future.

These, monks, are the other three causes for the origination of action.

(3:33)

21. Good Sleep

Thus have I heard. On one occasion when the Blessed One was dwelling in the Āḷavi country, he rested on a heap of leaves spread on a cattle track in a siṃsapa forest.

At that time Hatthaka of Āḷavi[16] passed that way while taking a walk and there he saw the Blessed One seated on the heap of leaves. Having approached the Blessed One and paid homage to him, Hatthaka sat down to one side and said to the Blessed One:

"Venerable sir, has the Blessed One slept well?"

"Yes, prince, I slept well. Among those in the world who always sleep well, I am one."

"But, Lord, the winter nights are cold and this is a week of frost. Hard is the ground trampled by the hoofs of cattle, thin is the spread of leaves, sparse are the leaves on the trees, thin are the tawny monk's robes and cold blows the wind. Yet the Blessed One says that he has slept well and that he is one of those in the world who always sleep well."

"Now, prince, I shall put a question to you about this and you may reply as you think fit. What do you think of this, prince? Suppose there is a householder or a householder's son living in a house with a gabled roof, plastered inside and out, protected against the wind, with fastened door bolts and windows closed. And there is a couch in the house, covered with a long-fleeced, black woollen rug, with a bedspread of white wool, a coverlet decorated with flowers, spread over with an exquisite antelope skin, having a canopy overhead, and scarlet cushions at both ends. Also a lamp is burning there and his four wives attend on him pleasantly. What do you think, prince: would that person sleep well or not, or what is your opinion about this?"

"He will surely sleep well, Lord. He will be one of those in the world who sleep well."

"What do you think, prince? Might there not arise in that householder or householder's son vexations of body or mind caused by lust, hatred, and delusion, which torment him so that he would sleep badly?"

"That may well be so, Lord."

"Now, prince, the lust, hatred, and delusion by which that householder is tormented, and which cause him to sleep badly, have been abandoned by the Tathāgata, cut off at the root, made barren like palm-tree stumps, obliterated so that they are no more subject to arise in the future. Therefore, prince, I have slept well."

The brahmin who is quenched within
Always sleeps happily;
He does not cling to sensual desires,
Free from props, one cool in mind.
Having cut all straps of attachment,
Removed care deep within the heart,
The Peaceful One sleeps happily,
Attained to perfect peace of mind.

(3:34)

22. The Divine Messengers

There are three divine messengers,[17] O monks. What three?

There is a person of bad conduct in body, speech, and mind. Being of such bad conduct, on the dissolution of the body, after death, he is reborn in the plane of misery, in a bad destination, in a lower world, in hell. There the warders of hell seize him by both arms and take him before Yama, the Lord of Death, saying: "This man, your majesty, had no respect for father and mother, nor for ascetics and brahmins, nor did he honour the elders of the family. May your majesty inflict due punishment on him!"

Then, monks, King Yama questions that man, examines and addresses him concerning the first divine messenger: "Didn't you ever see, my good man, the first divine messenger appearing among humankind?"

And he replies: "No, Lord, I did not see him."

Then King Yama says to him: "But, my good man, didn't you ever see a woman or a man, aged eighty, ninety or a hundred years, frail, bent like a roof bracket, crooked, leaning on a stick, shakily going along, ailing, youth and vigour gone, with broken teeth, with grey and scanty hair or none, wrinkled, with blotched limbs?"

And the man replies: "Yes, Lord, I have seen this."

Then King Yama says to him: "My good man, didn't it ever occur to you, an intelligent and mature person, 'I too am subject to old age and cannot escape it. Let me now do noble deeds by body, speech, and mind'?"

"No, Lord, I could not do it. I was negligent."

Then King Yama says: "Through negligence, my good man, you have failed to do noble deeds by body, speech, and mind. Well, you will be treated as befits your negligence. That evil action of yours was not done by mother or father, brothers, sisters, friends or companions, nor by relatives, devas, ascetics or brahmins. But you alone have done that evil deed, and you will have to experience the fruit."

When, monks, King Yama has questioned, examined and addressed him thus concerning the first divine messenger, he again questions, examines and addresses the man about the second one, saying: "Didn't you ever see, my good man, the second divine messenger appearing among humankind?"

"No, Lord, I did not see him."

"But, my good man, didn't you ever see a woman or a man who was sick and in pain, seriously ill, lying in his own filth, having to be lifted up by some and put to bed by others?"

"Yes, Lord, I have seen this."

"My good man, didn't it ever occur to you, an intelligent and mature person, 'I too am subject to illness and cannot escape it. Let me now do noble deeds by body, speech, and mind'?"

"No, Lord, I could not do it. I was negligent."

"Through negligence, my good man, you have failed to do noble deeds by body, speech, and mind. Well, you will be treated as befits your negligence. That evil action of yours was not done by mother or father, brothers, sisters, friends or companions, nor by relatives, devas, ascetics or brahmins. But you alone have done that evil deed, and you will have to experience the fruit."

When, monks, King Yama has questioned, examined and addressed him thus concerning the second divine messenger, he again questions, examines and addresses the man about the third one, saying: "Didn't you ever see, my good man, the third divine messenger appearing among humankind?"

"No, Lord, I did not see him."

"But, my good man, didn't you ever see a woman or a man one, two or three days dead, the corpse swollen, discoloured and festering?"

"Yes, Lord, I have seen this."

"Then, my good man, didn't it ever occur to you, an intelligent and mature person, 'I too am subject to death and cannot escape it. Let me now do noble deeds by body, speech, and mind'?"

"No, Lord, I could not do it. I was negligent."

"Through negligence, my good man, you have failed to do

noble deeds by body, speech, and mind. Well, you will be treated as befits your negligence. That evil action of yours was not done by mother or father, brothers, sisters, friends, or companions, nor by relatives, devas, ascetics, or brahmins. But you alone have done that evil deed, and you will have to experience the fruit."

Then, having questioned, examined, and addressed the man concerning the third divine messenger, King Yama becomes silent.

Thereupon the warders of hell inflict many kinds of torment on him on account of which he suffers grievous, severe, sharp, and bitter pain. Yet he does not die until that evil deed of his has been worked out.[18]

(3:35)

23. THREEFOLD PRIDE

I was delicately brought up, O monks; highly delicate, exceedingly delicate was my upbringing. At my father's house lotus ponds were made: in one of them blue lotuses bloomed, in another white lotuses, and in a third red lotuses, just for my enjoyment. I used only sandal unguent from Benares and my head dress, my jacket, my undergarment, and my tunic were made of Benares muslin. By day and by night a white canopy was held over me, lest cold and heat, dust, chaff or dew should trouble me. I had three palaces: one for the summer, one for the winter and one for the rainy season. In the palace for the rainy season, during the four months of the rains, I was waited upon by female musicians only, and I did not come down from the palace during these months. While in other people's homes servants and slaves receive a meal of broken rice together with sour gruel, in my father's house they were given choice rice and meat.

Amidst such splendour and an entirely carefree life, O monks, this thought came to me:[19] "An uninstructed worldling, though sure to become old himself and unable to escape ageing, feels repelled, humiliated and disgusted when seeing an old and decrepit person, being forgetful of his own situation. Now I too am sure to become old and cannot escape ageing. If, when seeing an old and decrepit person, I were to feel repelled, humiliated or disgusted, that would not be proper for one like myself." When I reflected thus, monks, all my pride in youthfulness vanished.

Again I reflected: "An uninstructed worldling, though sure to become ill himself and unable to escape illness, feels repelled, humiliated or disgusted when seeing a sick person, being forgetful of his own situation. Now I too am sure to become ill and cannot escape illness. If, when seeing a sick person, I were to feel repelled, humiliated or disgusted, that would not be proper for one like myself."

When I thus reflected, monks, all my pride in health vanished.

Again I reflected: "An uninstructed worldling is sure to die himself and cannot escape death; yet when seeing a dead person, he feels repelled, humiliated or disgusted, being forgetful of his own situation. Now I too am sure to die and cannot escape death. If, when seeing a dead person, I were to feel repelled, humiliated or disgusted, that would not be proper for one like myself." When I thus reflected, monks, all my pride in life vanished.[20]

(3:38)

24. The Conditioned and the Unconditioned

There are, O monks, three conditioned marks of the conditioned. What three? Its origination is discerned, its vanishing is discerned, its change while persisting is discerned.[21] These are the three conditioned marks of the conditioned.

There are, O monks, three unconditioned marks of the Unconditioned. What three? No origination is discerned, no vanishing is discerned, no change while persisting is discerned. These are the three unconditioned marks of the Unconditioned.[22]

(3:47)

25. AN ISLAND OF REFUGE

Once two frail and old brahmins, aged, advanced in years, at life's end, one hundred and twenty years of age, approached the Blessed One and said to him:

"We are brahmins, Master Gotama, frail and old ... one hundred and twenty years of age. But we have not done anything that is good and wholesome, we have not made a shelter for ourselves.[23] Let Master Gotama admonish us and exhort us, so that it may lead to our welfare and happiness for a long time!"

"Truly, brahmins, you are frail and old ... and you have not done anything good and wholesome, you have not made a shelter for yourselves. Indeed, brahmins, this world is swept away by old age, illness and death. Though the world is thus swept away by old age, illness and death, for one who departs from this world self-control in deeds, words, and thoughts will provide shelter and safety, an island of refuge and succour."

Life is swept away, brief is our span of years,
There are no shelters for one who has reached old age.
Perceiving the peril that lurks in death,
Perform good deeds that entail happiness.

When one is restrained in body,
Restrained by speech and by mind,
The deeds of merit one did while alive
Bring happiness when one departs.

When a house is burning, the goods removed from it,
Will be of use, but not what burns inside.
Thus, in this world aflame with age and death,
Save what you own by liberality—
Your goods given, are well removed and safe.

When one is restrained in body,
Restrained by speech and by mind,
The deeds of merit one did while alive
Bring happiness when one departs.

(3:51–52)

26. The Visible Nibbāna

Once the brahmin Jāṇussoṇi approached the Blessed One … and said to him:[24]

"It is said, Master Gotama, 'Nibbāna is directly visible.' In what way, Master Gotama, is Nibbāna directly visible, immediate, inviting one to come and see, worthy of application, to be personally experienced by the wise?"

"When, brahmin, a person is impassioned with lust … depraved through hatred … bewildered through delusion, overwhelmed and infatuated by delusion, then he plans for his own harm, for the harm of others, for the harm of both; and he experiences in his mind suffering and grief. But when lust, hatred, and delusion have been abandoned, he neither plans for his own harm, nor for the harm of others, nor for the harm of both; and he does not experience in his mind suffering and grief. In this way, brahmin, Nibbāna is directly visible, immediate, inviting one to come and see, worthy of application, to be personally experienced by the wise.

"Since he experiences the complete destruction of lust, hatred, and delusion, in this way, brahmin, Nibbāna is directly visible, immediate, inviting one to come and see, worthy of application, to be personally experienced by the wise."[25]

(3:55)

27. To Whom Should Gifts Be Given?

Once Vacchagotta the wanderer approached the Blessed One and said to him:[26]

"I have heard it said, Master Gotama, that the ascetic Gotama says: 'Gifts should be given only to me and not to others; they should be given only to my disciples and not to the disciples of others. Only what is given to me brings great fruit, not what is given to others; only what is given to my disciples brings great fruit, not what is given to the disciples of others.' Now, Master Gotama, do those who say so report Master

Gotama's actual words and not misrepresent him? Do they declare this in accordance with your teachings and will their assertion give no grounds for reproach? We certainly do not wish to misrepresent Master Gotama."

"Those who have said so, Vaccha, have not reported my words correctly, but misrepresent me. Their declarations do not accord with my teachings and their false assertion will certainly give cause for reproach.

"Vaccha, anyone who prevents another person from giving alms causes obstruction and impediment to three people: he obstructs the donor from doing a meritorious deed, he obstructs the recipient from getting the gift, and prior to that, he undermines and harms his own character. What I actually teach, Vaccha, is this: even if one throws away the rinsings from a pot or cup into a village pool or pond, wishing that the living beings there may feed on them—even this would be a source of merit, not to speak of giving a gift to human beings.

"However, I do declare that offerings made to the virtuous bring rich fruit, and not so much those made to the immoral.[27] The virtuous one has abandoned five qualities and possesses another five qualities. What are the five qualities he has abandoned? Sensual desire, ill will, sloth and torpor, restlessness and worry, and doubt: these are the five qualities he has abandoned. And what are the five qualities he possesses? He possesses the virtue, concentration, wisdom, liberation, and knowledge and vision of liberation of one perfect in training. These are the five qualities he possesses.

"What is given to one who has abandoned those five qualities and who possesses these five qualities—this, I declare, brings rich fruit."

(3:57)

28. Do Monks Benefit Others?

Once Saṅgārava the brahmin approached the Blessed One and said to him:[28]

"We are brahmins, Master Gotama: we sacrifice and enjoin others to make sacrifices. Now one who himself sacrifices and one who enjoins others to do so both engage in a meritorious practice, the offering of sacrifice that extends to many persons. But one of this or that family who goes forth from home into the homeless life, he tames himself alone, calms himself alone, attains Nibbāna for himself alone. If this is so, he then engages in a meritorious practice involving only one person, namely, the act of going forth into the homeless life."

"Well, brahmin, I shall ask you a question and you may answer as you think fit. Now, brahmin, what do you think of this: A Tathāgata arises in the world, an arahant, fully enlightened, accomplished in true knowledge and conduct, sublime, knower of the world, unsurpassed leader of persons to be tamed, teacher of devas and humans, the Enlightened One, the Blessed One. He speaks thus: 'Come! This is the way, this is the path treading which I have directly known and realized that highest consummation of the holy life which I now proclaim. Come! You too should practise thus, so that you too, by your own effort, may directly know and realize this highest consummation of the holy life and dwell in its attainment!'

"Thus this teacher shows the Dhamma and others too practise in that way. And of such who do so, there are many hundreds, many thousands, many hundreds of thousands. What do you think, brahmin: since this is so, is that act of going forth into homelessness a meritorious practice involving only one person or many people?"

"Since it is so, Master Gotama, the going forth is a meritorious practice extending to many people."

When this was said, the Venerable Ānanda spoke to the brahmin Saṅgārava thus:[29] "Of these two practices, brahmin, which appeals to you more as being simpler and less harmful, and as giving richer fruit and greater benefit?"

Thereupon the brahmin Saṅgārava said to the Venerable Ānanda: "I must honour and praise those like Master Gotama and Master Ānanda."

For a second time and third time, the Venerable Ānanda addressed the brahmin: "I do not ask you, brahmin, whom you honour and praise, but which of those two practices appeals to you more as being simpler and less harmful, and as giving richer fruit and greater benefit?"

But also for a second time and third time, the brahmin Saṅgārava replied: "I must honour and praise those like Master Gotama and Master Ānanda."

Then the Blessed One thought: "Even for a third time this brahmin Saṅgārava, on being asked by Ānanda a pertinent question, makes evasions and does not reply to it. Should I not release him from that situation?" And he spoke to the brahmin: "What might have been the topic of conversation, brahmin, among the king's courtiers when they sat together today in the royal palace?"

"The topic of conversation was this, Master Gotama: 'Formerly there were fewer monks, but there were more who displayed miracles of supernormal power transcending the human level. But now there are more monks, but fewer who display miracles of supernormal power transcending the human level.' This was the topic of conversation."

"There are three kinds of miracles, brahmin. What three? The miracle of supernormal power, the miracle of thought-reading, and the miracle of instruction.

"What now is the miracle of supernormal power? There is one who enjoys the various kinds of supernormal power: having been one, he becomes many; having been many, he becomes one; he appears and vanishes; he goes unhindered through a wall, through a rampart, through a mountain as if through space; he dives in and out of the earth as if it were water; he walks on water without sinking as if it were earth; while seated cross-legged he travels through the sky like a bird; with his hand he touches and strokes the sun and the moon, so powerful and mighty; he exercises mastery with his body even as far as the Brahma-world. This, brahmin, is called the miracle of psychic power.

"What now is the miracle of thought-reading? There is one who, by means of a sign,[30] declares: 'Thus is your mind, such and such is your mind, thus is your thought.' And however many such declarations he makes, they are exactly so and not otherwise.

"Another does not make his declarations by means of a sign, but after hearing voices of humans, of spirits or devas ... or by hearing the sound of a person's thought-vibrations ... or by mentally penetrating the direction of his mental dispositions when he is in a thought-free state of meditation.[31] And however many such declarations he makes, they are exactly so and not otherwise. This is called the miracle of thought-reading.

"And what, brahmin, is the miracle of instruction? There is one who instructs thus: 'You should think in this way and should not think in that way! You should attend to this and not to that! You should give up this and should dwell in the attainment of that!' This is called the miracle of instruction.[32]

"These, O brahmin, are the three kinds of miracles. Of these three miracles, which appeals to you as the most excellent and sublime?"

"As to the miracles of supernormal power and thought-reading, Master Gotama, only one who performs them will experience their outcome; they belong only to one who performs them. These two miracles, Master Gotama, appear to me as having the nature of a conjurer's trick. But as to the miracle of instruction-this, Master Gotama, appeals to me as the most excellent and sublime among these three.

"It is outstanding and remarkable how well this was spoken by Master Gotama. We shall remember Master Gotama as one endowed with these three miracles. For Master Gotama enjoys the various kinds of supernormal power. He mentally penetrates and knows the minds of others. And Master Gotama instructs others thus: 'You should think in this way and not in that way! You should attend to this and not to that! You should give up this and should dwell in the attainment of that! '"

"Indeed, brahmin, you have spoken strikingly befitting words. Hence I too shall confirm that I enjoy the various kinds of supernormal power ... that I mentally penetrate and know the minds of others ... and that I instruct others how to direct their minds."

"But is there, apart from Master Gotama, any other monk who is endowed with these three miracles?"

"Yes, brahmin. The monks endowed with these three miracles are not just one hundred, or two, three, four or five hundred, but even more monks than that are thus endowed."

"And where are these monks now dwelling, Master Gotama?"

"In this very Sangha of monks, brahmin."

"Excellent, Master Gotama! Excellent, Master Gotama! It is just as if one were to set upright what was overturned, or to reveal what was hidden, or to point out the way to one gone astray, or to hold a lamp in the darkness so that those who have eyes might see forms. Even so has the Dhamma been set forth in various ways by Master Gotama. I now go for refuge to Master Gotama, to the Dhamma, and to the Sangha of monks. Let Master Gotama accept me as a lay follower who has gone for refuge from today until life's end."

(3:60)

29. Three Sectarian Tenets

There are, O monks, three sectarian tenets which, if they are fully examined, investigated, and discussed, will end in a doctrine of inaction, even if adopted because of tradition.[33] What are these three tenets?

There are, monks, some ascetics and brahmins who teach and hold this view: "Whatever a person experiences, be it pleasure, pain or a neutral feeling, all that is caused by past action." There are others who teach and hold this view: "Whatever a person experiences ... all that is caused by God's creation." And there are still other ascetics and brahmins who teach and hold this view: "Whatever a person experiences ... is uncaused and unconditioned."[34]

(1) Now, monks, I approached those ascetics and brahmins (holding the first view) and said to them: "Is it true, as they say, that you venerable ones teach and hold the view that whatever a person experiences ... all that is caused by past action?" When they affirmed it, I said to them: "If that is so,

venerable sirs, then it is due to past action (done in a former life) that people kill, steal and engage in sexual misconduct; that they speak falsehood, utter malicious words, speak harshly and indulge in idle talk; that they are covetous and malevolent and hold false views.[35] But those who have recourse to past action as the decisive factor will lack the impulse and effort for doing this or not doing that. Since they have no real valid ground for asserting that this or that ought to be done or ought not to be done, the term 'ascetics' does not rightly apply to them, living without mindfulness and self-control."

This, monks, is my first justified rebuke to those ascetics and brahmins who teach and hold such a view.

(2) Again, monks, I approached those ascetics and brahmins (holding the second view) and said to them: "Is it true, as they say, that you venerable ones teach and hold the view that whatever a person experiences ... all that is caused by God's creation?" When they affirmed it, I said to them: "If that is so, venerable sirs, then it is due to God's creation that people kill ... and hold false views. But those who have recourse to God's creation as the decisive factor will lack the impulse and effort for doing this or not doing that. Since they have no real valid ground for asserting that this or that ought to be done or ought not to be done, the term 'ascetics' does not rightly apply to them, living without mindfulness and self-control."

This, monks, is my second justified rebuke to those ascetics and brahmins who teach and hold such a view.

(3) Again, monks, I approached those ascetics and brahmins (holding the third view) and said to them: "Is it true, as they say, that you venerable ones teach and hold the view that whatever a person experiences ... all that is uncaused and unconditioned?" When they affirmed it, I said to them: "If that is so, venerable sirs, then it is without cause and condition that people kill ... and hold false views. But those who have recourse to an uncaused and unconditioned (order of events) as the decisive factor will lack the impulse and effort for doing this or not doing that. Since they have no real valid ground for asserting that this or that ought to be done or ought not to be

done, the term 'ascetics' does not rightly apply to them, living without mindfulness and self-control."

This, monks, is my third justified rebuke to those ascetics and brahmins who teach and hold such a view.

These, monks, are the three sectarian tenets which, if fully examined, investigated, and discussed, will end in a doctrine of inaction, even if adopted because of tradition.

Now, monks, this Dhamma taught by me is unrefuted, untarnished, unblamed, and uncensored by intelligent ascetics and brahmins.[36] And what is that Dhamma?

"These are the six elements"—that is the Dhamma taught by me, which is unrefuted ... by intelligent ascetics and brahmins

"These are the six bases of contact" ... "These are the eighteen mental examinations" ... "These are the Four Noble Truths"—that is the Dhamma taught by me, which is unrefuted, untarnished, unblamed, and uncensured by intelligent ascetics and brahmins.

Now on account of what was it said that *the six elements* are the Dhamma taught by me? These are the six elements: the elements of earth, water, heat, air, space, and consciousness.[37]

Now on account of what was it said that *the six bases of contact* are the Dhamma taught by me? These are the six bases of contact: the eye, ear, nose, tongue, body, and mind as bases of contact.

Now on account of what was it said that *the eighteen mental examinations* are the Dhamma taught by me?[38] These are the eighteen mental examinations: Seeing a form with the eye, one examines a form that may give rise either to joy, sadness, or indifference. Hearing a sound with the ear ... Smelling an odour with the nose ... Tasting a flavour with the tongue ... Feeling a tactile object with the body ... Cognizing a mental object with the mind, one examines an object that may give rise either to joy, sadness or indifference. These are the eighteen mental examinations.

Now, on account of what was it said that *the Four Noble Truths* are the Dhamma taught by me? Based on the six elements there is descent into the womb.[39] Such descent taking place, there is name-and-form.[40] With name-and-form as condition there are the six sense bases; with the six sense bases as condition there is contact; with contact as condition there is feeling. Now it is for one who feels that I make known, "This is suffering," "This is the origin of suffering," "This is the cessation of suffering," "This is the way leading to the cessation of suffering."[41]

What now, monks, is the noble truth of suffering? Birth is suffering; ageing is suffering; illness is suffering; death is suffering; sorrow, lamentation, pain, grief, and despair are suffering; association with the unloved is suffering; separation from the loved is suffering; not to get what one wants is suffering; in brief, the five aggregates subject to clinging are suffering.[42]

And what, monks, is the noble truth of the origin of suffering? With ignorance as condition volitional formations come to be.[43] With the volitional formations as condition, consciousness; with consciousness as condition, name-and-form; with name-and-form as condition, the six sense bases; with the six sense bases as condition, contact; with contact as condition, feeling; with feeling as condition, craving; with craving as condition, clinging; with clinging as condition, the process of becoming; with the process of becoming as condition, birth; with birth as condition, ageing and death, sorrow, lamentation, pain, grief, and despair come to be. Such is the origin of this whole mass of suffering. This, monks, is called the noble truth of the origin of suffering.

And what, monks, is the noble truth of the cessation of suffering? With the entire fading away and cessation of this ignorance, the volitional formations cease. With the cessation of the volitional formations, consciousness ceases. With the cessation of consciousness, name-and-form ceases. With the cessation of name-and-form, the six sense bases cease. With the cessation of the six sense bases, contact ceases. With the cessation of contact, feeling ceases. With the cessation of feeling, craving ceases. With the cessation of craving, clinging ceases. With the cessation of clinging, the process of becoming ceases. With the cessation of the process of becoming, birth ceases. With the cessation of birth, ageing and death, sorrow, lamentation, pain, grief, and despair cease. Such is the cessation of this whole mass of suffering. This, monks, is called the noble truth of the cessation of suffering.

And what, monks, is the noble truth of the way leading to the cessation of suffering? It is just this Noble Eightfold Path, namely, right view, right intention, right speech, right action, right livelihood, right effort, right mindfulness, and right concentration. This, monks, is called the noble truth of the way leading to the cessation of suffering.

These Four Noble Truths are the Dhamma taught by me, which is unrefuted, untarnished, unblamed, and uncensured by intelligent ascetics and brahmins.

(3:61)

30. TO THE KĀLĀMAS

Thus have I heard. On one occasion the Blessed One was wandering on tour together with a large Sangha of monks when he arrived at a town of the Kālāmas named Kesaputta.[44] Now the Kālāmas of Kesaputta heard: "It is said that the ascetic Gotama, the Sakyan son who went forth from a Sakyan family, has arrived at Kesaputta. Now a good report about that master Gotama has been circulating thus: "That Blessed One is an arahant, fully enlightened, accomplished in true knowledge and conduct, sublime, knower of the world, unsurpassed leader of persons to be tamed, teacher of devas and humans, the Enlightened One, the Blessed One. He makes known this world with its devas, with Māra, with Brahmā, this generation with its ascetics and brahmins, with its devas and humans, having realized it through his own direct knowledge. He teaches a Dhamma that is good in the beginning, good in the middle and good in the end, with the right meaning and expression; he reveals a holy life that is perfectly complete and purified.' Now it is good to see arahants such as this."

Then the Kālāmas of Kesaputta approached the Blessed One. Some paid homage to him and sat down to one side; some exchanged greetings with him and, after their greetings and cordial talk, sat down to one side; some saluted him reverentially and sat down to one side; some remained silent and sat down to one side. Then the Kālāmas said to the Blessed One:

"There are, Lord, some ascetics and brahmins who come to Kesaputta. They explain and elucidate their own doctrines, but disparage, debunk, revile and vilify the doctrines of others. But then some other ascetics and brahmins come to Kesaputta, and they too explain and elucidate their own doctrines, but disparage, debunk, revile and vilify the doctrines of the others. For us, Lord, there is perplexity and doubt as to which of these good ascetics speak truth and which speak falsehood."

"It is fitting for you to be perplexed, O Kālāmas, it is fitting for you to be in doubt. Doubt has arisen in you about a perplexing matter. Come, Kālāmas. Do not go by oral tradition, by lineage of teaching, by hearsay, by a collection of scriptures, by logical reasoning, by inferential reasoning, by reflection on reasons, by the acceptance of a view after pondering it, by the seeming competence of a speaker, or because you think, 'The ascetic is our teacher.'[45] But when you know for yourselves, 'These things are unwholesome, these things are blamable; these things are censured by the wise; these things, if undertaken and practised, lead to harm and suffering,' then you should abandon them.

"What do you think, Kālāmas? When greed, hatred, and delusion arise in a person, is it for his welfare or harm?"[46]—"For his harm, Lord."—"Kālāmas, a person who is greedy, hating and deluded, overpowered by greed, hatred, and delusion, his thoughts controlled by them, will destroy life, take what is not given, engage in sexual misconduct and tell lies; he will also prompt others to do likewise. Will that conduce to his harm and suffering for a long time?"—"Yes, Lord."

"What do you think, Kālāmas? Are these things wholesome or unwholesome?—"Unwholesome, Lord."—"Blamable or blameless?"—"Blamable, Lord."—"Censured or praised by the wise?"—"Censured, Lord."—"Undertaken and practised, do they lead to harm and suffering or not, or how is it in this case?"—"Undertaken and practised, these things lead to harm and suffering. So it appears to us in this case."

"It was for this reason, Kālāmas, that we said: Do not go by oral tradition....

"Come, Kālāmas. Do not go by oral tradition, by lineage of teaching, by hearsay, by a collection of scriptures, by logical reasoning, by inferential reasoning, by reflection on reasons, by the acceptance of a view after pondering it, by the seeming competence of a speaker, or because you think, "The ascetic is our teacher.' But when you know for yourselves, "These things are wholesome, these things are blameless; these things are praised by the wise; these things, if undertaken and practised, lead to welfare and happiness,' then you should engage in them.

"What do you think, Kālāmas? When non-greed, non-hatred, and non-delusion arise in a person, is it for his welfare or harm?"—"For his welfare, Lord."—"Kālāmas, a person who is without greed, without hatred, without delusion, not overpowered by greed, hatred, and delusion, his thoughts not controlled by them, will abstain from the destruction of life, from taking what is not given, from sexual misconduct and from false speech; he will also prompt others to do likewise. Will that conduce to his welfare and happiness for a long time?"—"Yes, Lord."

"What do you think, Kālāmas? Are these things wholesome or unwholesome?—"Wholesome, Lord."—"Blamable or blameless?"—"Blameless, Lord."—"Censured or praised by the wise?"—"Praised, Lord."—"Undertaken and practised, do they lead to welfare and happiness or not, or how is it in this case?"—"Undertaken and practised, these things lead to welfare and happiness. So it appears to us in this case."

It was for this reason, Kālāmas, that we said: Do not go upon oral tradition....

"Then, Kālāmas, that noble disciple—devoid of covetousness, devoid of ill will, unconfused, clearly comprehending, ever mindful—dwells pervading one quarter with a mind imbued with loving-kindness, likewise the second quarter, the third and the fourth.[47] Thus above, below, across and everywhere, and to all as to himself, he dwells pervading the entire world with a mind imbued with loving-kindness, vast, exalted, measureless, without hostility, and without ill will.

"He dwells pervading one quarter with a mind imbued with compassion ... with altruistic joy ... with equanimity, likewise the second quarter, the third and the fourth. Thus above, below, across and everywhere, and to all as to himself, he dwells pervading the entire world with a mind imbued with equanimity, vast, exalted, measureless, without hostility, and without ill will.

""When, Kālāmas, this noble disciple has thus made his mind free of enmity, free of ill will, uncorrupted and pure, he has won four assurances in this very life.

"The first assurance he has won is this: "If there is another world, and if good and bad deeds bear fruit and yield results, it is possible that with the breakup of the body, after death, I shall arise in a good destination, in a heavenly world.'

"The second assurance he has won is this: "If there is no other world, and if good and bad deeds do not bear fruit and yield results, still right here, in this very life, I live happily, free of enmity and ill will.

"The third assurance he has won is this: "Suppose evil befalls the evil-doer. Then, as I do not intend evil for anyone, how can suffering afflict me, one who does no evil deed?'

"The fourth assurance he has won is this: "Suppose evil does not befall the evil-doer. Then right here I see myself purified in both respects.'[48]

"When, Kālāmas, this noble disciple has thus made his mind free of enmity, free of ill will, uncorrupted and pure, he has won these four assurances in this very life."

"So it is, Blessed One! So it is, Sublime One! When this noble disciple has thus made his mind free of enmity, free of ill will, uncorrupted, and pure, he has won these four assurances in this very life.

"Excellent, Lord!... (as in Text 28) ... Let the Blessed One accept us as lay followers who have gone for refuge from today until life's end."

(3:65)

31. LUST, HATRED, AND DELUSION

"O monks, wandering ascetics of other sects might question you thus: 'Friends, there are these three qualities: lust,[49] hatred, and delusion. Now, friends, what is the distinction between these three qualities, what are their disparity and their difference?' If questioned thus, monks, how would you answer those wandering ascetics of other sects?"

"For us, Lord, the teachings are rooted in the Blessed One and have the Blessed One as guide and resort. It would be good, Lord, if the Blessed One himself would clarify the meaning of this statement. Having listened to the Blessed One, the monks will keep it in mind."

"Listen then, monks, pay careful attention. I will speak."

"Yes, Lord," the monks replied. The Blessed One said this:

"If those wandering ascetics of other sects should ask you about the distinction, disparity, and difference between these three qualities, you should answer them thus: 'Lust is less blamable but hard to remove. Hatred is more blamable but easier to remove. Delusion is very blamable and hard to remove.'[50]

"If they ask: 'Now, friends, what is the cause and reason for the arising of unarisen lust, and for the increase and strengthening of arisen lust?' you should reply: 'A beautiful object: for one who attends improperly to a beautiful object, unarisen lust will arise and arisen lust will increase and become strong.'[51]

"If they ask: 'And what, friends, is the cause and reason for the arising of unarisen hatred, and for the increase and strengthening of arisen hatred?' you should reply: 'A repulsive object: for one who attends improperly to a repulsive object, unarisen hatred will arise and arisen hatred will increase and become strong.'

"If they ask: 'And what, friends, is the cause and reason for the arising of unarisen delusion, and for the increase and strengthening of arisen delusion?' you should reply: 'Improper attention: for one who attends improperly to things, unarisen delusion will arise and arisen delusion will increase and become strong.'

"If they ask: 'But what, friends, is the cause and reason for the non-arising of unarisen lust, and for the abandoning of arisen lust?' you should reply: 'A foul object: for one who attends properly to a foul object, unarisen lust will not arise and arisen lust will be abandoned.'

"If they ask: 'And what, friends, is the cause and reason for the non-arising of unarisen hatred, and for the abandoning of arisen hatred?' you should reply: 'The liberation of the mind by loving-kindness: for one who attends properly to the liberation of the mind by loving-kindness, unarisen hatred will not arise and arisen hatred will be abandoned.'

"If they ask: 'And what, friends, is the cause and reason for the non-arising of unarisen delusion, and for the abandoning of arisen delusion?' you should reply: 'Proper attention: for one who attends properly to things, unarisen delusion will not arise and arisen delusion will be abandoned.'"

(3:68)

32. Becoming

Once the Venerable Ānanda came to see the Blessed One and said to him: "One speaks, Lord, of 'becoming, becoming.' How does becoming taking place?"[52]

"If, Ānanda, there were no kamma ripening in the sense-sphere realm, would there appear any sense-sphere becoming?"[53]

"Surely not, Lord."

"Therefore, Ānanda, kamma is the field, consciousness the seed and craving the moisture for the consciousness of beings hindered by ignorance and fettered by craving to become established in a lower realm. Thus there is re-becoming in the future.[54]

"If, Ānanda, there were no kamma ripening in the form realm, would there appear any form-sphere becoming?"[55]

"Surely not, Lord."

"Therefore, Ānanda, kamma is the field, consciousness the seed and craving the moisture for the consciousness of beings hindered by ignorance and fettered by craving to become established in an intermediate realm. Thus there is re-becoming in the future.

"If, Ānanda, there were no kamma ripening in the formless realm, would there appear any formless-sphere becoming?"[56]

"Surely not, Lord."

"Therefore, Ānanda, kamma is the field, consciousness the seed and craving the moisture for the consciousness of beings hindered by ignorance and fettered by craving to become established in a lofty realm. Thus there is re-becoming in the future.

"It is in this way, Ānanda, that there is becoming."

(3:76)

33. THE THREEFOLD TRAINING

On one occasion the Blessed One was dwelling at Vesālī in the Great Wood in the Hall with the Peaked Roof. Then a certain monk from the Vajjian clan approached him ... and said to him:

"Lord, I am unable to train in the more than a hundred and fifty training rules that come for recitation every forthnight."[57]

"Then, monk, there are these three trainings: the training in the higher virtue, the training in the higher mind, and the training in the higher wisdom.[58]

"And what is the training in the higher virtue? Here, a monk is virtuous, restrained by the restraint of the Pātimokkha, perfect in conduct and resort, seeing danger in the slightest faults. Having undertaken the training rules, he trains himself in them. This is called the training in the higher virtue.

"And what is the training in the higher mind? Here, secluded from sensual pleasures, secluded from unwholesome states, a monk enters and dwells in the first jhāna, which is accompanied by thought and examination, with rapture and happiness born of seclusion. With the subsiding of thought and examination, he enters and dwells in the second jhāna, which has internal confidence and unification of the mind, is without thought and examination, and has rapture and happiness born of concentration. With the fading away as well of rapture, he dwells equanimous and, mindful and clearly comprehending, he experiences happiness with the body; he enters and dwells in the third jhāna of which the noble ones declare: 'He is equanimous, mindful, one who dwells happily.' With the abandoning of pleasure and pain, and with the previous passing away of joy and sadness, he enters and dwells in the fourth jhāna, which is neither painful nor pleasant and includes the purification of mindfulness by equanimity. This is the training in the higher mind.

"And what is the training in the higher wisdom? Here, a monk understands as it really is: 'This is suffering. This is the origin of suffering. This is the cessation of suffering. This is the way leading to the cessation of suffering.' This is the higher wisdom.[59]

"Are you able, monk, to train in these three trainings?"

"I am, Lord."

"Well then, monk, train in these three trainings: the higher virtue, the higher mind and the higher wisdom. When you train thus you will abandon lust, hatred, and delusion. With their abandoning you will not do anything unwholesome or resort to anything evil."

Then afterwards that monk trained in the training in the higher virtue, in the training in the higher mind, and in the training in the higher wisdom. As he so trained, he abandoned lust, hatred, and delusion. With their abandoning he did not do anything unwholesome or resort to anything evil.

(3:83 & 88; combined)

34. THE REFINEMENT OF THE MIND-I

There are, O monks, gross impurities in gold, such as earth and sand, gravel and grit. Now the goldsmith or his apprentice first pours the gold into a trough and washes, rinses and cleans it thoroughly. When he has done this, there still remain moderate impurities in the gold, such as fine grit and coarse sand. Then the goldsmith or his apprentice washes, rinses and cleans it again. When he has done this, there still remain minute impurities in the gold, such as fine sand and black dust. Now the goldsmith or his apprentice repeats the washing, and thereafter only the gold dust remains.

He now pours the gold into a melting pot, smelts it and melts it together. But he does not yet take it out from the vessel, as the dross has not yet been entirely removed[60] and the gold is not yet quite pliant, workable, and bright; it is still brittle and does not yet lend itself easily to moulding. But a time comes when the goldsmith or his apprentice repeats the melting thoroughly, so that the flaws are entirely removed. The gold is now quite pliant, workable, and bright, and it lends itself easily to moulding. Whatever ornament the goldsmith now wishes to make of it, be it a diadem, earrings, a necklace or a golden chain, the gold can now be used for that purpose.

It is similar, monks, with a monk devoted to the training in the higher mind: there are in him gross impurities, namely, bad conduct of body, speech, and mind. Such conduct an earnest, capable monk abandons, dispels, eliminates, and abolishes.

When he has abandoned these, there are still impurities of a moderate degree that cling to him, namely, sensual thoughts, thoughts of ill will, and violent thoughts.[61] Such thoughts an earnest, capable monk abandons, dispels, eliminates, and abolishes.

When he has abandoned these, there are still some subtle impurities that cling to him, namely, thoughts about his relatives, his home country, and his reputation. Such thoughts an earnest, capable monk abandons dispels, eliminates, and abolishes.

When he has abandoned these, there still remain thoughts about higher mental states experienced in meditation.[62] That concentration is not yet peaceful and sublime; it has not attained to full tranquillity, nor has it achieved mental unification; it is maintained by strenuous suppression of the defilements.

But there comes a time when his mind becomes inwardly steadied, composed, unified, and concentrated. That concentration is then calm and refined; it has attained to full tranquillity and achieved mental unification; it is not maintained by strenuous suppression of the defilements.

Then, to whatever mental state realizable by direct knowledge he directs his mind, he achieves the capacity of realizing that state by direct knowledge, whenever the necessary conditions obtain.[63]

"If he wishes: 'May I wield the various kinds of spiritual power: having been one, may I become many; having been many, may I become one; may I appear and vanish; go unhindered through a wall, through a rampart, through a mountain as if through space; dive in and out of the earth as if it were water; walk on water without sinking as if it were earth; travel through the sky like a bird while seated cross-legged; touch and stroke with my hand the moon and sun, so powerful and mighty; exercise mastery with my body even as far as the Brahma-world'—he achieves the capacity of realizing that state by direct knowledge, whenever the necessary conditions obtain.

"If he wishes: 'With the divine ear element, which is purified and surpasses the human, may I hear both kinds of sounds, the divine and human, those that are far as well as near'—he achieves the capacity of realizing that state by direct knowledge, whenever the necessary conditions obtain.

If he wishes: "May I understand the minds of other beings, of other persons, having encompassed them with my own mind. May I understand a mind with lust as a mind with lust; a mind without lust as a mind without lust; a mind with hatred as a mind with hatred; a mind without hatred as a mind without hatred; a mind with delusion as a mind with delusion; a mind without delusion as a mind without delusion; a contracted mind as contracted and a distracted mind as distracted; an exalted mind as exalted and an unexalted mind as unexalted; a surpassable mind as surpassable and an unsurpassable mind as unsurpassable; a concentrated mind as concentrated and an unconcentrated mind as unconcentrated; a liberated mind as liberated and an unliberated mind as unliberated"—he achieves the capacity of realizing that state by direct knowledge, whenever the necessary conditions obtain.

If he wishes, "May I recollect my manifold past abodes, that is, one birth, two births, three births, four births, five births, ten births, twenty births, thirty births, forty births, fifty births, a hundred births, a thousand births, a hundred thousand births, many aeons of world-contraction, many aeons of world-expansion, many aeons of world-contraction and expansion thus: 'There I was so named, of such a clan, with such an appearance, such was my food, such my experience of pleasure and pain, such my lifespan; passing away from there, I was reborn elsewhere, and there too I was so named, of such a clan, with such an appearance, such was my food, such my experience of pleasure and pain, such my lifespan; passing away from there, I was reborn here.' May I thus recollect my manifold past abodes with their modes and details"—he achieves the capacity of realizing that state by direct knowledge, whenever the necessary conditions obtain.

If he wishes, "With the divine eye, which is purified and surpasses the human, may I see beings passing away and being reborn, inferior and superior, beautiful and ugly, fortunate and unfortunate, and understand how beings fare on in accordance with their kamma thus: 'These beings who engaged in misconduct of body, speech, and mind, who reviled the noble ones, held wrong view, and undertook actions based on wrong view, with the breakup of the body, after death, have been reborn in the plane of misery, in a bad destination, in the lower world, in hell; but these beings who engaged in good conduct of body, speech, and mind, who did not revile the noble ones, who held right view, and undertook action based on right view, with the breakup of the body, after death, have been reborn in a good destination, in the heavenly world.' Thus with the divine eye, which is purified and surpasses the human, may I see beings passing away and being reborn, inferior and superior, beautiful and ugly, fortunate and unfortunate, and understand how beings fare on in accordance with their kamma"—he achieves the capacity of realizing that state by direct knowledge, whenever the necessary conditions obtain.

If he wishes, "By the destruction of the taints, may I in this very life enter and dwell in the taintless liberation of mind, liberation by wisdom, realizing it for myself with direct knowledge"—he achieves the capacity of realizing that state by direct knowledge, whenever the necessary conditions obtain.

(3:100.1–10)

35. The Refinement of the Mind-II

A monk devoted to the training in the higher mind should from time to time give attention to three items.[64] He should from time to time give attention to the item of concentration, from time to time to the item of energetic effort, from time to time to the item of equanimity.[65]

If a monk devoted to the training in the higher mind should give exclusive attention to the item of concentration, it is possible that his mind may fall into indolence. If he should give exclusive attention to the item of energetic effort, it is possible that his mind may fall into restlessness. If he should give exclusive attention to the item of equanimity, it is possible that his mind will not be well concentrated for the destruction of the taints.

But if, from time to time, he gives attention to each of these three items, then his mind will be pliant, workable, lucid, and not unwieldy, and it will be well concentrated for the destruction of the taints.

Suppose a goldsmith or his apprentice builds a furnace, lights a fire in its opening, takes the gold with a pair of tongs, and puts it into the furnace. From time to time he blows on it, from time to time he sprinkles water on it, from time to time he just looks on.[66] If the goldsmith were to blow on the gold continuously it might be heated too much. If he continuously sprinkled water on it, it would be cooled. If he were only to look at it, the gold would not come to perfect refinement. But if, from time to time, the goldsmith attends to each of these three functions, the gold will become pliant, workable, and bright, and it can easily be moulded. Whatever ornaments the goldsmith wishes to make of it, be it a diadem, earrings, a necklace, or a golden chain, the gold can now be used for that purpose.

Similarly there are those three items to which a monk devoted to the training in the higher mind should give attention from time to time, namely, the items of concentration, energetic effort, and equanimity. If he gives regular attention to each of them, then his mind will become pliant, workable, lucid, and not unwieldy, and it will be well concentrated for the destruction of the taints.

To whatever mental state realizable by direct knowledge he directs his mind, he achieves the capacity of realizing that state by direct knowledge, whenever the necessary conditions obtain.

(3:100.11–15)

36. GRATIFICATION, DANGER AND ESCAPE-1

Before my enlightenment, O monks, when I was still a bodhisatta, this thought occurred to me: "What is the gratification in the world, what is the danger in the world, and what is the escape from the world?"[67] Then I thought: "Whatever joy and happiness there is in the world, that is the gratification in the world; that the world is impermanent, pervaded by suffering and subject to change, that is the danger in the world; the removal and abandoning of desire and lust for the world, that is the escape from the world."

So long, monks, as I did not fully understand, as they really are, the world's gratification as gratification, its danger as danger, and the escape from the world as escape, for so long I did not claim that I had awakened to the unsurpassed perfect enlightenment in this world with its devas, Māra and Brahmā, in this generation with its ascetics and brahmins, its devas and humans.

But when I had fully understood all this, then I claimed that I had awakened to the unsurpassed perfect enlightenment in this world with … its devas and humans. The knowledge and vision arose in me: "Unshakeable is the liberation of my mind; this is my last birth; there is now no further re-becoming."

(3:101.1–2)

37. Gratification, Danger and Escape-II

I went in search of the gratification in the world, O monks. Whatever gratification there is in the world, that I have found; and in how far there is gratification in the world, that I have clearly seen by wisdom.

I went in search of the danger in the world. Whatever danger there is in the world, that I have found; and in how far there is danger in the world, that I have clearly seen by wisdom.

I went in search of an escape from the world. That escape from the world I have found; and in how far there is an escape from the world, that I have clearly seen by wisdom.

(3:101.3)

38. Gratification, Danger and Escape-III

If, monks, there were no gratification in the world, beings would not become attached to the world. But as there is gratification in the world, beings become attached to it.

If there were no danger in the world, beings would not become disenchanted with the world. But as there is danger in the world, beings become disenchanted with it.

If there were no escape from the world, beings could not escape from the world. But as there is an escape from the world, beings can escape from it.

(3:102)

39. At the Gotamaka Shrine

On one occasion the Blessed One was dwelling at the Gotamaka Shrine, near Vesālī. There the Blessed One addressed the monks thus:

"On the basis of direct knowledge I teach the Dhamma, O monks, not without direct knowledge. On good grounds I teach the Dhamma, not without good grounds. Convincingly I teach the Dhamma, not unconvincingly. Therefore, monks, my advice should be followed and my instruction accepted. This, monks, is sufficient for your satisfaction, sufficient for your gladness, sufficient for your joy: fully enlightened is the Blessed One; well proclaimed is the Blessed One's Dhamma; well conducted is the Sangha."

Thus spoke the Blessed One. Gladdened, those monks approved the Blessed One's words. While this discourse was being spoken, the thousandfold world system shook.[68]

(3:123)

40. THE THREE CHARACTERISTICS OF EXISTENCE

Whether Tathāgatas arise in the world or not, it still remains a fact, a firm and necessary condition of existence, that all formations are impermanent ... that all formations are subject to suffering ... that all things are non-self.[69]

A Tathāgata fully awakens to this fact and penetrates it. Having fully awakened to it and penetrated it, he announces it, teaches it, makes it known, presents it, discloses it, analyses it and explains it: that all formations are impermanent, that all formations are subject to suffering, that all things are non-self.

(3:134)

41. HAPPY DAYS

Whatever beings, O monks, behave righteously by body, speech, and mind during the morning, a happy morning will be theirs.

Whatever beings behave righteously by body, speech, and mind at noon, a happy noon will be theirs.

Whatever beings behave righteously by body, speech, and mind during the evening, a happy evening will be theirs.

Truly auspicious and a festive time,
A happy morning and a joyful rising,
A precious moment and a blissful hour
Will come for those who offer alms
To the ones who lead the holy life.

On such a day, right acts in words and deeds,
Right thoughts and noble aspirations,
Bring gain to those who practise them;
Happy are those who reap such gain,
For they have grown in the Buddha's Teaching.
May you and all your relatives
Be happy and enjoy good health!

(3:150)

IV. The Chapter of the Fours

42. The Stream

These four kinds of persons, O monks, are to be found in the world. What four? The person who goes with the stream; one who goes against the stream; one who stands firm; and one who has crossed over and gone to the far shore, a brahmin who stands on dry land.[1]

Of what nature is the person going with the stream? It is one who indulges his sensual desire and commits wrong deeds.[2]

Of what nature is one who goes against the stream? It is one who does not indulge sensual desire and commit wrong deeds. He lives the holy life, though in painful struggle, with difficulty, sighing and in tears.[3]

Of what nature is one who stands firm? It is one who, with the utter destruction of the five lower fetters, is due to be reborn spontaneously (in a celestial realm) and there attain final Nibbāna, without ever returning from that world.[4]

Of what nature is one who has crossed over and gone to the far shore, a brahmin who stands on dry land? It is one who, with the destruction of the taints, in this very life enters and dwells in the taintless liberation of mind, liberation by wisdom, having realized it for himself by direct knowledge.[5]

These, monks, are the four kinds of persons to be found in the world.

(4:5)

43. Training for Enlightenment

If while walking, standing, sitting or reclining when awake, a sensual thought, a thought of ill will, or a violent thought arises in a monk, and he tolerates it, does not abandon it, dispel it, eliminate it and abolish it, that monk—who in such a manner is ever and again lacking in earnest endeavour and moral shame—is called indolent and devoid of energy.

If while a monk is walking, standing, sitting or reclining while awake, a sensual thought, a thought of ill will, or a violent thought arises in him, and he does not tolerate it but abandons it, dispels it, eliminates it and abolishes it, that monk—who in such a manner ever and again shows earnest endeavour and moral shame—is called energetic and resolute.

Whether walking or standing,
Whether sitting or lying down,
One who cherishes evil thoughts
Connected with the worldly life
Is travelling down a treacherous path,
Beguiled by delusive things.
Such a monk cannot attain
Enlightenment, the supreme goal.

Whether walking or standing,
Whether sitting or lying down,
One who overcomes these thoughts
Finds delight in stilling the mind.
Such a monk may well attain
Enlightenment, the supreme goal.

(4:11)

44. Training in Determination and Insight

You should dwell, O monks, devoted to virtue, restrained by the restraint of the Pātimokkha, perfect in conduct and resort, seeing danger in the slightest faults. Having undertaken the training rules, you should train yourselves in them. But if a monk lives like that, what further should he do?

If while he is walking, standing, sitting, or reclining, a monk is free from greed and ill will, from sloth and torpor, from restlessness and worry, and has discarded doubt,[6] then his will has become strong and impregnable; his mindfulness is alert and unclouded; his body is calm and unexcited; his mind is concentrated and collected.

A monk who in such a manner ever and again shows earnest endeavour and moral shame is called energetic and resolute.

Controlled when walking, controlled when standing,
Controlled when sitting and lying down,
Controlled when drawing in the limbs,
Controlled when stretching out the limbs:
Above, across and below,
As far as the world extends,
A monk observes how things occur,
How aggregates arise and fall.[7]

When one thus lives ardently
Calm and quiet in demeanour,
Ever mindful, training oneself
In the practice of calming the mind,
They call a monk of such behaviour
"One who is ever resolute."

(4:12)

45. The Four Right Efforts

There are four right efforts, O monk.[8] What four?

Herein a monk rouses his will not to permit the arising of evil, unwholesome states that have not arisen—to abandon evil, unwholesome states already arisen—to arouse wholesome states that have not yet arisen—to maintain wholesome states already arisen and not allow them to disappear; he makes an effort (for it), stirs up his energy exerts his mind and strives.

(4:13)

46. The Tathāgata

Monks, the world is fully understood by the Tathāgata; the Tathāgata is released from the world.[9]

The origin of the world is fully understood by the Tathāgata; the origin of the world is abandoned by the Tathāgata.

The cessation of the world is fully understood by the Tathāgata; the cessation of the world has been realized by the Tathāgata.

The path to the cessation of the world is fully understood by the Tathāgata; the path to the cessation of the world has been developed by the Tathāgata.

Monks, in the world with its devas, Māra and Brahmā, in this generation with its ascetics and brahmins, devas and humans, whatever is seen, heard, sensed and cognized, attained, searched into, pondered over by the mind—all that is fully understood by the Tathāgata. That is why he is called the Tathāgata.

Moreover, monks, whatever the Tathāgata speaks, utters, and proclaims from the day of his perfect enlightenment up to the day when he utterly passes away into the Nibbāna-element without residue left[10]—all that is just so and not otherwise. Therefore he is called the Tathāgata.

Monks, as the Tathāgata speaks, so he acts; as he acts, so he speaks. Therefore he is called the Tathāgata.

Monks, in the whole world with its devas, Māra and Brahmā, in this generation with its ascetics and brahmins, devas and humans, the Tathāgata is the conqueror, unconquered, one who sees-at-will, the wielder of power. Therefore he is called the Tathāgata.

By comprehending all the world,
All in the world just as it is,
From all the world he is released;
In all the world he clings to nothing.

He is the all-victorious sage,
The liberator from all bonds,
By him the highest peace was won:
Nibbāna that is free of fear.

A taintless Enlightened One,
Free from all woe, with doubt destroyed,
Has made an end to all kamma,
Set free in the destruction of life's props.

Exalted One, he is the Buddha,
The lion without compare;
For the divine and human worlds
He has set rolling the Supreme Wheel.

Therefore devas and human beings
Who go for refuge to the Buddha,
Meet him full of reverence,
The mighty one free from self-doubt.

"Tamed, of the tamed he is the best;
Calmed, of the calm he is the first;
Freed, of the free he is supreme;
Crossed over, the best of those who cross."

So saying, they pay him reverence,
The mighty one free from self-doubt;
In all the worlds of devas and humans
There is none who ever equals you!

(4:23)

47. The Lion

Monks, the lion, the king of beasts, comes forth from his lair in the evening. Then he stretches himself, surveys the four directions all around, and roars three times his lion's roar, after which he sets out in search of prey.

Now whatever animals hear the lion's roar are for the most part gripped by fear, excitement and terror. Those animals which live in holes hide in their holes; those which live in the forest resort to the forest; and the birds rise into the sky. All the royal elephants living in villages, towns or capital cities, tethered with strong leather thongs, burst and break those thongs and, voiding urine and excrement, they run here and there full of fear. So much power, O monks, has the lion, the king of beasts, over the animals, so mighty is his influence and majesty.

Just so, monks, the Tathāgata arises in the world, an arahant, fully enlightened, accomplished in true knowledge and conduct, sublime, knower of the world, unsurpassed leader of persons to be tamed, teacher of devas and humans, the Enlightened One, the Blessed One. He teaches the Dhamma thus: "Such is personality, such is the origin of personality, such is the cessation of personality, such is the path leading to the cessation of personality."[11]

Then, monks, whatever devas there be—long-lived, lovely, full of happiness, living for a long time in their lofty celestial abodes—they too, when hearing the Tathāgata's teaching of the Dhamma, are for the most part[12] gripped by fear, excitement and terror, and exclaim: "Oh, we who thought ourselves to be permanent are really impermanent. We who thought ourselves to be secure are really insecure. We who thought ourselves to be eternal are really non-eternal. So indeed we are impermanent, insecure, and non-eternal, and are within the sphere of personality."[13]

So much power, O monks, has the Tathāgata over the world with its devas, so mighty is his influence and majesty.

(4:33)

48. THE BEST KINDS OF FAITH

Monks, there are four best kinds of faith. What four?

Monks, among all living beings—be they footless or two-footed, with four feet or many feet, with form or formless, percipient, non-percipient or neither-percipient-nor-non-percipient[14]—the Tathāgata, the Arahant, the Fully Enlightened One, is reckoned the best of them all. Those who have faith in the Buddha have faith in the best; and for those who have faith in the best, the best result will be theirs.[15]

Monks, among all things conditioned, the Noble Eightfold Path is reckoned to be the best of them all.[16] Those who have faith in the Noble Eightfold Path have faith in the best; and for those who have faith in the best, the best result will be theirs.

Monks, among things conditioned and unconditioned, dispassion is reckoned to be the best of them all: the crushing of all infatuation, the removal of thirst, the uprooting of attachment, the cutting off of the round (of rebirth), the destruction of craving, dispassion, Nibbāna.[17] Those who have faith in the Dhamma of dispassion have faith in the best; and for those who have faith in the best, the best result will be theirs.

Monks, among all (religious) orders or communities, the Sangha of the Tathāgata's disciples is reckoned to be the best, that it to say, the four pairs of noble persons, the eight noble individuals; this Sangha of the Blessed One's disciples is worthy of gifts, worthy of hospitality, worthy of offerings, worthy of reverential salutation, an unsurpassed field of merit for the world.[18] Those who have faith in the Sangha have faith in the best; and for those who have faith in the best, the best result will be theirs.

These, O monks, are the four best kinds of faith.

(4:34)

49. DOṆA THE BRAHMIN

On one occasion the Blessed One was walking on the highway between Ukkaṭṭhā and Setavyā. And it happened that the brahmin Doṇa was also walking along that road. Doṇa the brahmin saw on the footprints of the Blessed One the wheel marks with their thousand spokes, with felly and hub, perfect in every respect.[19] Seeing these marks, he thought to himself: "It is truly wonderful, it is astonishing! These certainly cannot be the footprints of a human being!"

Meanwhile the Blessed One had left the highway and had sat down under a tree not far off, with legs crossed, keeping his body erect, having set up mindfulness before him. Then Doṇa the brahmin, following the Blessed One's footprints, saw him seated under a tree, of pleasing appearance, inspiring confidence, with calm features and calm mind, in perfect composure and equipoise, controlled and restrained (like) a well-trained bull elephant.

Seeing the Blessed One, Doṇa approached him and said: "Will your reverence become a deva?"[20]

"No, brahmin, I shall not become a deva."

"Then your reverence might become a gandhabba?"[21]

"No, brahmin, I shall not become a gandhabba."

"Then will your reverence become a yakkha?"

"No, brahmin, I shall not become a yakkha."

"Then will your reverence become a human being?"

"No, brahmin, I shall not become a human being."

"Now when I asked whether your reverence will become a deva or a gandhabba or a yakkha or a human being, you replied, 'I shall not.' What, then, will your reverence become?"

"Brahmin, those taints whereby, if they were not abandoned, I might become a deva—these taints are abandoned by me, cut off at the root, made barren like palm-tree stumps, obliterated so that they are no more subject to arise in the future.

"Those taints whereby, if they were not abandoned, I might become a gandhabba, a yakkha or a human being—these taints are abandoned by me, cut off at the root, made barren like palm-tree stumps, obliterated so that they are no more subject to arise in the future.

"Just as, brahmin, a blue, red or white lotus, though born and grown in the water, rises up and stands unsoiled by the water, so, brahmin, though born and grown in the world, I have overcome the world and dwell unsoiled by the world. Consider me, O brahmin, a Buddha."[22]

(4:36)

50. Seeking the End of the World

On one occasion the Blessed One was dwelling at Sāvatthī, in Jeta's Grove, Anāthapiṇḍika's monastery. At an advanced hour of the night Rohitassa, a son of the devas,[23] approached the Blessed One, and in resplendent beauty shed his brilliant light over the entire Jeta Grove. Having come to the Blessed One, he paid homage to him, stood at one side, and said:

"Is it possible, O Lord, that by going one can know, see, or reach the end of the world, where one is not born, does not age, does not die, does not pass away, and is not reborn?"

"I declare, O friend, that by going it is not possible to know, see or reach the end of the world, where one is not born, does not age, does not die, does not pass away, and is not reborn."[24]

"It is wonderful, Lord! It is amazing, Lord, how well it was said by the Blessed One that by going it is not possible to know, see or reach the end of the world, where one is not born, does not age, does not die, does not pass away, and is not reborn. Once in a former life I was a seer named Rohitassa, Bhoja's son. Endowed with supernormal power I could walk through the sky. Such, Lord, was my speed that in the time needed for a strong, skilled, experienced and trained archer to shoot easily, with a swift arrow, across the shadow of a palm tree—in such time I could take a step as long as the distance between the eastern and the western sea. Endowed with such speed and such a stride, I wanted to reach the end of the world by walking. And with my lifespan of a hundred years, except the time needed to eat and drink, to urinate and defecate, to sleep and rest, I walked for a hundred years, and without reaching the world's end I died along the way.

"It is wonderful, Lord! It is amazing, Lord, how well it was said by the Blessed One that by going it is not possible to know, see or reach the end of the world, where one is not born, does not age, does not die, does not pass away, and is not reborn."

"Indeed, friend, so do I declare. But I do not say that one can make an end to suffering without having reached the end of the world. And I further proclaim, friend, that it is in this fathom-long body with its perceptions and thoughts that there is the world, the origin of the world, the cessation of the world, and the path leading to the cessation of the world."[25]

By walking one can never reach
The end and limit of the world,
Yet there is no release from suffering
Without reaching the world's end.

Hence the wise one who knows the world,
The one who has lived the holy life,
Will reach the end of the world,
Knowing the world's end, at peace.
He no more longs for this world
Nor for any other.

(4:45)

51. DISTORTIONS OF PERCEPTION

Monks, there are these four distortions of perception, four distortions of thought and four distortions of views.[26] What four?

To hold that in the impermanent there is permanence: this is a distortion of perception, thought and views.

To hold that in suffering there is happiness: this is a distortion of perception, thought and views.

To hold that in what is non-self there is a self: this is a distortion of perception, thought and views.

To hold that in the foul there is beauty: this is a distortion of perception, thought and views.

These, monks, are the four distortions of perception, thought and views.

Monks, there are four non-distortions of perception, thought and views. What four?

To hold that in the impermanent there is impermanence ... that in suffering there is suffering ... that in what is non-self there is no self ... that in the foul there is foulness—these are the four non-distortions of perception, thought and views.

Those who perceive the changeful to be permanent,
Suffering as bliss, a self in the selfless,
And who see in the foul the mark of beauty—
Such folk resort to distorted views,
Mentally deranged, subject to illusions.
Caught by Māra, not free from bonds,
They are still far from the secure state.
Such beings wander through the painful round
And go repeatedly from birth to death.

But when the Buddhas appear in the world,
The makers of light in a mass of darkness,
They reveal this Teaching, the noble Dhamma,
That leads to the end of suffering.
When people with wisdom listen to them,
They at last regain their sanity.
They see the impermanent as impermanent,
And they see suffering just as suffering.
They see the selfless as void of self,
And in the foul they see the foul.
By this acceptance of right view,
They overcome all suffering.

(4:49)

52. How to Be United in Future Lives

On one occasion the Blessed One was dwelling among the Bhagga people, near Suṃsumāragiri, in the Deer Park of the Bhesakalā Grove. One morning the Blessed One dressed, took his upper robe and bowl, and went to the dwelling of the householder Nakulapitā.[27] Having arrived there, he sat down on the seat prepared for him. Then the householder Nakulapitā and the housewife Nakulamātā approached the Blessed One and, after paying homage to him, sat down to one side. So seated, the householder Nakulapitā said to the Blessed One:

"Lord, ever since the young housewife Nakulamātā was brought home to me when I too was still young, I am not aware of having wronged her even in my thoughts, still less in my deeds. Lord, our wish is to be in one another's sight so long as this life lasts and in the future life as well."

Then Nakulamātā the housewife, addressed the Blessed One thus: "Lord, ever since I was taken to the home of my young husband Nakulapitā, while being a young girl myself, I am not aware of having wronged him even in my thoughts, still less in my deeds. Lord, our wish is to be in one another's sight so long as this life lasts and in the future life as well."

Then the Blessed One spoke thus: "If householders, both wife and husband wish to be in one another's sight so long as this life lasts and in the future life as well, they should have the same faith, the same virtue, the same generosity, the same wisdom; then they will be in one another's sight so long as this life lasts and in the future life as well."

When both are faithful and bountiful,
Self-restrained, of righteous living,
They come together as husband and wife
Full of love for each other.

Many blessings come their way,
They dwell together in happiness,
Their enemies are left dejected,
When both are equal in virtue.

Having lived by Dhamma in this world,
The same in virtue and observance,
They rejoice after death in the deva-world,
Enjoying abundant happiness.

(4:55)

53. THE GIFT OF FOOD

On one occasion the Blessed One was dwelling among the Koliyans, at a town called Sajjanela. One morning the Blessed One dressed, took his upper robe and bowl, and went to the dwelling of Suppavāsā, a Koliyan lady.[28] Having arrived there, he sat down on the seat prepared for him. Suppavāsā the Koliyan lady attended to the Blessed One personally and served him with various kinds of delicious food. When the Blessed One had finished his meal and had withdrawn his hand from the bowl, Suppavāsā the Koliyan lady sat down to one side and the Blessed One addressed her as follows:

"Suppavāsā, a noble woman-disciple, by giving food, gives four things to those who receive it. What four? She gives long life, beauty, happiness, and strength. By giving long life, she herself will be endowed with long life, human or divine. By giving beauty, she herself will be endowed with beauty, human or divine. By giving happiness, she herself will be endowed with happiness, human or divine. By giving strength, she herself will be endowed with strength, human or divine. A noble woman-disciple, by giving food, gives those four things to those who receive it."

(4:57)

54. Respect for Parents

Those families, O monks, dwell with Brahmā where at home the parents are respected by their children. Those families dwell with the ancient teachers where at home the parents are respected by their children. Those families dwell with the ancient deities where at home the parents are respected by the children. Those families dwell with those worthy of worship where at home the parents are respected by their children.[29]

"Brahmā," monks, is a term for father and mother. "The early teachers" is a term for father and mother. "The early deities" is a term for father and mother. "Those worthy of worship" is a term for father and mother. And why? Parents are of great help to their children, they bring them up, feed them and show them the world.

(4:63)

55. A Superior Person

Monks, one who has four qualities should be considered an inferior person. What are these four?

Even unasked, an inferior person reveals the faults of others, how much more so when he is asked. When asked, however, and led on by questions, he speaks of others' faults without omitting anything, without holding back, fully and in detail. He should be considered an inferior person.

Further: even when asked, an inferior person does not reveal what is praiseworthy in others, and still less so when not asked. When asked, however, and obliged to reply to questions, he speaks of what is praiseworthy in others with omissions and hesitatingly, incompletely and not in detail. He should be considered an inferior person.

Further: an inferior person does not reveal his own faults even when asked, still less so when not asked. When asked, however, and obliged to reply to questions, he speaks of his own faults with omissions and hesitatingly, incompletely and not in detail. He should be considered an inferior person.

Further: an inferior person reveals his own praiseworthy qualities even unasked, how much more so when asked. When asked, however, and led on by questions, he speaks of his own praiseworthy qualities without omissions and without hesitation, fully and in detail. He should be considered an inferior person.

One who has these four qualities should be considered an inferior person.

Monks, one who has four qualities should be considered a superior person.[30] What are these four?

Even when asked, a superior person does not reveal the faults of others, and still less so when not asked. When asked, however, and led on by questions, he speaks of others' faults with omissions and hesitatingly, incompletely and not in detail. He should be considered a superior person.

Further: even unasked, a superior person reveals what is praiseworthy in others, how much more so when he is asked. When asked, however, and obliged to reply to questions, he speaks of what is praiseworthy in others without omitting anything, without holding back, fully and in detail. He should be considered a superior person.

Further: even unasked, a superior person reveals his own faults, how much more so when he is asked. When asked, however, and obliged to reply to questions, he speaks of his own faults without omitting anything, without holding back, fully and in detail. He should be considered a superior person.

Further: even when asked, a superior person does not reveal his own praiseworthy qualities, still less so when not asked. When asked, however, and obliged to reply to questions, he speaks of his own praiseworthy qualities with omissions and hesitatingly, incompletely and not in detail. He should be considered a superior person.

One who has these four qualities should be considered a superior person.

(4:73)

56. The Four Unthinkables

Monks, there are these four unthinkables,[31] not to be pondered upon; which if pondered upon, would lead one to insanity and distress. What are the four?

The range of a Buddha,[32] O monk, is an unthinkable, not to be pondered upon; which, if pondered upon, would lead one to insanity and distress.

The range of the meditative absorptions ... the results of Kamma... speculations about the world[33] are unthinkables, not to be pondered upon, which if pondered upon, would lead to insanity and distress.

(4:77)

57. One's Own Good and Another's

These four kinds of persons, O monks, are found existing in the world. What four? There is one who lives for his own good but not for the good of others; one who lives for the good of others but not for his own good; one who lives neither for his own good nor for the good of others; and one who lives for both his own good and for the good of others.

(1) (AN 4:96) And how, monks, does a person live for his own good and not for the good of others? He practises for the removal of lust, hatred, and delusion in himself, but does not encourage others in the removal of lust, hatred, and delusion.

(AN 4:99) He himself abstains from killing, stealing, sexual misconduct, false speech, and intoxicants, but he does not encourage others in such restraint.

(2) (AN 4:96) And how, monks, does a person live for the good of others but not for his own? He encourages others in the removal of lust, hatred, and delusion, but he himself does not practise for their removal.

(AN 4:99) He encourages others in abstention from killing, stealing, sexual misconduct, false speech and intoxicants, but he himself does not practise such restraint.

(3) (AN 4:96) And how, monks, does a person live neither for his own good nor for the good of others? He neither practises for the removal of lust, hatred, and delusion himself, nor does he encourage others to do so.

(AN 4:99) He neither practises abstention from killing and so forth himself, nor does he encourage others in such restraint.

(4) (AN 4:96) And how, monks, does a person live both for his own good and for the good of others? He himself practises for the removal of lust, hatred, and delusion, and also encourages others to do so.

(AN 4:99) He himself practises abstention from killing and so forth, and also encourages others in such restraint.[34]

(4:96, 99)

58. FOUR THOROUGHBREDS

Four good, thoroughbred horses, O monks, are found existing in the world. What four?

There is one good, thoroughbred horse which just on seeing the shadow of the goad is alerted and feels stirred, thinking, "What task will my trainer set me today? Shouldn't I obey him?" This is the first good, thoroughbred horse found in the world.

Again, monks, there is one good, thoroughbred horse that is not alerted and stirred by merely seeing the shadow of the goad, but when his hair is touched with the goad he is alerted and stirred, thinking, "What task will my trainer set me today?…" This is the second good, thoroughbred horse found in the world.

Again, monks, there is one good, thoroughbred horse that is not yet alerted and stirred by seeing the shadow of the goad nor when his hair is touched by it, but when his skin is pricked by the goad he becomes alerted and stirred, thinking, "What task will my trainer set me today?..." This is the third good, thoroughbred horse found in the world.

Again, monks, there is one good, thoroughbred horse that is not yet alerted and stirred by seeing the shadow of the goad nor when his hair is touched or his skin pricked by it; but when pierced by the goad to the very bone, he is alerted and stirred, thinking, "What task will my trainer set me today?..." This is the fourth good, thoroughbred horse found in the world.

These, monks, are the four good, thoroughbred horses found existing in the world.

Similarly, O monks, four good, thoroughbred persons can be found existing in the world. What four?

In this case, monks, there is a good, thoroughbred person who hears it said, "In such a village or town, a woman or man is ailing or has died." Thereby he is moved and stirred. Being moved, he strives earnestly. With his mind fully dedicated, he realizes in his own person the supreme truth (Nibbāna) and sees it by penetrating it with wisdom. This good, thoroughbred person, I say, is similar to the good, thoroughbred horse that is alerted and stirred when he sees the shadow of the goad. This is the first good, thoroughbred person found in the world.

Again, monks, there is another good, thoroughbred person who does not hear it said, but who sees for himself that in such a village or town a woman or man is ailing or has died. Thereby he is moved and stirred ... he realizes in his own person the supreme truth and sees it by penetrating it with wisdom. This good, thoroughbred person, I say, is similar to the good, thoroughbred horse that is alerted and stirred only when his hair is touched. This is the second good, thoroughbred person found in the world.

Again, monks, there is another good, thoroughbred person who neither hears nor sees that some woman or man is ailing or has died; but a kinsman of his, a close relation, is ailing or has died. Thereby he is moved and stirred ... he realizes in his own person the supreme truth and sees it by penetrating it with wisdom. This good, thoroughbred person, I say, is similar to the good, thoroughbred horse that is alerted and stirred only when his skin is pricked. This is the third good, thoroughbred person found in the world.

Again, monks, there is another good, thoroughbred person who neither hears it said nor sees that some woman or man is ailing or has died, nor did this happen to a kinsman of his, a close relation; but he himself becomes afflicted with great bodily pains that are severe, sharp, piercing, utterly unpleasant and disagreeable, endangering his life. Thereby he is moved and stirred. Being moved, he strives earnestly. With his mind fully dedicated, he realizes in his own person the supreme truth and sees it by penetrating it with wisdom. This good, thoroughbred person, I say, is similar to the good, thoroughbred horse that is alerted and stirred only when he is pierced by the goad to the very bone. This, is the fourth good, thoroughbred person found in the world.

These, monks, are the four good, thoroughbred persons found existing in the world.

(4:113)

59. Four Occasions for Diligence

To four matters, O monks, diligence should be applied.[35] What four?

You should give up bad conduct in deeds and cultivate good conduct in deeds. Do not be negligent in that.

You should give up bad conduct in speech and cultivate good conduct in speech. Do not be negligent in that.

You should give up bad conduct in thought and cultivate good conduct in thought. Do not be negligent in that.

You should give up wrong view and cultivate right view. Do not be negligent in that.

If a monk has given up bad conduct in deeds, speech and thought, and has cultivated good conduct in deeds, speech and thought; if he has given up wrong view and cultivated right view, he need not fear death in a future existence.

(4:116)

60. For One's Own Sake

For one's own sake, O monks, digilent mindfulness should be made the mind's guard, and this for four reasons:

"May my mind not harbour lust for anything inducing lust!"—for this reason diligent mindfulness should be made the mind's guard, for one's own sake.

"May my mind not harbour hatred towards anything inducing hatred!"—for this reason diligent mindfulness should be made the mind's guard, for one's own sake.

"May my mind not harbour delusion concerning anything inducing delusion!"—for this reason diligent mindfulness should be made the mind's guard, for one's own sake.

"May my mind not be infatuated by anything inducing infatuation!"[36]—for this reason diligent mindfulness should be made the mind's guard, for one's own sake.

When, monks, a monk's mind does not harbour lust for lust-inducing objects, because he is free from lust; when his mind does not harbour hatred towards hate-inducing objects, because he is free from hatred; when his mind does not harbour delusion concerning anything inducing delusion, because he is free from delusion; when his mind is not infatuated by anything inducing infatuation, because he is free from infatuation—then such a monk will not waver, shake or tremble, he will not succumb to fear, nor will he adopt the views of other ascetics.[37]

(4:117)

61. Four Wonderful Things

Monks, on the manifestation of a Tathāgata, an Arahant, a Fully Enlightened One, four wonderful and marvellous things are manifested. What four?

People generally find pleasure in attachments, take delight in attachments and enjoy attachments. But when the Dhamma of non-attachment is taught by the Tathāgata, people wish to listen to it, give ear, and try to understand it. This is the first wonderful and marvellous thing that appears on the manifestation of a Tathāgata, an Arahant, a Fully Enlightened One.

People generally find pleasure in conceit, take delight in conceit and enjoy conceit. But when the Dhamma is taught by the Tathāgata for the abolition of conceit, people wish to listen to it, give ear, and try to understand it. This is the second wonderful and marvellous thing that appears on the manifestation of a Tathāgata, an Arahant, a Fully Enlightened One.

People generally find pleasure in a life of excitement, take delight in excitement and enjoy excitement. But when the peaceful Dhamma is taught by the Tathāgata, people wish to listen to it, give ear, and try to understand it. This is the third wonderful and marvellous thing that appears on the manifestation of a Tathāgata, an Arahant, a Fully Enlightened One.

People generally live in ignorance, are blinded by ignorance, and fettered by ignorance. But when the Dhamma is taught by the Tathāgata for the abolition of ignorance, people wish to listen to it, give ear, and try to understand it. This is the fourth wonderful and marvellous thing that appears on the manifestation of a Tathāgata, an Arahant, a Fully Enlightened One.

On the manifestation of a Tathāgata, an Arahant, a Fully Enlightened One, these four wonderful and marvellous things become manifest.

(4:128)

62. THE NUN

On one occasion the Venerable Ānanda was dwelling at Kosambī in Ghosita's monastery. Now on that occasion a certain nun summoned a man and told him: "Go, my good man, and meet the Venerable Ānanda. Salute him on my behalf and speak to him thus: 'Venerable sir, a nun of such and such a name has fallen sick, she is in pain and gravely ill. She pays her homage at the feet of the Venerable Ānanda.' And you may add: 'It would be good, sir, if the Venerable Ānanda would visit the nunnery and meet that nun, out of compassion.'"[38]

"Yes, venerable sister," that man replied, and he went to the Venerable Ānanda and delivered his message. The Venerable Ānanda consented in silence. In the early morning he dressed, took his bowl and robe, and went to the nunnery where that nun lived. When the nun saw the Venerable Ānanda approaching in the distance, she lay down on her couch, and drew her covering over her head.

When the Venerable Ānanda arrived at the nun's place, he sat down on a prepared seat and spoke to her thus:[39] "Sister, this body has come into being through food; yet based on food, food can be abandoned. This body has come into being through craving; yet based on craving, craving can be abandoned. This body has come into being through conceit; yet based on conceit, conceit can be abandoned. This body has come into being through the sexual act; but in regard to the sexual act the Blessed One has advised the destruction of the bridge.[40]

"It has been said: 'Sister, this body has come into being through food; yet based on food, food can be abandoned.' With reference to what was this said? Here, sister, a monk or nun, reflecting wisely, takes food neither for enjoyment, nor for indulgence, nor for physical beauty and attractiveness, but only for the upkeep and sustenance of this body, for avoiding harm to it and for supporting the holy life, thinking: 'Thus I shall put a stop to old feelings (of hunger) and shall not arouse new feelings, and I shall be healthy and blameless and live in comfort.' Then some time later, based on food, he abandons food.[41] It is on account of this that it was said: 'This body has come into being through food; yet based on food, food can be abandoned.'

"It has been said: 'Sister, this body has come into being through craving; yet based on craving, craving can be abandoned.' With reference to what was this said? In this case, a monk hears it said: 'They say that a monk of such and such a name, by the destruction of the taints, in this very life enters and dwells in the taintless liberation of mind, liberation by wisdom, having realized it for himself by direct knowledge.' Then he thinks, 'Oh, when shall I too realize the taintless liberation of mind, liberation by wisdom?' Then, some time later, based on that craving, he abandons craving.[42] It is on account of this that it was said: 'This body has come into being through craving; yet based on craving, craving can be abandoned.'

"It has been said: 'Sister, this body has come into being through conceit; yet based on conceit, conceit can be abandoned.' With reference to what was this said? In this case, a monk hears it said: 'They say that a monk of such and such a name, by the destruction of the taints, in this very life enters and dwells in the taintless liberation of mind, liberation by wisdom, having realized it for himself by direct knowledge.' Then he thinks, 'Oh, when shall I too realize the taintless liberation of mind, liberation by wisdom?' Then, some time later, based on that conceit, he abandons conceit. It is on account of this that it was said: 'This body has come into being through conceit; yet based on conceit, conceit can be abandoned.'

"This body, sister, has come into being through the sexual act; but in regard to the sexual act the Blessed One has advised the destruction of the bridge."

Thereupon that nun rose from her couch, arranged her upper robe on one shoulder, fell at the feet of the Venerable Ānanda, and said:

"Oh, venerable sir, I committed an offence when I behaved so foolishly, stupidly and unskilfully! Let the Venerable Ānanda accept my admission of the offence and pardon me, and I shall practise restraint in the future."[43]

"Truly, sister, you committed an offence when you behaved so foolishly, stupidly and unskilfully. But as you have recognized your offence as such and make amends for it according to the rule, we pardon you. For it is a sign of growth in the Discipline of the Noble One that one recognizes one's offence, makes amends for it according to the rule, and in future practises restraint."

(4:159)

63. Four Ways of Behaviour

There are, O monks, four ways of behaviour. What four? The way of impatience, the way of patience, the way of taming, and the way of calming.

And what, monks, is the way of impatience? If scolded, one scolds in return; if insulted, one insults in return; if abused, one abuses in return.

And what, monks, is the way of patience? If scolded, one does not scold in return; if insulted, one does not insult in return; if abused, one does not abuse in return.

And what is the way of taming? Here, on seeing a visible form with the eye, or hearing a sound with the ear, or smelling an odour with the nose, or tasting a flavour with the tongue, or touching a tactile object with the body, or cognizing a mental object with the mind, a monk does not seize upon the object's general appearance or its details. Since, if he left his sense faculties unguarded, evil and unwholesome states of covetousness and grief might invade him, he applies himself to the restraint of the sense faculties, he guards them and achieves control over them.

And what is the way of calming? Here, a monk does not tolerate in himself any sensual thoughts, or thoughts of ill will, or thoughts of violence, nor any other evil, unwholesome states that may have arisen in him. He abandons them, dispels them, eliminates them, and abolishes them.

These, monks, are the four ways of behaviour.

(4:165)

64. Ways to Arahantship

Thus have I heard. On one occasion the Venerable Ānanda was dwelling at Kosamb" in Ghosita's monastery. There the Venerable Ānanda addressed the monks thus:

"Friends!"

"Yes, friend," the monks replied. Thereupon the Venerable Ānanda said:

"Friends, whatever monks or nuns declare before me that

they have attained the final knowledge of arahantship, all these do so in one of four ways. What four?

"Here, friends, a monk develops insight preceded by tranquillity.[44] While he thus develops insight preceded by tranquillity, the path arises in him. He now pursues, develops, and cultivates that path, and while he is doing so the fetters are abandoned and the underlying tendencies eliminated.[45]

"Or again, friends, a monk develops tranquillity preceded by insight.[46] While he thus develops tranquillity preceded by insight, the path arises in him. He now pursues, develops, and cultivates that path, and while he is doing so the fetters are abandoned and the underlying tendencies eliminated.

"Or again, friends, a monk develops tranquillity and insight joined in pairs.[47] While he thus develops tranquillity and insight joined in pairs, the path arises in him. He now pursues, develops, and cultivates that path, and while he is doing so the fetters are abandoned and the underlying tendencies eliminated.

"Or again, friends, a monk's mind is seized by agitation caused by higher states of mind.[48] But there comes a time when his mind becomes internally steadied, composed, unified and concentrated; then the path arises in him. He now pursues, develops, and cultivates that path, and while he is doing so the fetters are abandoned and the underlying tendencies eliminated.

"Friends, whatever monks or nuns declare before me that they have attained the final knowledge of arahantship, all these do so in one of these four ways."

(4:170)

65. VOLITION

Monks, when there is the body, there arise in oneself pleasure and pain caused by bodily volition.[49] When there is speech, there arise in oneself pleasure and pain caused by verbal volition. When there is mind, there arise in oneself pleasure and pain caused by mental volition. And all this is conditioned by ignorance.[50]

Monks, either on one's own accord one constructs that bodily volitional formation whereby pleasure and pain arise in oneself; or one does so when induced by others. Either clearly knowing one constructs that bodily volitional formation whereby pleasure and pain arise in oneself; or one does so not clearly knowing.[51]

Either on one's own accord one constructs that verbal volitional formation whereby pleasure and pain arise in oneself; or one does so when induced by others. Either clearly knowing one constructs that verbal volitional formation whereby pleasure and pain arise in oneself; or one does so not clearly knowing.

Either on one's own accord one constructs that mental volitional formation whereby pleasure and pain arise in oneself; or one does so when induced by others. Either clearly knowing one constructs that mental volitional formation whereby pleasure and pain arise in oneself; or one does so not clearly knowing.

In all these states, monks, ignorance is involved.[52] But with the complete fading away and cessation of ignorance, there is no longer that body, speech or mind conditioned by which pleasure and pain may arise in oneself. There is no longer a field, a site, a base or a foundation conditioned by which pleasure and pain may arise in oneself.[53]

(4:171)

66. No Guarantee

Against four things, O monks, there can be no guarantee, whether from an ascetic, a brahmin, a deva or Māra or Brahmā, or anyone else in the world. What are those four things?

That what is liable to decay should not decay; that what is liable to illness should not fall ill; that what is liable to die should not die; and that no fruit should come forth from one's own evil deeds, which are defiling, productive of re-becoming, fearful, having painful results, leading to future birth, decay, and death.

Against these four things there can be no guarantee, whether from an ascetic, a brahmin, a deva or Māra or Brahmā, or anyone else in the world.

(4:182)

67. FEAR OF DEATH

Once the brahmin Jāṇussoṇi approached the Blessed One and addressed him thus:

"I maintain, Master Gotama, and hold the view that there is no mortal who does not fear death, who is not afraid of death."

"There is indeed, brahmin, such a mortal who fears death, who is afraid of death. But there is also a mortal who has no fear of death, who is not afraid of death. And who is the one who fears death and the other who does not fear death?

"There is, brahmin, a person who is not free from lust for sensual pleasures, not free from the desire and affection for them, not free from thirsting and fevering after them, not free from craving for sensual pleasures. Then it happens that a grave illness befalls him. Thus afflicted by a grave illness, he thinks: 'Oh, those beloved sensual pleasures will leave me, and I shall have to leave them!' Thereupon he grieves, moans, laments, weeps beating his breast, and becomes deranged. This mortal is one who fears death, who is afraid of death.

"Further, brahmin, there is a person who is not free from lust for this body, not free from desire and affection for it, not free from thirsting and fevering after it, not free from craving for the body. Then it happens that a grave illness befalls him. Thus afflicted by a grave illness, he thinks: 'Oh, this beloved body will leave me, and I shall have to leave it.' Thereupon he grieves ... and becomes deranged. This mortal too is one who fears death, who is afraid of death.

"Further, brahmin, there is a person who has not done anything good and wholesome, who has not made a shelter for himself; but he has done what is evil, cruel and wicked. Then it happens that a grave illness befalls him. Thus afflicted by a grave illness, he thinks: 'Oh, I have not done anything good and wholesome, I have not made a shelter for myself; but I have done what is evil, cruel and wicked. I shall go hereafter to the destiny of those who do such deeds.' Thereupon he grieves ... and becomes deranged. This mortal too is one who fears death, who is afraid of death.

"Further, brahmin, there is a person who has doubts and perplexity about the good Dhamma and has not come to certainty in it. Then it happens that a grave illness befalls him. Thus afflicted by a grave illness, he thinks: 'Oh, I am full of doubts and perplexity about the good Dhamma and have not come to certainty in it!' Thereupon he grieves, moans, laments, weeps beating his breast and becomes deranged. This mortal too is one who fears death, who is afraid of death.

"These, brahmin, are the four mortals who fear death and are afraid of death.

"But which mortal, brahmin, does not fear death?

"There is, brahmin, a person who is free from lust for sensual pleasures, free from desire and affection for them, free from thirsting and fevering after them, free from craving for sensual pleasures. When a grave illness befalls him, no such thoughts come to him: 'Oh, these beloved sensual pleasures will leave me and I shall have to leave them!' Hence he does not grieve or moan, lament or weep beating his breast, nor does he become deranged. This mortal is one who does not fear death, who is not afraid of death.

"Further, brahmin, there is a person who is free from lust for this body .... When a grave illness befalls him, no such thoughts come to him: 'Oh, this beloved body will leave me and I shall have to leave it!' Hence he does not grieve ... nor does he become deranged. This mortal too is one who does not fear death, who is not afraid of death.

"Further, brahmin, there is a person who has not done anything evil, cruel or wicked, but has done what is good and wholesome, who has made a shelter for himself. When a grave illness befalls him, these thoughts come to him 'I have not done anything evil, cruel, or wicked, but have done what is good and wholesome, I have made a shelter for myself. I shall go hereafter to the destiny of those who do such deeds.' Hence he does not grieve ... nor does he become deranged. This mortal too is one who does not fear death, who is not afraid of death.

"Further, brahmin, there is a person who has no doubts and perplexity about the good Dhamma and has gained certainty in it. When a grave illness befalls him, this thought comes to him: 'I am free of doubt and perplexity about the good Dhamma and have gained certainty in it.' Hence he does not grieve or moan, lament or weep beating his breast, nor does he become deranged. This mortal too is one who does not fear death, who is not afraid of death.

"These, brahmin, are the four mortals who do not fear death and are not afraid of death."[54]

"Excellent, Master Gotama! ... Let Master Gotama accept me as a lay follower who has gone for refuge from today until life's end."

(4:184)

68. HOW TO JUDGE A PERSON'S CHARACTER

Four facts about a person, O monks, can be known from four circumstances. What are these four?

By living together with a person his virtue can be known, and this too only after a long time, not casually; by close attention, not without attention; by one who is wise, not by one who is stupid.

By having dealings with a person his integrity can be known, and this too only after a long time, not casually; by close attention, not without attention; by one who is wise, not by one who is stupid.

In misfortune a person's fortitude can be known, and this too only after a long time, not casually; by close attention, not without attention; by one who is wise, not by one who is stupid.

By conversation a person's wisdom can be known, and this too only after a long time, not casually; by close attention, not without attention; by one who is wise, not by one who is stupid.

(1) It was said: "By living together with a person, his virtue can be known." On account of what was this said?

Living together with a person, one comes to know him thus: "For a long time the actions of this fellow have shown weaknesses, defects, taints and blemishes as to his morals; and he was morally inconsistent in his actions and conduct. This fellow is an immoral person; he is not virtuous."

In another case, when living together with a person, one comes to know him thus: "For a long time the actions of this fellow have shown no weaknesses, defects, taints, or blemishes as to his morals; and he is morally consistent in his actions and conduct. This fellow is virtuous; he is not an immoral person."

It was on account of this that it was said: "By living together with a person, his virtue can be known."

(2) Further it was said: "By having dealings with a person, his integrity can be known." On account of what was this said?

Having dealings with a person, one comes to know him thus: "This fellow behaves in one way if he has to do with one person and in different ways with two, three, or more persons.[55] His earlier behaviour deviates from his later behaviour. The behaviour of this fellow is dishonest; he is not of honest behaviour."

In another case, when dealing with a person, one comes to know him thus: "In the same way as he behaves towards one, he behaves towards two, three, or more people. His earlier behaviour does not deviate from his later behaviour. The behaviour of this fellow is honest; he is not a dishonest man."

It was on account of this that it was said: "By having dealings with a person, his integrity can be known."

(3) Further it was said: "In misfortune a person's fortitude can be known." On account of what was this said?

There is a person afflicted with the loss of relatives, wealth or health, but he does not reflect thus: "Of such nature is life in this world, of such nature is the uptake of individual existence, that the eight worldly conditions keep the world turning around, and the world turns around these eight worldly conditions, namely: gain and loss, fame and disrepute, praise and blame, pleasure and pain."[56] Not considering this, he is grieved and worried, he laments and beats his breast, and is deeply perturbed when afflicted with loss of relatives, wealth or health.

In another case, a person when afflicted with the loss of relatives, wealth or health, reflects thus: "Of such nature is life in this world ... and the world turns around these eight worldly conditions, namely: gain and loss, fame and disrepute, praise and blame, pleasure and pain." Considering this, he neither grieves nor worries, nor does he lament or beat his breast, nor is he perturbed when afflicted with the loss of relatives, wealth, or health.

It was on account of this that it was said: "In misfortune a person's fortitude can be known."

(4) Further it was said: "By conversation a person's wisdom can be known." On account of what was this said?

When conversing with a person, one comes to know: "Judging from the way this fellow examines, formulates and brings up a problem,[57] he is a stupid person, not a wise one. And why? He does not utter words that are profound, calming, sublime, beyond ordinary reasoning, subtle, intelligible to the wise. When he speaks of the Dhamma, he is not able to explain its meaning, be it briefly or in detail. He is a stupid person, not a wise one."

Just as if, monks, a man with good sight, standing on the bank of a pond, were to see a small fish emerging and would think: "Judging from its emergence,[58] from the ripples caused by it and from its speed, this is a small fish, not a big one"—similarly, when conversing with a person, one comes to know: "This is a stupid person, not a wise one."

In another case, when conversing with a person, one comes to know: "Judging from the way this fellow examines, formulates, and brings up a problem, he is a wise person, not a stupid one. He utters words that are profound, calming, sublime, beyond ordinary reasoning, subtle, intelligible to the wise. When he speaks of the Dhamma, he is able to explain its meaning, be it briefly or in detail. He is a wise person, not a stupid one."

Just as if, monks, a man with good sight, standing on the bank of a pond, were to see a big fish emerging and would think: "Judging from its emergence, from the ripples caused by it and from its speed, this is not a small fish but a big one"—similarly, when conversing with a person, one comes to know: "He is a wise person, not a stupid one."

It was on account of this that it was said: "By conversation a person's wisdom can be known."

These, monks, are the four facts about a person that can be known from the above four circumstances.

(4:192)

69. The Growth of Wisdom

These four things, O monks, are conducive to the growth of wisdom. What four?

Association with superior persons, hearing the good Dhamma, proper attention, and practice in accordance with the Dhamma. These four things are conducive to the growth of wisdom.[59]

These four things are also a great help to a human being.[60]

(4:246)

V. The Chapter of the Fives

70. The Trainee's Powers

Monks, there are five powers of one in higher training.[1] What five?

The trainee's powers of faith, shame, moral dread, energy, and wisdom.

And what is the power of faith? Here, monks, a noble disciple has faith; he places faith in the enlightenment of the Tathāgata: "The Blessed One is an arahant, fully enlightened, accomplished in true knowledge and conduct, sublime, knower of the world, unsurpassed leader of persons to be tamed, teacher of devas and humans, the Enlightened One, the Blessed One."

And what is the power of shame? Here, monks, a noble disciple has a sense of shame; he feels ashamed of bad behaviour by body, speech, and mind; he feels ashamed of anything evil and unwholesome.[2]

And what is the power of moral dread? Here, monks, a noble disciple has moral dread; he dreads bad behaviour by body, speech, and mind; he dreads anything evil and unwholesome.

And what is the power of energy? Here, monks, a noble disciple lives with energy set upon the abandoning of everything unwholesome and the acquiring of everything wholesome; he is steadfast and strong in his effort, not shirking his task in regard to wholesome qualities.

And what is the power of wisdom? Here, monks, a noble disciple is wise; he possesses that wisdom which sees into the rise and fall of phenomena, which is noble and penetrating, and leads to the complete destruction of suffering.[3]

These, monks, are the five powers of one in higher training.

Therefore, O monks, you should train yourselves thus: "We will acquire the powers of faith, shame, moral dread, energy, and wisdom possessed by one in higher training!" Thus should you train yourselves.

(5:2)

71. Conditions of Good and Evil

So long, O monks, as faith exists in wholesome qualities, then what is unwholesome will not gain entry. But when faith (in the wholesome) has vanished and disbelief takes a hold and prevails, then what is unwholesome will gain entry.[4]

So long, O monks, as a sense of shame exists in regard to wholesome qualities, then what is unwholesome will not gain entry. But when such a sense of shame has vanished and shamelessness takes a hold and prevails, then what is unwholesome will gain entry.

So long, O monks, as moral dread exists in regard to wholesome qualities, then what is unwholesome will not gain entry. But when such moral dread has vanished and moral recklessness takes a hold and prevails, then what is unwholesome will gain entry.

So long, O monks, as there is energy directed to wholesome qualities, then what is unwholesome will not gain entry. But when such energy has vanished and indolence takes a hold and prevails, then what is unwholesome will gain entry.

So long, O monks, as there is wisdom concerning wholesome qualities, then what is unwholesome will not gain entry. But when such wisdom has vanished and stupidity takes a hold and prevails, then what is unwholesome will gain entry.

(5:6)

72. The Simile of the Infant

Generally, monks, beings find sensual pleasures enjoyable. Now if a young man of good family has discarded sickle and carrying-pole[5] and has gone forth from home into the homeless life, one may rightly suppose that he has done so out of faith. And why can this be assumed? Because for the young, sensual pleasures are easily accessible. Of whatsoever kind, coarse, average or refined—they all count as sensual pleasures.

Now suppose, monks, there is a tender infant lying on its back. Through the nurse's negligence, the child has put a little stick or a shard into its mouth. Then the nurse very quickly would consider what has happened, and very quickly she would remove the object. But if she is unable to remove it quickly, she would hold the infant's head with her right hand, and crooking a finger, she would extract the object, even if she had to draw blood. And why? Though certainly it hurts the infant—and I do not deny this—yet the nurse had to act like this, wishing the best for the child, being concerned with its welfare, out of pity, for compassion's sake. But when the child has grown up and is sensible enough, the nurse can be unconcerned about the child, knowing that now it can watch over itself and will no longer be negligent.

Similarly, monks, as long as a monk has not yet proved his faith in things wholesome, not yet proved his sense of shame and moral dread, his energy and wisdom as to things wholesome, so long do I have to watch over him. But when he has proved himself in all these things, I can be unconcerned about that monk, knowing that he can now watch over himself and will no longer be negligent.[6]

(5:7)

73. ANOTHER FIVE POWERS

There are, O monks, another five powers: the powers of faith, energy, mindfulness, concentration and wisdom.[7]

What, monks, is the power of faith? (As in Text 70.)

What is the power of energy? (As in Text 70.)

What is the power of mindfulness? Here, monks, a noble disciple is mindful; he is equipped with the keenest mindfulness and circumspection; he remembers well and keeps in mind what has been said and done long ago.[8]

What is the power of concentration? Here, monks, secluded from sensual pleasures, secluded from unwholesome states, a noble disciple enters and dwells in the first jhāna ... (as in Text 33) ... in the fourth jhāna, which is neither painful nor pleasant and includes the purification of mindfulness by equanimity.

What is the power of wisdom? (As in Text 70.)

(5:14)

74. Criteria of the Five Powers

There are, O monks, these five powers: the powers of faith, energy, mindfulness, concentration and wisdom.

Where, monks, can the power of faith be seen? In the four factors of stream-entry.[9]

Where can the power of energy be seen? In the four right kinds of effort.[10]

Where can the power of mindfulness be seen? In the four foundations of mindfulness.[11]

Where can the power of concentration be seen? In the four jhānas.

Where can the power of wisdom be seen? In the Four Noble Truths.[12]

(5:15)

75. The Five Helpers of Right View

Right view, O monks, if it is helped by five things, has liberation of mind as its fruit and is rewarded by the fruit of liberation of mind; it has liberation by wisdom as its fruit and is rewarded by the fruit of liberation by wisdom.[13] What are those five things?

Here, monks, right view is helped by virtue, by wide learning, by discussion (of what was learned), by tranquillity and by insight.[14]

(5:25)

76. The Bliss of Detachment

Thus have I heard. On one occasion the Blessed One was wandering on tour in the Kosala country together with a large company of monks when he arrived at a brahmin village called Icchānaṅgala. There the Blessed One dwelt in a woodland near Icchānaṅgala.

Now the brahmin householders of Icchānaṅgala heard: "It is said that the ascetic Gotama, the Sakyan son who went forth from a Sakyan family, has arrived at Icchānaṅgala. Now a good report about that master Gotama has been circulating thus: 'That Blessed One is an arahant ... (as at AN 3:65) ... he reveals a holy life that is perfectly complete and purified.' Now it is good to see arahants such as this."

And when the night had passed, the brahmin householders went to the woodland where the Blessed One was dwelling, taking with them ample hard and soft food. Having arrived, they stopped outside the entrance, making an uproar and a racket.

Now at that time, the Venerable Nāgita was the Blessed One's personal attendant. And the Blessed One said to the Venerable Nāgita: "Who is it, Nāgita, that is making this uproar and racket? One would think they were fishermen making a haul of fish."

"These, Lord, are brahmin householders of Icchānaṅgala. They stand at the entrance with ample provisions of food for the Blessed One and for the Sangha of monks."

"May I have nothing to do with fame, Nāgita, nor may fame come upon me! Whosoever cannot obtain at will, easily and without difficulty, this happiness of renunciation, this happiness of seclusion, this happiness of peace, this happiness of enlightenment as I obtain it, let him enjoy this filthy and slothful happiness, this happiness gotten of gains, homage and publicity."

"Please, Lord, let the Blessed One with forbearance accept the offering, may the Sublime One accept it! It is now timely for the Blessed One to accept it in forbearance. Wherever the Blessed One now goes, there the brahmin householders of town and countryside will be inclined to go. Just as, when it rains in big drops, the water tends to flow downhill, similarly wherever the Blessed One now goes, there people will tend to go. And why is that so? Because of the Blessed One's virtue and wisdom."

"May I have nothing to do with fame, Nāgita, nor may fame come upon me! Whosoever cannot obtain at will, easily and without difficulty, this happiness of renunciation ... this happiness of enlightenment, as I obtain it, let him enjoy this filthy and slothful happiness, this happiness gotten of gains, homage, and publicity.

"Truly, Nāgita: eating, drinking, chewing and savouring end in excrement and urine; this is their outcome.

"Through change and alteration in what one loves there arise sorrow, lamentation, pain, grief, and despair; this is its outcome.

"But whosoever, Nāgita, applies himself to meditation on the foulness (of attractive things), in him revulsion towards attractive objects will be firmly established; this is its outcome.

"Whosoever, Nāgita, dwells contemplating the impermanence in the six bases of sensory contact, in him revulsion towards sensory contact will be firmly established; this is its outcome.

"Whosoever, Nāgita, dwells contemplating rise and fall in the five aggregates of clinging, in him revulsion towards clinging will be firmly established; this is its outcome."

(5:30)

77. THE BENEFITS OF ALMS-GIVING

On one occasion the Blessed One was dwelling at Sāvatthī in Jeta's Grove, Anāthapiṇḍika's monastery. At that time Princess Sumanā, with a following of five hundred court ladies in five hundred chariots, came to see the Blessed One. Having arrived, she paid homage to the Blessed One, sat down to one side, and said:

"Lord, suppose there are two disciples of the Blessed One who are equal in faith, equal in virtue and equal in wisdom. But one is a giver of alms and the other is not. Then these two, with the body's breakup, after death, would be reborn in a happy state, in a heavenly world. Having thus become devas, O Lord, would there be any distinction or difference between them?"

"There would be, Sumanā," said the Blessed One. "The one who has given alms, having become a deva, will surpass the non-giver in five ways: in divine lifespan, divine beauty, divine happiness, divine fame and divine power."

"But if these two, Lord, pass away from there and return to this world here, would there still be some distinction or difference between them when they become humans again?"

"There would be, Sumanā," said the Blessed One. "The one who has given alms, having become a human being, will surpass the non-giver in five ways: in human lifespan, human beauty, human happiness, human fame and human power."

"But if these two, Lord, should go forth from home into the homeless life of monkhood, will there still be any distinction or difference between them when they are monks?"

"There would be, Sumanā," said the Blessed One. "The one who has given alms, having become a monk, will surpass the non-giver in five ways: he is often asked to accept robes, and it is rare that he is not asked; he is often asked to accept alms-food ... a dwelling ... and medicine, and it is rare that he is not asked. Further, his fellow monks are usually friendly towards him in deeds, words, and thoughts; it is rare that they are unfriendly. The gifts they bring him are mostly pleasing, and it is rare that they are not."

"But, Lord, if both attain arahantship, would there still be some distinction or difference between them?"

"In that case, Sumanā, I declare, there will not be any difference between one liberation and the other."

"It is wonderful, Lord, it is marvellous! One has, indeed, good reason to give alms, good reason to do meritorious deeds, if they will be of help to one as a deva, of help as a human, of help as a monk."

(5:31)

78. Five Desirable Things

Once the Blessed One addressed the householder Anāthapiṇḍika thus:

"There are, O householder, five things that are wished for, loved and agreeable yet rarely gained in the world. What five? Long life, beauty, happiness, fame, and rebirth in heaven. But of those five things, householder, I do not teach that they are to be obtained by prayer or by vows. If one could obtain them by prayer or vows, who would not obtain them?

"For a noble disciple, householder, who wishes to have long life, it is not befitting that he should pray for long life or take delight in so doing. He should rather follow a path of life that is conducive to longevity.[15] By following such a path he will obtain long life, be it divine or human.

"For a noble disciple, householder, who wishes to have beauty, happiness, fame, and rebirth in heaven, it is not befitting that he should pray for them or take delight in so doing. He should rather follow a path of life that is conducive to beauty, happiness, fame, and rebirth in heaven. By following such a path he will obtain beauty, happiness, fame, and rebirth in heaven."

(5:43)

79. Five Contemplations for Everyone

There are five facts, O monks, which ought to be often contemplated upon by everyone—whether man or woman, householder or one gone forth as a monk. What five?

"I am sure to become old; I cannot avoid ageing."

"I am sure to become ill; I cannot avoid illness."

"I am sure to die; I cannot avoid death."

"I must be separated and parted from all that is dear and beloved to me."

"I am the owner of my actions, heir of my actions, actions are the womb (from which I have sprung), actions are my relations, actions are my protection. Whatever actions I do, good or bad, of these I shall become the heir."[16]

Now for what good reason should a man or woman, a householder or monk, often contemplate the fact that they are sure to become old and cannot avoid ageing? Beings while young take pride in youth; and infatuated by that pride in youth they lead an evil life in deeds, words, and thoughts. But in one who often contemplates the certainty of old age, the pride of youth will either vanish entirely or will be weakened. For that good reason the fact of ageing should often be contemplated.[17]

For what good reason should a man or woman, a householder or monk, often contemplate the fact that they are sure to become ill and cannot avoid illness? Beings while healthy take pride in their health; and infatuated by that pride in health they lead an evil life in deeds, words, and thoughts. But in one who often contemplates the certainty of illness, the pride in health will either vanish entirely or will be weakened. For that good reason the fact of illness should often be contemplated.

For what good reason should a man or woman, a householder or monk, often contemplate the fact that they are sure to die and cannot avoid death? Beings while alive take pride in life; and infatuated by that pride in life they lead an evil life in deeds, words, and thoughts. But in one who often contemplates the certainty of death, the pride in life will either vanish entirely or will be weakened. For that good reason the fact of death should often be contemplated.

For what good reason should a man or woman, a householder or monk, often contemplate the fact that they must be separated and parted from all that dear and beloved to them? Beings have lustful desire for what is dear and beloved; and inflamed by lust, they lead an evil life in deeds, words, and thoughts. But in one who often contemplates separation from things dear and beloved, lustful desire for what is dear and beloved will either vanish entirely or will be weakened. For that good reason separation from what is beloved should often be contemplated.

For what good reason should a man or woman, a householder or monk, often contemplate the fact that they are owners of their actions, and that whatever actions they do, good or bad, of these they will become the heirs? There are beings who lead an evil life in deeds, words, and thoughts. But in one who often contemplates one's responsibility for one's actions, such evil conduct will either vanish entirely or will be weakened. For that good reason the fact of responsibility for one's actions should often be contemplated.

Now, O monks, the noble disciple contemplates thus: "I am not the only one who is sure to become old, to fall ill, and to die. But wherever beings come and go, pass away and re-arise, they all are subject to old age, illness and death." In one who often contemplates these facts, the path arises. He now regularly pursues, develops and cultivates that path, and while he is doing so the fetters are abandoned and the underlying tendencies eliminated.[18]

Further, the noble disciple contemplates thus: "I am not the only one who must be separated and parted from what is dear and beloved; I am not the only one who is the owner and heir of his actions. But wherever beings come and go, pass away and re-arise, all must be separated and parted from what is dear and beloved; and all are owners and heirs of their actions." In one who often contemplates these facts, the path arises. He now regularly pursues, develops and cultivates that path, and while he is doing so the fetters are abandoned and the underlying tendencies eliminated.

Worldlings are disgusted by other beings [19]
Who share in our common nature,
By those afflicted with ageing and illness,
By those on the verge of death.
When I live for a higher aim, it is unfitting
For me to loathe such pitiful beings.
While dwelling thus, I will defeat
The pride in health, youth and life,
Having known the state free from props,
Seeing security in renunciation.[20]

As I gazed towards Nibbāna, zeal arose in me:
"Now I can never pursue sensual pleasures!
Never again shall I turn back,
The holy life is now my highest goal."

(5:57)

80. THE REPULSIVE AND THE UNREPULSIVE

In the Tikaṇḍaki Grove near Sāketa, the Blessed One said:

"Monks, it is good for a monk:

(1) to abide from time to time perceiving the repulsive in the unrepulsive;

(2) to abide from time to time perceiving the unrepulsive in the repulsive;

(3) to abide from time to time perceiving the repulsive in the unrepulsive as well as in the repulsive;

(4) to abide from time to time perceiving the unrepulsive in the repulsive as well as in the unrepulsive;

(5) to reject both the repulsive and the unrepulsive and to abide in equanimity, mindful and clearly comprehending.[21]

(1) "But for what reason should a monk abide perceiving the repulsive in the unrepulsive? (He should do so with the thought:) 'May no lust arise in me for lust-inducing objects!'

(2) "And for what reason should he abide perceiving the unrepulsive in the repulsive? (He should do so with the thought:) 'May no hatred arise in me towards hate-inducing objects!'

(3) "And for what reason should he abide perceiving the repulsive in the unrepulsive as well as in the repulsive? (He should do so with the thought:) 'May no lust arise in me for lust-inducing objects, and may no hatred arise in me towards hate-inducing objects!'

(4) "And for what reason should he abide perceiving the unrepulsive in the repulsive as well as in the unrepulsive? (He should do so with the thought:) 'May no hatred arise in me towards hate-inducing objects, and may no lust arise in me for lust-inducing objects!'

(5) "And for what reason should he reject both the repulsive and the unrepulsive and abide in equanimity, mindful and clearly comprehending? (He should do so with the thought:) 'In any situation, anywhere and to any extent, may lust never arise in me for lust-inducing objects, nor hatred towards hate-inducing objects, nor delusion towards objects liable to cause delusion!'"[22]

(5:144)

81. The Right Way of Teaching Dhamma

On one occasion while the Blessed One was dwelling at Kosambī, in Ghosita's monastery, the Venerable Udāyī was seated there in the midst of a large gathering of layfolk and taught the Dhamma to them. The Venerable Ānanda, seeing this, went to the Blessed One and reported this to him. (The Blessed One then said:)

"It is not easy, Ānanda, to teach the Dhamma to others. To teach the Dhamma to others one should set up in oneself five standards for doing so. What five?

"'I shall give a gradual discourse':[23] in that way should the Dhamma be taught to others.

"'I shall give a well-reasoned discourse': in that way should the Dhamma be taught to others.

"'Moved by sympathy I shall speak':[24] in that way should the Dhamma be taught to others.

"'Not for the sake of worldly advantage I shall speak': in that way should the Dhamma be taught to others.

"'Without alluding to myself or to others I shall speak':[25] in that way should the Dhamma be taught to others.

"Truly, Ānanda, it is not easy to teach the Dhamma to others. When doing so one should set up in oneself these five standards."

(5:159)

82. How to Remove Grudges

There are, O monks, five ways of getting rid of a grudge, by means of which a monk can remove all grudges that have arisen within him. What five?

If a grudge arises towards any person, then one should cultivate loving-kindness towards him … or compassion … or equanimity.[26] In that way one can remove the grudge towards that person.

Or one should pay no attention to him and give no thought to him. In that way one can remove the grudge.

Or one may apply to that person the fact of ownership of kamma: "This worthy person is the owner of his actions, the heir of his actions; his actions are the womb (from which he has sprung), his relations, and his protection. Whatever he does, good or bad, he will be heir to that."

These are the five ways of getting rid of a grudge, by means of which a monk can remove all grudges that have arisen within him.

(5:161)

83. WRONG LIVELIHOOD

These five trades, O monks, should not be taken up by a lay follower: trading with weapons, trading in living beings, trading in meat, trading in intoxicants, trading in poison.[27]

(5:177)

84. PRAISING THE BUDDHA

On one occasion the Blessed One was dwelling at Vesālī in the Great Forest, in the Hall with the Peaked Roof. At that time, a brahmin named Kāraṇapāli was engaged in supervising building work for the Licchavis. He saw another brahmin named Piṅgiyāni approaching in the distance, and addressed him: "Where are you coming from at high noon?"

"I am coming from the ascetic Gotama."

"Well, what do you think of the ascetic Gotama's accomplishment in wisdom? Do you think he is a wise man?"

"Who am I honourable sir, that I should comprehend the ascetic Gotama's accomplishment in wisdom? Certainly, only one who equals him could comprehend it."

"It is very high praise, indeed, by which you extol the ascetic Gotama."

"Who am I honourable sir, that I should praise him? Master Gotama is praised by the praised as best among devas and humans."[28]

"But what has the honourable Piṅgiyāni noticed in the ascetic Gotama that he has such great faith in him?"

"Just as a man who has found satisfaction in the choicest of tastes will not yearn for other tastes of an inferior kind; so too, dear sir, one will no longer have a liking for the doctrines of those many other ascetics and brahmins, after one has listened to Master Gotama's Dhamma, be it discourses, mixed prose, expositions or marvellous accounts.

"Just as a man weakened by hunger who comes upon a honey cake, wherever he eats of it he will enjoy a sweet, delicious taste; so too, dear sir, whatever one hears of Master Gotama's Dhamma, be it discourses, mixed prose, expositions or marvellous accounts, one will derive from it satisfaction and confidence in one's heart.

"Just as a man who comes upon a piece of yellow or red sandalwood, wherever he smells it—be it at the top, the middle or the lower end—he will enjoy a fragrant, delicious scent; so too, dear sir, whatever one hears of Master Gotama's Dhamma, be it discourses, mixed prose, expositions or marvellous accounts, one will derive from it happiness and joy.

"Just as a capable physician might instantly cure a patient who is afflicted, in pain and gravely ill; so too, dear sir, whatever one hears of the Master Gotama's Dhamma, be it discourses, mixed prose, expositions or marvellous accounts, one's sorrow, lamentation, pain, grief, and despair will vanish.

"Just as if there were a beautiful pond with a pleasant shore, its water clear, agreeable, cool and limpid, and a man came by, scorched and exhausted by the heat, fatigued, parched and thirsty, and he would step into the pond, bathe and drink, and thus all his affliction, fatigue and feverishness would be allayed; so too, dear sir, whenever one hears Master Gotama's Dhamma, be it discourses, mixed prose, expositions or marvellous accounts, all one's affliction, fatigue and feverish burning are allayed."

When Piṅgiyāni had thus spoken, the brahmin Kāraṇapāli rose from his seat, arranged his upper robe over one shoulder, and placing his right knee on the ground, he extended his hands in reverential salutation towards the Blessed One and uttered three times these inspired words:

"Homage to him, the Blessed One, the Arahant, the Fully Enlightened One!

"Homage to him, the Blessed One, the Arahant, the Fully Enlightened One!

"Homage to him, the Blessed One, the Arahant, the Fully Enlightened One!

"Excellent, Master Piṅgiyāni! Excellent, Master Pingiyāni! It is just as if one were to set upright what was overturned, or to reveal what was hidden, or to point out the way to one gone astray, or to hold a lamp in the darkness so that those who have eyes might see forms. Even so has the Dhamma been set forth in various ways by Master Piṅgiyāni.

"Now, Piṅgiyāni, I go for refuge to that Master Gotama, to the Dhamma and to the Sangha of monks. Let Master Piṅgiyāni accept me as a lay follower who has gone for refuge from today until life's end."

(5:194)

85. THE FIVE DREAMS OF THE BODHISATTA

Monks, before the Tathāgata, the Arahant, the Fully Enlightened One attained enlightenment, while he was still a bodhisatta, five great dreams appeared to him. What five?

He dreamt that this mighty earth was his great bedstead; the Himālaya, king of mountains, was his pillow; his left hand rested on the eastern sea, his right hand on the western sea; his two feet on the southern sea. This, monks, was the first dream that appeared to the Tathāgata while he was still a bodhisatta.

Again, he dreamt that from his navel arose a kind of grass called *tiriyā* and continued growing until it touched the clouds. This, monks, was the second great dream....

Again, he dreamt that white worms with black heads crawled on his legs up to his knees, covering them. This, monks, was the third great dream....

Again, he dreamt that four birds of different colours came from the four directions, fell at his feet and turned all white. This, monks, was the fourth great dream....

Again, he dreamt that he climbed up a huge mountain of dung without being soiled by the dung. This, monks, was the fifth great dream....

Now when the Tathāgata, while still a bodhisatta, dreamt that the mighty earth was his bedstead, the Himālaya, king of mountains, his pillow ... this first dream was a sign that he would awaken to unsurpassed, perfect enlightenment.

When he dreamt of the *tiriyā* grass growing from his navel up to the clouds, this second great dream was a sign that he would fully understand the Noble Eightfold Path and would proclaim it well among devas and humans.

When he dreamt of the white worms with black heads crawling on his legs up to his knees and covering them, this third great dream was a sign that many white-clad householders would go for refuge to the Tathāgata until the end of their lives.

When he dreamt of four birds of different colours coming from all four directions and, falling at his feet, turning white, this fourth great dream was a sign that members of the four castes—nobles, brahmins, commoners and menials—would go forth into homelessness in the Doctrine and Discipline taught by the Tathāgata and would realize the unsurpassed liberation.

When he dreamt of climbing up a huge mountain of dung without being soiled by it, this fifth great dream was a sign that the Tathāgata would receive many gifts of robes, alms-food, dwellings and medicines, and he would make use of them without being tied to them, without being infatuated with them, without being committed to them, seeing the danger and knowing the escape.

These are the five great dreams that appeared to the Tathāgata, the Arahant, the Fully Enlightenment One, before he attained enlightenment, while he was still a bodhisatta.

(5:196)

86. WELL-SPOKEN WORDS

If speech has five marks, O monks, it is well spoken, not badly spoken, blameless and above reproach by the wise. What are these five marks?

It is speech that is timely, true, gentle, purposeful, and spoken with a mind of loving-kindness.

(5:198)

87. FIVE ROUTES OF ESCAPE

There are, O monks, five routes of escape.[29] What five?

There is one monk who, when attending to sensuality,[30] feels no urge towards sensuality, is not pleased with it, does not dwell on it, and has no inclination for sensuality. But when attending to renunciation he feels an urge towards renunciation, is pleased with it, dwells on it mentally, and inclines to it. His mind is well directed and well developed, has risen above sensuality, is free of it, untrammelled; and as to those disturbing and tormenting passions caused by sensuality, he is rid of them and has no such feelings. This is called the escape from sensuality.[31]

Again, there is one monk who, when attending to ill will,[32] feels no urge towards ill will, is not pleased with it, does not dwell on it and has no inclination for ill will. But when attending to non-ill will,[33] he feels an urge towards it, he is pleased with it, dwells on it and inclines to it. His mind is well directed and well developed, has risen above ill will, is free of it, untrammelled; and as to those disturbing and tormenting passions caused by ill will, he is rid of them and has no such feelings. This is called the escape from ill will.

Again, there is one monk who, when attending to cruelty, feels no urge towards cruelty,[34] is not pleased with it, does not dwell on it, has no inclination for cruelty. But when attending to non-cruelty, he feels an urge towards it, is pleased with it, dwells on it and inclines to it. His mind is well directed and well developed, has risen above cruelty, is free of it, untrammelled; and as to those disturbing and tormenting passions caused by cruelty, he is rid of them and has no such feelings. This is called the escape from cruelty.

Again, there is one monk who, when attending to form, feels no urge towards form,[35] is not pleased with it, does not dwell on it, has no inclination for it. But when attending to the formless, he feels an urge towards it, is pleased with it, dwells on it mentally, and inclines to it. His mind is well directed and well developed, has risen above form, is free of it, untrammelled; and as to those disturbing and tormenting passions caused by form, he is rid of them and has no such feelings. This is called the escape from form.

Again, there is one monk who, when attending to personality,[36] , feels no urge towards personality, is not pleased with it, does not dwell on it, has no inclination for it. But when attending to the cessation of personality, he feels an urge towards that cessation, is pleased with it, dwells on it mentally, and inclines to it. His mind is well directed and well developed, has risen above personality, is free of it, untrammelled; and as to those disturbing and tormenting passions caused by personality, he is rid of them and has no such feelings. This is called the escape from personality.

For such a one no relishing of sensuality lies within, no relishing of ill will lies within, no relishing of violence lies within, no relishing of form lies within, no relishing of personality lies within. Therefore such a monk is called "one without underlying tendencies."[37] He has cut off craving, has discarded the fetter, and by completely breaking through conceit, he has made an end to suffering.

These, monks, are the five basic routes of escape.

(5:200)

VI. The Chapter of the Sixes

88. Sensual Desire

Monks, "peril" is a name for sensual desire, "pain" is a name for sensual desire, "disease" is a name for sensual desire "tumour" ... "fetter" ... "morass" is a name for sensual desire.

And why, monks, is "peril" a name for sensual desire? Inflamed by sensual passions and in bondage to lustful desire, one is free neither of the perils of this world nor of the perils of the next world.

Inflamed by sensual passions and in bondage to lustful desire, one is free neither of the pain, the disease, the tumour, the fetter, and the morass of this world nor of the next world.

(6:23)

89. The Six Things Unsurpassed

There are, O monks, these six things unsurpassed.[1] What are the six?

The seeing unsurpassed, the hearing unsurpassed, the gain unsurpassed, the training unsurpassed, the service unsurpassed and the recollection unsurpassed.

And what is the seeing unsurpassed? Some here, O monks, go to see the elephant-treasure, the horse-treasure, the jewel-treasure, or to see this and that; or else they go to see an ascetic or brahmin of wrong views, of wrong practice.[2] And is that, monks, called "seeing"? No, I say it is not, for that seeing is indeed low, common, worldly, ignoble, and unbeneficial; nor does it lead to disenchantment, dispassion, cessation, peace, direct knowledge, enlightenment and Nibbāna. But when one goes to see the Tathāgata or the Tathāgata's disciple, established in faith, established in love, gone surely for refuge, serenely assured: that, O monks, is seeing unsurpassed for the purification of beings, for passing beyond sorrow and lamentation, for the destruction of suffering and grief, for reaching the noble path, for the realization of Nibbāna.[3] This, monks, is called the seeing unsurpassed.

Such is the seeing unsurpassed, but what is the hearing unsurpassed? Some here, O monks, go to hear the sound of drums, the sound of lutes, the sound of singing, or to hear this or that; or else they go to hear an ascetic or brahmin of wrong views, of wrong practice. And is that, monks, called "hearing"? No, I say it is not, for that hearing is indeed low ... nor does it lead to disenchantment ... and Nibbāna. But when one goes to hear the Dhamma from the Tathāgata or the Tathāgata's disciple, established in faith, established in love, gone surely for refuge, serenely assured: that, O monks, is hearing unsurpassed for the purification of beings, for passing beyond sorrow and lamentation, for the destruction of suffering and grief, for reaching the noble path, for the realization of Nibbāna. This, monks, is called the hearing unsurpassed.

Such is the seeing unsurpassed and the hearing unsurpassed; but what is the gain unsurpassed? Some here, O monks, gain a child, gain a wife, gain wealth, gain this or that; or else they gain faith in an ascetic or brahmin of wrong views, of wrong practice. And is that, monks, called "gain"? No, I say it is not, for that gain is indeed low ... nor does it lead to disenchantment ... and Nibbāna. But when one gains faith in the Tathāgata or in the Tathāgata's disciple, established in faith, established in love, gone surely for refuge, serenely assured: that, O monks, is gain unsurpassed for the purification of beings, for passing beyond sorrow and lamentation, for the destruction of suffering and grief, for reaching the noble path, for the realization of Nibbāna. This, monks, is called the gain unsurpassed.

"Such is the seeing unsurpassed, the hearing unsurpassed and the gain unsurpassed; but what is the training unsurpassed? Some here, O monks, train in elephantry, in horsemanship, in charioteering, in archery, in swordsmanship, or in this or that; or else they train under an ascetic or brahmin of wrong views, of wrong practice. And is that, monks, called "training"? No, I say it is not, for that training is indeed low ... nor does it lead to disenchantment ... and Nibbāna. But when one trains in the higher virtue, the higher mind and the higher wisdom as taught in the Dhamma and Discipline made known by the Tathāgata, established in faith, established in love, gone surely for refuge, serenely assured: that, O monks, is training unsurpassed for the purification of beings, for passing beyond sorrow and lamentation, for the destruction of suffering and grief, for reaching the noble path, for the realization of Nibbāna. This, monks, is called the training unsurpassed.

"Such is the seeing unsurpassed, the hearing unsurpassed, the gain unsurpassed and the training unsurpassed; but what is the service unsurpassed? Some here, O monks, serve kings, brahmins, householders, or this or that person; or else they serve an ascetic or brahmin of wrong views, of wrong practice. And is that, monks, called "service"? No, I say it is not, for that service is indeed low ... nor does it lead to disenchantment ... and Nibbāna. But when one serves the Tathāgata or the Tathāgata's disciple, established in faith, established in love, gone surely for refuge, serenely assured: that, O monks, is service unsurpassed for the purification of beings, for passing beyond sorrow and lamentation, for the destruction of suffering and grief, for reaching the noble path, for the realization of Nibbāna. This, monks, is called the service unsurpassed.

"Such is the seeing unsurpassed, the hearing unsurpassed, the gain unsurpassed, the training unsurpassed and the service unsurpassed; but what is the recollection unsurpassed? Some here, O monks, recollect the gain of a child, the gain of a wife, the gain of wealth, or recollect this and that; or else recollect an ascetic or brahmin of wrong views, of wrong practice. And is that, monks, called "recollection"? No, I say it is not, for that recollection is indeed low, common, worldly, ignoble, and unbeneficial; nor does it lead to disenchantment, dispassion, cessation, peace, direct knowledge, enlightenment and Nibbāna. But when one recollects the Tathāgata or the Tathāgata's disciple, established in faith, established in love, gone surely for refuge, serenely assured: that, O monks, is the recollection unsurpassed for the purification of beings, for passing beyond sorrow and lamentation, for the destruction of suffering and grief, for reaching the noble path, for the realization of Nibbāna. This, monks, is called the recollection unsurpassed.

These, O monks, are the six things unexcelled.

> "They who have gained the seeing unexcelled,
> The hearing unexcelled, as well the gain
> Called unexcelled, they rejoicing too
> In the training unexcelled, established too
> In service, they develop in recollectedness—
> And they being to solitude attached—
> The Path to the Deathless and to the Secure,
> In heedfulness joyful, wise and well-restrained:
> In time, for certain, they shall come to know
> Where it is that dukkha is destroyed."

(6:30)

90. Causes for the Origination of Actions

There are three causes for the origination of actions.[4] Greed is a cause for the origination of actions. Hatred is a cause for the origination of actions. Delusion is a cause for the origination of actions.

It is not non-greed, O monks, that arises from greed; it is rather greed that arises again from greed. It is not non-hatred that arises from hatred; it is rather hatred that arises again from hatred. It is not non-delusion that arises from delusion; it is rather delusion that arises again from delusion.

It is not through actions born of greed, hatred, and delusion that there is the appearance of devas, of humans or of any other creatures belonging to a good destination; it is rather beings of the hells, of the animal realm, of the sphere of ghosts or any others of a bad destination that appear through actions born of greed, hatred, and delusion.

These are the three causes for the origin of unwholesome actions.

There are three other causes for the origination of actions. Non-greed is a cause for the origination of actions, non-hatred is a cause for the origination of actions, non-delusion is a cause for the origination of actions.

It is not greed, O monks, that arises from non-greed; it is rather non-greed that arises again from non-greed. It is not hatred that arises from non-hatred; it is rather non-hatred that arises again from non-hatred. It is not delusion that arises from non-delusion; it is rather non-delusion that arises again from non-delusion.

It is not through actions born of non-greed, non-hatred, and non-delusion that there is the appearance of beings of the hells, of the animal realm, of the sphere of ghosts or any others of a bad destination; it is rather devas, humans or any other creatures belonging to a good destination that appear through actions born of non-greed, non-hatred, and non-delusion.

These are the three causes for the origin of wholesome actions.

(6:39)

91. DON'T JUDGE OTHERS!

Once the Venerable Ānanda, having dressed in the morning, took his bowl and went to the house of the female lay disciple Migasālā, where he sat down on the seat prepared for him. The female lay disciple Migasālā, after having paid homage to him, sat down to one side and said to him:

"Please, venerable sir, how ought one to understand this teaching taught by the Blessed One: namely, that one who leads the pure, celibate life and one who does not should both have the very same status after death? My father Purāṇa, venerable sir, was (in his later years) a celibate, living remote from sensuality, abstaining from the low sexual life; and when my father died, the Blessed One declared that he had attained to the state of a once-returner and had been reborn among the Tusita devas.[5]

"But then, venerable sir, there was my father's brother Isidatta, who was not a celibate but lived a contented married life. When he died the Blessed One said that he too was a once-returner and had been reborn among the Tusita devas.

"Now, Venerable Ānanda, how ought one to understand this statement of the Blessed One, that both had the very same status?"

"Well, sister, it was just in that way that the Blessed One had declared it."

When the Venerable Ānanda had taken his alms-food at the house of the female lay disciple Migasālā, he rose from his seat and left. And in the afternoon, after meal time, he went to the Blessed One, paid homage to him, and sat down to one side. So seated, he told the Blessed One what had occurred.

The Blessed One said: "Who, indeed, is this female lay disciple Migasālā, this foolish, inexperienced woman with a woman's wit? And who (in comparison) are those who have the knowledge of other persons' different qualities?[6]

"There are, Ānanda, six types of persons found existing in the world. What six?

(1) "There is one person, Ānanda, who is gentle, a pleasant companion, with whom his fellow monks gladly live together. But he has not heard the teachings and acquired much learning, he has no keen understanding nor has he attained even temporary liberation of mind.[7] With the breakup of the body, after death, he will be set for decline, not for progress; he will deteriorate and not rise higher.

(2) "Then there is one who is gentle, a pleasant companion, with whom his fellow monks gladly live together. And he has heard the teachings and acquired much learning; he has a keen understanding and has attained temporary liberation of mind. With the breakup of the body, after death, he is set for progress, not for decline; he will rise higher and will not deteriorate.

"Then, Ānanda, the critics will pass such judgement: 'This one has the same qualities as the other. Why, then, should one be inferior and the other better?' Such judgement, indeed, will for a long time cause harm and suffering to those critics.

"Now, Ānanda, one who has heard the teachings and acquired much learning, who has a keen understanding and attains a temporary liberation of mind—such a one surpasses and excels the other person. And why? Because the Dhamma-stream carries him along. But who can be aware of these differences except a Tathāgata, a Perfect One?

"Therefore, Ānanda, you should not be a hasty critic of people, should not lightly pass judgement on people. One who passes judgement on people harms himself. I alone, Ānanda, or one like me, can judge people.

(3) "Further, there is a person prone to anger and pride, and from time to time states of greed rise up in him. And he has not heard the teachings or acquired much learning; he has no keen understanding, nor has he attained even temporary liberation of mind. With the breakup of the body, after death, he will be set for decline, not for progress; he will deteriorate and not rise higher.

(4) "Then there is one likewise prone to anger and pride, and from time to time states of greed rise up in him. But he has heard the teachings and acquired much learning; he has keen understanding and has attained temporary liberation of mind. With the breakup of the body, after death, he is set for progress, not for decline; he will rise higher and will not deteriorate.

"Then, Ānanda, the critics will pass such judgement: 'This one has the same qualities as the other. Why, then, should one be inferior and the other better?' Such judgement, indeed, will for a long time cause harm and suffering to those critics.

"Now, Ānanda, one who has heard the teachings ... surpasses and excels the other person. And why? Because the Dhamma-stream carries him along. But who can be aware of these differences except a Tathāgata, a Perfect One?

"Therefore, Ānanda, you should not be a hasty critic of people....

(5) "Further, there is another person prone to anger and pride, and from time to time verbosity rises up in him. And he has not heard the teachings and acquired much learning; he has no keen understanding nor has he attained even temporary liberation of mind. With the breakup of the body, after death, he will be set for decline, not for progress; he will deteriorate and not rise higher.

(6) "Then there is one likewise prone to anger and pride, and from time to time verbosity rises up in him. But he has heard the teachings and acquired much learning; he has keen understanding and has attained temporary liberation of mind. With the breakup of the body, after death, he is set for progress, not for decline; he will rise higher and will not deteriorate.

"Then, Ānanda, the critics will pass such judgement: 'This one has the same qualities as the other. Why, then, should one be inferior and the other better?' Such judgement, indeed, will for a long time cause harm and suffering to those critics.

"Now, Ānanda, one who has heard the teachings and acquired much learning, who has keen understanding and attains temporary liberation of mind—such a one surpasses and excels the other person. And why? Because the Dhamma-stream carries him along. But who can be aware of these differences except a Tathāgata, a Perfect One?

"Therefore, Ānanda, you should not be a hasty critic of people, should not lightly pass judgement on people. He who passes judgement on people harms himself. I alone, Ānanda, or one like me, can judge people.

"Who, indeed, Ānanda, is this female lay disciple Migasālā, this foolish, inexperienced woman, with a woman's wit? And who (in comparison) are those who have the knowledge of other persons' different qualities?

"These, Ānanda, are the six types of persons to be found in this world.

"If Isidatta had possessed the same degree of virtue that Purāṇa had, Purāṇa could not have equalled Isidatta's status. And if Purāṇa had possessed the same wisdom that Isidatta had, Isidatta could not have equalled Purāṇa's status.[8] These two persons, however, were each deficient in one respect."

(6:44)

92. Poverty

"Poverty, O monks, is suffering in the world for one who enjoys sensual pleasures."—"So it is, Lord."

"And if a pauper, one destitute and indigent, gets into debt, his indebtedness, too, is suffering in the world for one who enjoys sensual pleasures."—"So it is Lord."

"And if that poor man, being indebted, promises to pay interest, this payment of interest, too, is suffering in the world for one who enjoys sensual pleasures."—"So it is Lord."

"And if that poor man cannot pay the interest that falls due and he is pressed by the creditors, such pressure, too, is suffering in the world for one who enjoys sensual pleasures."—"So it is Lord."

"And if, being pressed, that poor man still cannot pay and the creditors are constantly after him, such harassment, too, is suffering in the world for one who enjoys sensual pleasures."—"So it is Lord."

"And if, being harassed and still unable to pay, that poor man is thrown into jail, this imprisonment too is suffering in the world for one who enjoys sensual pleasures."—"So it is Lord."

"Thus, O monks, poverty, indebtedness, the paying of interest, being pressed and harassed by creditors, and imprisonment—all these are suffering in the world for one who enjoys sensual pleasures.

"Similar, O monks, is it with anyone who lacks faith in wholesome qualities, who has no sense of shame or moral dread in regard to wholesome qualities, no energy or wisdom in regard to wholesome qualities. Such a one is called poor, destitute, and indigent in the Discipline of the Noble One.

"If now such a man who is poor, destitute and indigent through his lack of faith, shame, moral dread, energy and wisdom concerning wholesome qualities, conducts himself badly in deeds, words, and thoughts, this I call his getting into debt.

"If, to cover up his bad conduct in deeds, words, and thoughts, he harbours in himself evil wishes; if he desires, plans, chooses his words, and tries to act in such a way that nobody may come to know his nature—this I call the interest (to be paid on his moral debts).[9]

"Then virtuous monks speak about him thus: 'This venerable monk acts thus; he behaves in such and such a way.' This I call the pressure on him.

"If he resorts to the forest, the foot of a tree or a solitary place, he is pursued by evil, unwholesome thoughts connected with remorse. This I call his being harassed.

"Such a (morally) poor, destitute, and indigent person of bad conduct, with the breakup of the body, after death, will be bound by the bonds of hell or the bonds of the animal realm. And I know of no other imprisonment, monks, that is so cruel, so harsh, so painful and such an obstacle to attaining the unsurpassed security from bondage as the bonds of hell and of the animal realm."

(6:45)

93. Scholars and Meditators

Thus have I heard. On one occasion the Venerable Mahācunda was dwelling at Sahājāti among the Ceti people. There he addressed the monks thus:

"Friends, there are monks who are keen on Dhamma[10] and they disparage those monks who are meditators, saying: 'Look at those monks! They think, "We are meditating, we are meditating!" And so they meditate to and meditate fro, meditate up and meditate down![11] What, then, do they meditate about and why do they meditate?' Thereby neither these monks keen on Dhamma nor the meditators will be pleased, and they will not be practising for the welfare and happiness of the multitude, for the good of the multitude, for the welfare and happiness of devas and humans.[12]

"Then, friends, there are meditating monks who disparage the monks who are keen on Dhamma, saying: 'Look at those monks! They think, "We are Dhamma-experts, we are Dhamma-experts!" And therefore they are conceited, puffed up and vain; they are talkative and voluble. They are devoid of mindfulness and clear comprehension, and they lack concentration; their thoughts wander and their senses are uncontrolled. What then makes them Dhamma-experts, why and how are they Dhamma-experts?' Thereby neither these meditating monks nor those keen on Dhamma will be pleased, and they will not be practising for the welfare and happiness of the multitude, for the good of the multitude, for the welfare and happiness of devas and humans.

"There are Dhamma-experts who praise only monks who are also Dhamma-experts but not those who are meditators. And there are meditators who praise only those monks who are also meditators but not those who are Dhamma-experts. Thereby neither of them will be pleased, and they will not be practising for the welfare and happiness of the multitude, for the good of the multitude, for the welfare and happiness of devas and humans.

"Therefore, friends, you should train yourselves thus: 'Though we ourselves are Dhamma-experts, we will praise also those monks who are meditators.' And why? Such outstanding persons are rare in the world who have personal experience of the deathless element (Nibbāna).

"And the other monks, too, should train themselves thus: 'Though we ourselves are meditators, we will praise also those monks who are Dhamma-experts.' And why? Such outstanding persons are rare in the world who can by their wisdom clearly understand a difficult subject."

(6:46)

94. THE VISIBLE TEACHING

Once a wandering ascetic, Moliya Sīvaka, addressed the Blessed One as follows:

"It is said, venerable sir, 'The Dhamma is directly visible.' In what way, venerable sir, is the Dhamma directly visible, immediate, inviting one to come and see, worthy of application, to be personally experienced by the wise?"[13]

"Well, Sīvaka, I shall in return question you about this. You may answer as you see fit.

"What do you think, Sīvaka: when there is greed in you, will you know, 'There is greed in me'? And when there is no greed in you, will you know, 'There is no greed in me'?"—"Yes, venerable sir, I shall know."

"If you thus know of the greed present in you that it is there; and when greed is absent that it is absent—that is a way the Dhamma is directly visible.

"What do you think, Sīvaka: when there is hatred or delusion in you, will you know, 'There is hatred ... There is delusion in me'? And when there is no hatred ... no delusion in you, will you know, 'There is no hatred ... no delusion in me'?"—"Yes, venerable sir, I shall know."

"If you thus know of the hatred or delusion present in you that they are there; and when hatred or delusion are absent that they are absent—that is a way the Dhamma is directly visible.[14]

"In this way, Sīvaka, the Dhamma is directly visible, immediate, inviting one to come and see, worthy of application, to be personally experienced by the wise"

(6:47)

95. Professing Enlightenment

On one occasion the Blessed One was dwelling at Sāvatthī in Jeta's Grove, Anāthapiṇḍika's monastery. At that time the Venerable Khema and the Venerable Sumana were dwelling in the Dark Forest near Sāvatthī. One day both went to see the Blessed One. Having arrived, they paid homage to the Blessed One and sat down to one side, and the Venerable Khema addressed the Blessed One as follows:

"A monk, Lord, who is an arahant, one with taints destroyed, who has lived the holy life, done his task, laid down the burden, attained his goal, discarded the fetters of becoming, and is liberated by final knowledge—he has no such thought, 'There is one better than I; there is one who is equal; there is one who is worse.'"[15]Thus the Venerable Khema spoke and the Teacher approved. Knowing the Teacher's approval, the Venerable Khema rose from his seat, paid homage to the Blessed One and left.

Soon after he had left, the Venerable Sumana addressed the Blessed One thus:

"A monk, O Lord, who is an arahant, one with taints destroyed, who has lived the holy life, done his task, laid down the burden, attained his goal, discarded the fetters of becoming and is liberated by final knowledge—he has no such thought, 'There is none better than I; there is none who is equal; there is none worse.'" Thus the Venerable Sumana spoke and the Teacher approved. Knowing the Teacher's approval, the Venerable Sumana rose from his seat, paid homage to the Blessed One and left.

Soon after the Venerable Khema and the Venerable Sumana had left, the Blessed One addressed the monks, saying:

"It is in such a way, monks, that noble sons declare final knowledge: the fact is mentioned, but there is no allusion to self. Yet there are some foolish persons who declare in a rather lighthearted manner that they have attained final knowledge. But afterwards distress will befall them."

They do not consider themselves better,
Nor equal, nor worse.
With birth destroyed, free from fetters,
They live the pure holy life.

(6:49)

96. Step by Step

If there is no sense control, O monks, then the basis for virtue is destroyed for one who lacks sense control. If there is no virtue, then the basis for right concentration is destroyed for one who lacks virtue. If there is no right concentration, then the basis for knowledge and vision of things as they really are is destroyed for one who lacks right concentration. If there is no knowledge and vision of things as they really are, then the basis for revulsion and dispassion is destroyed for one who lacks such knowledge and vision. If there is no revulsion and dispassion, then the basis for the knowledge and vision of liberation is destroyed for one who lacks revulsion and dispassion.[16]

This is like a tree without branches and foliage: the buds will not mature; nor will the bark, the greenwood, and the heartwood mature. Similarly, if sense control is absent, there will be no basis for virtue ... for knowledge and vision of liberation.

But if there is sense control, O monks, virtue will have a basis for one who possesses sense control. If there is virtue, right concentration will have a basis for one who possesses virtue. If there is right concentration, knowledge and vision of things as they really are will have a basis for one who possesses right concentration. If there is knowledge and vision of things as they really are, revulsion and dispassion will have basis for one who possesses such knowledge and vision of things as they really are. If there is revulsion and dispassion, the knowledge and vision of liberation will have a basis for one who possesses revulsion and dispassion.

This is like a tree with branches and foliage intact: the buds will mature, and so also the bark, the greenwood and the heartwood will mature. Similarly, if sense control is present, this will provide a basis for virtue ... for knowledge and vision of liberation.

(6:50)

97. THE AIMS OF PEOPLE

Once the brahmin Jāṇussoṇi approached the Blessed One and asked:

"What, Master Gotama, is a noble's aim, what is his quest, his mainstay, his desire and his ideal?"[17]

"Wealth, O brahmin, is a noble's aim, his quest is for knowledge, his mainstay is power, his desire is to rule the earth and his ideal is sovereignty."[18]

"And what, Master Gotama, is a brahmin's aim?"

"Wealth, O brahmin, is a brahmin's aim, his quest is for knowledge, his mainstay is his sacred texts, his desire is for sacrifices and his ideal is the Brahma-world."

"And what, Master Gotama, is a householder's aim?"

"Wealth, O brahmin, is a householder's aim, his quest is for knowledge, his mainstay is his craft, his desire is for work and his ideal is to bring his work to an end."

"And what Master Gotama, is a woman's aim?"

"A man, O brahmin, is a woman's aim, her quest is for adornments, her mainstay is sons,[19] her desire is to be without a co-wife and her ideal is domination."

"And what, Master Gotama, is a thief's aim?"

"Robbery, O brahmin, is a thief's aim, his quest is for a hiding-place, his mainstay is weapons, his desire is darkness, and his ideal is not to be found out."

"And what, Master Gotama, is an ascetic's aim?"

"Patience and purity, O brahmin, are an ascetic's aim, his quest is for knowledge, his mainstay is virtue, his desire is to be unencumbered and his ideal is Nibbāna."

"It is wonderful, Master Gotama! It is marvellous, Master Gotama! Truly, Master Gotama knows the aim, quest, mainstay, desire, and ideal of nobles, brahmins, householders, women, thieves and ascetics. Excellent, Master Gotama!... Let Master Gotama accept me as a lay follower who has gone for refuge from this day until life's end."

(6:52)

98. THE SIMILE OF THE LUTE

Thus have I heard. On one occasion the Blessed One was dwelling at Rājagaha on Mount Vulture Peak. On that occasion the Venerable Soṇa was dwelling in the Cool Forest, near Rājagaha.[20]

While the Venerable Soṇa dwelt there alone and secluded, this thought occurred to him: "I am one of the most energetic disciples of the Blessed One, yet my mind has not attained liberation from the taints by non-clinging. Now my family is wealthy, and I can enjoy my wealth and do meritorious deeds. Let me then give up the training, return to the lower state (of a layman), enjoy my wealth and do meritorious deeds."

Then the Blessed One, perceiving in his own mind the Venerable Soṇa's thoughts, left Mount Vulture Peak; and, as speedily as a strong man might stretch his bent arm or bend his stretched arm, he appeared in the Cool Forest before the Venerable Soṇa. There he sat down on a seat prepared for him. The Venerable Soṇa, having paid homage to the Blessed One, sat down to one side, and the Blessed One said to him:

"Soṇa, weren't you just now thinking of giving up the training and returning to lay life?"

"Yes, Lord."

"Tell me, Soṇa, when in earlier days you lived at home, were you not skilled in playing the lute?"—"Yes, Lord."

"And, Soṇa, when the strings of your lute were too taut, was your lute well tuned and easy to play?"—"No, Lord."

"And when the strings of your lute were too loose, was your lute well tuned and easy to play?"—"No, Lord."

"But, Soṇa, when the strings of your lute were neither too taut nor too loose, but adjusted to an even pitch, was your lute then well tuned and easy to play?"—"Yes, Lord."

"Similarly, Soṇa, if energy is applied too forcefully it will lead to restlessness, and if energy is too lax it will lead to lassitude. Therefore, Soṇa, keep your energy in balance, penetrate to a balance of the spiritual faculties, and there seize your object."[21]

"Yes, Lord," the Venerable Soṇa replied in assent.

When the Blessed One had admonished the Venerable Soṇa with this exhortation, he vanished instantly from the Cool Forest and appeared again on Mount Vulture Peak.

Afterwards the Venerable Soṇa kept his energy balanced, penetrated to a balance of the spiritual faculties, and there seized his object. And the Venerable Soṇa, living alone and secluded, diligent, ardent and resolute, soon realized here and now, by his own direct knowledge, that unsurpassed goal of the holy life for the sake of which sons of good family rightly go forth from home to the homeless life, and entering upon it he dwelt therein. And he knew: "Destroyed is birth, the holy life has been lived, what had to be done has been done, there is no more for this world." And the Venerable Soṇa became one of the arahants.

Having reached arahantship, the Venerable Soṇa thought: "Let me go to the Blessed One and in his presence declare final knowledge." And the Venerable Soṇa went to the Blessed One, paid homage to him, and sat down to one side. So seated, he said to the Blessed One:

"A monk, O Lord, who is an arahant, one with taints destroyed, who has lived the holy life, done his task, laid down the burden, attained his goal, discarded the fetters of becoming, and is liberated by final knowledge—he is dedicated to six things: he is dedicated to renunciation, to solitude, to non-harming, to the destruction of craving, to the destruction of clinging and to non-confusion.

"Perhaps, Lord, one of the venerables here might think: 'Could it be that this venerable one is dedicated to renunciation just by relying on faith alone?' But one should not see it in that way. A monk with taints destroyed, who has lived the holy life, done his task and does not see in himself anything still to be done or to be added to what was done—such a one is dedicated to renunciation because he is free from lust through the destruction of lust; because he is free from hatred through the destruction of hatred; because he is free from delusion through the absence of delusion.

"Perhaps, Lord, one of the venerable ones here might think: 'Could it be that this venerable one is dedicated to solitude because he hankers after gain, honour and fame?... And could it be that he is dedicated to non-harming because he thinks it essential to adhere to rules and vows?' But one should not see it in that way. A monk with taints destroyed, who has lived the holy life, done his task and does not see in himself anything still to be done or to be added to what was done—such a one is dedicated to solitude ... dedicated to non-harming because he is free from lust through the destruction of lust; because he is free from hatred through the destruction of hatred; because he is free from delusion through the absence of delusion.

"It is because of his destruction of lust, hatred, and delusion, because of their absence, that he is dedicated to the destruction of craving, dedicated to the destruction of clinging, dedicated to non-confusion.

"Lord, even if forms cognizable by the eye strongly impinge on the eye faculty of a monk with a fully liberated mind, they do not overpower his mind; his heart remains untinged by them; firm and imperturbable he contemplates their transience. Even if sounds cognizable by the ear ... odours cognizable by the nose ... tastes cognizable by the tongue ... tactile objects cognizable by the body ... mind-objects cognizable by the mind strongly impinge on the mind faculty of a monk with a fully liberated mind, they do not overpower his mind; his heart remains untinged by them; firm and imperturbable he contemplates their transience.

"If, Lord, there were a rocky mountain of one solid mass, without clefts or fissures, and from any of the four directions a tempestuous rainstorm should lash down upon it, that rock could not be moved by it, could not be shaken, could not be stirred. Similarly, even very strong sense impressions will not overpower a monk whose mind is fully liberated; his mind remains untinged by them; firm and imperturbable he contemplates their transience."

If one is bent on renunciation and solitude,
Intent on harmlessness, on the end of clinging;
If one is bent on an end to craving,
Dedicated to unconfused vision,
When one has seen the arising of the sense bases,
One's mind will be entirely released.
For the monk thus freed, with peaceful mind,
There is no need to add to what he has done,
No further task or duty to perform.

Just as a rocky mountain is not moved by storms,
So sights, sounds, tastes, smells, contacts and ideas,
Whether desirable or undesirable,
Will never stir one of steady nature,
Whose mind is firm and free,
Who sees how all things pass.

(6:55)

99. A PENETRATIVE EXPOSITION

"I shall teach you, monks, a penetrative exposition,[22] a Dhamma exposition. Listen to it and attend carefully. I shall speak."—"Yes, Lord," the monks replied. The Blessed One then spoke thus:

"What now, O monks, is that penetrative exposition, that Dhamma exposition?

Sensual desires should be known; the conditioned origin of sensual desires should be known; their diversity, their outcome, their cessation, and the way leading to their cessation should be known.

Feelings should be known; the conditioned origin of feelings should be known; their diversity, their outcome, their cessation, and the way leading to their cessation should be known.

Perceptions ... The taints ... Kamma ... Suffering should be known; the conditioned origin of suffering should be known; its diversity, its outcome, its cessation, and the way leading to its cessation should be known.

(1) It was said that *sensual desires* should be known, their conditioned origin, and so forth should be known.[23] Because of what was this said?

There are five cords of sensual pleasure, namely: forms cognizable by the eye that are desirable, attractive, pleasant, endearing, associated with sensuality, and tantalizing; sounds cognizable by the ear ... odours cognizable by the nose ... tastes cognizable by the tongue ... tactile objects cognizable by the body that are desirable, attractive, pleasant, endearing, associated with sensuality, and tantalizing. These, however, are not truly sensuality; in the Noble One's Discipline they are called merely 'cords of sensual pleasure.' A man's sensuality lies in thoughts of passion.

> Sensuality does not lie in the world's pretty things;
> A man's sensuality lies in thoughts of passion.
> While the world's pretty things remain as they are,
> The wise remove the desire for them.[24]

And what, monks, is the conditioned origin of sensual desires? It is contact that is their conditioned origin.[25]

And what, monks, is the diversity of sensual desires? There is one sensual desire for forms, another for sounds, for odours, for tastes, and for tactile objects. This is called the diversity of sensual desires.

And what, monks, is the outcome of sensual desires? One motivated by sensual desire produces personalized existence born of this or that desire, belonging either to the meritorious or the demeritorious. This is called the outcome of sensual desires.[26]

And what, monks, is the cessation of sensual desires? Through the cessation of contact there is cessation of sensual desires.

And it is this Noble Eightfold Path that is the way leading to the cessation of sensual desires, namely, right view, right intention, right speech, right action, right livelihood, right effort, right mindfulness, and right concentration.

If, monks, a noble disciple in such a way knows sensual desires; if in such a way he knows the conditioned origin, the diversity, the outcome and the cessation of sensual desires, and the way leading to their cessation— he knows this penetrative holy life as the cessation of sensual desires.[27]

Because of this it was said that sensual desires should be known, their conditioned origin and so forth should be known.

(2) It was said that *feelings* should be known, their conditioned origin and so forth should be known. Because of what was this said?

There are, monks, these three kinds of feeling: pleasant feeling, painful feeling, and neither-painful-nor-pleasant feeling.

And what, monks, is the conditioned origin of feelings? It is contact that is their conditioned origin.

And what, monks, is the diversity of feelings? There are pleasant feelings that are carnal or non-carnal; unpleasant feelings that are carnal or non-carnal; and neither-painful-nor-pleasant feelings that are carnal or non-carnal. This is called the diversity of feelings.

And what, monks, is the outcome of feelings? One who

feels produces personalized existence born of this or that feeling,[28] belonging either to the meritorious or the demeritorious. This is called the outcome of feelings.

And what, monks, is the cessation of feelings? Through the cessation of contact there is cessation of feelings.

And it is this Noble Eightfold Path that is the way leading to the cessation of feelings, namely, right view ... right concentration.

If, monks, a noble disciple in such a way knows feelings; if in such a way he knows the conditioned origin, the diversity, the outcome and the cessation of feelings, and the way leading to their cessation—he knows this penetrative holy life as the cessation of feelings.

Because of this it was said that feelings should be known, their conditioned origin and so forth should be known.

(3) It was said that *perceptions* should be known, their conditioned origin and so forth should be known. Because of what was this said?

There are, monks, these six kinds of perception: perception of forms, of sounds, of odours, of tastes, of tactile objects, and of mind-objects.

And what, monks, is the conditioned origin of perceptions? It is contact that is their conditioned origin.

And what, monks, is the diversity of perceptions? There is one perception pertaining to forms, and others pertaining to sounds, odours, tastes, tactile objects, and mind-objects.

And what, monks, is the outcome of perceptions? Perceptions, I say, have communication by speech as their outcome. As one perceives a thing, so one expresses it, saying: 'So I have perceived it.'

And what, monks, is the cessation of perceptions? Through the cessation of contact there is cessation of perceptions.

And it is this Noble Eightfold Path that is the way leading to the cessation of perceptions, namely, right view ... right concentration.

If, monks, a noble disciple in such a way knows perceptions; if in such a way he knows the conditioned origin, the diversity, the outcome and the cessation of perceptions, and the way leading to their cessation—he knows this penetrative holy life as the cessation of perceptions.

Because of this it was said that perceptions should be known, their conditioned origin and so forth should be known.

(4) It was said that the *taints* should be known, their conditioned origin and so forth should be known. Because of what was this said?

There are, monks, these three taints: the taint of sensual desire, the taint of desire for becoming, and the taint of ignorance.

And what, monks, is the conditioned origin of the taints? It is ignorance that is their conditioned origin.[29]

And what, monks, is the diversity of taints? There are taints leading to the hells, to the animal realm, to the sphere of ghosts, to the human world, and to the heavenly realms.

And what, monks, is the outcome of the taints? One immersed in ignorance produces personalized existence born of this or that taint, belonging either to the meritorious or the demeritorious. This is called the outcome of the taints.

And what, monks, is the cessation of the taints? Through the cessation of ignorance there is cessation of the taints.

And it is this Noble Eightfold Path that is the way leading to the cessation of the taints, namely, right view ... right concentration.

If, monks, a noble disciple in such a way knows the taints; if in such a way he knows the conditioned origin, the diversity, the outcome and the cessation of the taints, and the way leading to their cessation—he knows this penetrative holy life as the cessation of the taints.

Because of this it was said that the taints should be known, their conditioned origin and so forth should be known.

(5) It was said that *kamma* should be known, its conditioned origin and so forth should be known. Because of what was this said?

It is volition, monks, that I declare to be kamma.[30] Having willed, one performs an action by body, speech or mind.

And what, monks, is the conditioned origin of kamma? It is contact that is its conditioned origin.

And what, monks, is the diversity of kamma? There is kamma leading to the hells, to the animal realm, to the sphere of ghosts, to the human world, and to the heavenly realms.

And what, monks, is the outcome of kamma? Kamma, I declare, has a threefold outcome: in this life, in the next life, or in subsequent future lives.[31]

And what, monks, is the cessation of kamma? Through the cessation of contact there is cessation of kamma.

And it is this Noble Eightfold Path that is the way leading to the cessation of kamma, namely, right view … right concentration.

If, monks, a noble disciple in such a way knows kamma; if in such a way he knows the conditioned origin, the diversity, the outcome and the cessation of kamma, and the way leading to its cessation—he knows this penetrative holy life as the cessation of kamma.

Because of this it was said that kamma should be known, its conditioned origin and so forth should be known.

(6) It was said that *suffering* should be known, its conditioned origin and so forth should be known. Because of what was this said?

Birth is suffering; ageing is suffering; illness is suffering; death is suffering; sorrow, lamentation, pain, grief, and despair are suffering; not to get what one wants is suffering; in brief, the five aggregates subject to clinging are suffering.

And what, monks, is the conditioned origin of suffering? Craving is the conditioned origin of suffering.

And what, monks, is the diversity of suffering? There is intense suffering and moderate suffering; there is suffering that fades away slowly and suffering that fades away quickly.

And what, monks, is the outcome of suffering? There is a person who is overwhelmed by suffering, his mind in the grip of suffering: he grieves, moans, laments, beats his breast, weeps and becomes deranged; or in his misery he searches outside for a remedy: 'Who knows a word or two for bringing my suffering to an end?' Hence I say, the outcome of suffering is either derangement or search.

And what, monks, is the cessation of suffering? With the cessation of craving there is cessation of suffering.

And it is this Noble Eightfold Path that is the way leading to the cessation of suffering, namely, right view, right intention, right speech, right action, right livelihood, right effort, right mindfulness, and right concentration.

If, monks, a noble disciple in such a way knows suffering; if in such a way he knows the conditioned origin, the diversity, the outcome and the cessation of suffering, and the way leading to its cessation—he knows this penetrative holy life as the cessation of suffering.

Because of this it was said that suffering should be known, its conditioned origin and so forth should be known.

This, O monks, is the penetrative exposition, a Dhamma exposition."

(6:63)

100. Non-returning

Without having given up six qualities, O monks, one will be incapable of realizing the fruit of non-returning.[32] What six? Lack of faith, lack of moral shame, lack of moral dread, laziness, lack of mindfulness and lack of wisdom. But by giving up these six qualities one will be capable of realizing the fruit of non-returning.

(6:65)

101. Arahantship

Without having given up six qualities, O monks, one will be incapable of realizing arahantship. What six?

(AN 6:66) Sloth, torpor, restlessness, worry, lack of faith, and negligence.

(AN 6:76) Conceit, inferiority-conceit, superiority-conceit, self-overrating, obstinacy, and servility.

But by giving up these six qualities one will be capable of realizing arahantship.

(6:66, 76)

102. SIX RARITIES

These six things, O monks, rarely appear in the world: Rare in the world is the appearance of a Tathāgata. Rare in the world is the appearance of one who teaches the Dhamma and Discipline proclaimed by the Tathāgata. Rare in the world is it to be reborn in the land of the noble ones. Rare in the world is the possession of unimpaired physical and mental faculties. Rare in the world is absence of stupidity and dullness. Rare in the world is a desire for wholesome qualities.[33]

(6:96)

103. THE BLESSINGS OF STREAM-ENTRY

There are, O monks, these six blessings in realizing the fruit of stream-entry: One is firm in the good Dhamma. One is unable to fall back. One has set a limit to suffering. One is endowed with uncommon knowledge. One has clearly understood causes and the phenomena arisen by causes.[34]

(6:97)

104. CONVICTION IN CONFORMITY WITH THE DHAMMA

Truly, O monks, that a monk who considers any formation as permanent; any formation as pleasant; anything as a self; Nibbāna as suffering, can have a conviction that conforms with the Dhamma,[35] that cannot be; and that one who is without a conviction that conforms with the Dhamma should enter into the certainty of rightness, that too cannot be; and that one who has not entered into the certainty of rightness should realize the fruits of stream-entry, once-returning, non-returning, or arahantship, that too cannot be.[36]

(6:98–101; combined)

105. Advantages of Contemplating Impermanence

When a monk sees six advantages, it should be enough for him to establish the perception of impermanence in all formations without exception. What six?

"All formations will appear to me as transient. My mind will not delight in anything worldly. My mind will emerge from all the world. My mind will incline to Nibbāna. The fetters will be discarded by me. And I shall be endowed with the status of a supreme ascetic."[37]

(6:102)

106. Advantages of Contemplating Suffering

When a monk sees six advantages, it should be enough for him to establish the perception of suffering in all formations without exception. What six?

"A perception of revulsion will be present in me towards all formations, as towards a murderer with raised sword. My mind will emerge from all the world. I shall come to see the peace in Nibbāna. The underlying tendencies will come to be uprooted. I shall be one who has completed his task. And I shall have served the Master with loving-kindness."[38]

(6:103)

107. Advantages of Contemplating Non-self

When a monk sees six advantages, it should be enough for him to establish the perception of non-self in all things without exception.[39] What six?

"I shall be aloof from all the world. Notions of 'I' will vanish in me. Notions of 'mine' will vanish in me. I shall be endowed with uncommon knowledge. I shall clearly understand causes and the phenomena arisen from causes."

(6:104)

VII. The Chapter of the Sevens

108. Getting Rid of Drowsiness

Thus have I heard. On one occasion the Blessed One was dwelling in the Bhagga country near the town of Suṃsumāragiri, in the Deer Park at the Bhesakalā Grove. On that occasion the Venerable Mahāmoggallāna, dwelling in Māgadha near the village of Kallavāḷamutta, was nodding in his seat.[1]

The Blessed One saw this with the divine eye, purified and superhuman. Having seen this, he vanished from the Deer Park at the Bhesakalā Grove and, as speedily as a strong man might stretch his bent arm or bend his stretched arm, he appeared before the Venerable Mahāmoggallāna. The Blessed One sat down on the seat prepared for him and said to the Venerable Mahāmoggallāna:

"Are you nodding, Moggallāna, are you nodding?"—"Yes, Lord."

(1) "Well then, Moggallāna, at whatever thought drowsiness befalls you, you should not give attention to that thought. Then, by doing so, it is possible that your drowsiness will vanish.

(2) "But if, by doing so, your drowsiness does not vanish, then you should ponder the Dhamma as you have learnt it and mastered it, you should examine it and investigate it closely in your mind. Then, by doing so, it is possible that your drowsiness will vanish.

(3) "But if, by doing so, your drowsiness does not vanish, then you should recite in detail the Dhamma as you have learnt it and mastered it. Then, by doing so, it is possible that your drowsiness will vanish.

(4) "But if, by doing so, your drowsiness does not vanish, then you should pull both ear-lobes and rub your limbs with your hand. Then, by doing so, it is possible that your drowsiness will vanish.

(5) "But if, by doing so, your drowsiness does not vanish, you should get up from your seat and, after washing your eyes

with water, you should look around in all directions and upwards to the stars and constellations. Then, by doing so, it is possible that your drowsiness will vanish.

(6) "But if, by doing so, your drowsiness does not vanish, then you should attend to the perception of light, resolve upon the perception of daytime: as by day, so at night, as at night, so by day. Thus, with an open and unencumbered heart, you should develop a luminous mind. Then, by doing so, it is possible that your drowsiness will vanish.

(7) "But if, by doing so, your drowsiness does not vanish, then, with your senses turned inward and your mind not straying outward, you should take to walking up and down, being aware of going to and fro. Then, by doing so, it is possible that your drowsiness will vanish.

"But if, by doing so, your drowsiness does not vanish, then, mindful and clearly comprehending, you may lie down, lion-like, on your right side, placing one foot on the other, keeping in mind the thought of rising; and on awakening, you should quickly get up, thinking, 'I must not indulge in the pleasure of resting and reclining, in the pleasure of sleep.'

"Thus, Moggallāna, should you train yourself.

"Further, Moggallāna, you should train yourself by thinking: You should think, 'When calling at families (on the alms round), I shall not be given to pride.' Thus should you train yourself.

"For in families it may happen that people are busy with work and may not notice that a monk has come. Then a monk (if given to pride) may think, 'Who, I wonder, has estranged me from this family? These people seem to be displeased with me.' Thus, by not receiving (alms-food from them), he is perturbed; being perturbed, he becomes excited; being excited, he loses self-control; and if he is uncontrolled, his mind will be far from concentration.

"Further, Moggallāna, you should train yourself in this way: 'I shall not speak contentious talk.' Thus should you train yourself. If there is contentious talk, there is sure to be much wordiness; with much wordiness, there will be excitement; he who is excited will loose self-control; and if he is uncontrolled, his mind will be far from concentration.

"I do not, Moggallāna, praise all companionship, nor do I blame all companionship. I do not praise companionship with monks and lay folk. But companionship with dwellings where there are few sounds and little noise, which are fanned by cool breezes, remote from human habitation, suitable for seclusion—this do I praise."

After these words the Venerable Mahāmoggallāna said to the Blessed One: "In what way, Lord, can it be explained briefly how a monk is liberated through the elimination of craving—one who has reached the final end, the final security from bondage, the final holy life, the final consummation, and is foremost among devas and humans?"[2]

"Here, Moggallāna, a monk has learnt this: 'Nothing is fit to be clung to.'[3] If a monk has learnt that nothing is fit to be clung to, he directly knows everything; by directly knowing everything, he fully understands everything; when he fully understands everything, whatever feeling he experiences, be it pleasant, painful or neither-painful-nor-pleasant, in regard to those same feelings he dwells contemplating impermanence, contemplating dispassion, contemplating cessation, contemplating relinquishment.[4] When he thus abides contemplating impermanence, dispassion, cessation, and relinquishment in regard to those feelings, he does not cling to anything in the world; without clinging he is not agitated; being unagitated, he personally attains Nibbāna. He understands: 'Destroyed is birth, the holy life has been lived, what had to be done has been done, there is no more for this world.'

"That, Moggallāna, briefly put, is how a monk is liberated through the elimination of craving—one who has reached the final end, the final security from bondage, the final holy life, the final consummation, and is foremost among devas and humans."[5]

(7:58A)

109. Loving-kindness[6]

Monks, do not be afraid of deeds of merit![7] They are equivalent to happiness, these deeds of merit. For I know very well that for a long time I have experienced desirable, pleasant and agreeable results from meritorious deeds often performed.

For seven years I cultivated thoughts of loving-kindness. Having cultivated a heart full of loving-kindness for seven years, I did not return to this world for seven aeons of world-contraction and world-expansion.[8] Whenever a world was destroyed, I entered (by way of rebirth) among the devas of Streaming Radiance, and when the world unfolded again, I was reborn in an empty Brahma-palace.[9] And there I was Mahābrahmā, the unvanquished victor, all-powerful. And thirty-six times I was Sakka, ruler of the devas, and many hundred times I was a universal monarch, a just and righteous king.

(7:58B; selected)

110. Seven Kinds of Wives

On one occasion the Blessed One was dwelling at Sāvatthī in Jeta's Grove, Anāthapiṇḍika's monastery. In the morning the Blessed One dressed, took his bowl and robe, and went to Anāthapiṇḍika's house, where he sat down in a seat prepared for him. On that occasion people in the house were making an uproar and a racket. The householder Anāthapiṇḍika approached the Blessed One, paid homage to him, and sat down to one side. The Blessed One then said to him: "Why are people in your house making this uproar and racket, householder? One would think they were fishermen making a haul of fish."

"That, Lord, is our daughter-in-law Sujātā. She is rich and has been brought here from a rich family. She does not obey her father-in-law and mother-in-law, nor her husband. She does not even honour, respect, esteem and venerate the Blessed One."

Then the Blessed One called the daughter-in-law Sujātā, saying, "Come, Sujātā."

"Yes, Lord," she replied, and she went to the Blessed One, paid homage to him, and sat down to one side. The Blessed One then said to her: "There are these seven kinds of wives, Sujātā. What seven? One like a slayer, one like a thief, one like a tyrant, one like a mother, one like a sister, one like a friend, and one like a handmaid. These are the seven kinds of wives. Now which of these seven are you?"

"I do not understand in detail the meaning of the Blessed One's brief statement. It would be good, Lord, if the Blessed One would teach me the Dhamma in such a way that I might understand the meaning in detail."

"Then listen, Sujātā, and attend carefully. I will speak."

"Yes, Lord," the daughter-in-law Sujātā replied. The Blessed One said this:

With hateful mind, cold and heartless,
Lusting for others, despising her husband;
Who seeks to kill the one who bought her—
Such a wife is called *a slayer.*

When her husband acquires wealth
By his craft or trade or farm work,
She tries to filch a little for herself—
Such a wife is called *a thief.*

The slothful glutton, bent on idling,
Harsh, fierce, rough in speech,
A woman who bullies her own supporter—
Such a wife is called *a tyrant.*

One who is always helpful and kind,
Who guards her husband as a mother her son,
Who carefully protects the wealth he earns—
Such a wife is called *a mother.*

She who holds her husband in high regard
As younger sister holds the elder born,
Who humbly submits to her husband's will—
Such a wife is called *a sister.*

One who rejoices at her husband's sight
As one friend might welcome another,
Well raised, virtuous, devoted –
Such a wife is called *a friend*.

One without anger, afraid of punishment,
Who bears with her husband free of hate,
Who humbly submits to her husband's will—
Such a wife is called *a handmaid*.[10]

The types of wives here called a slayer,
A thief, and the wife like a tyrant,
These kinds of wives, with the body's breakup,
Will be reborn deep in hell.

But wives like mother, sister, friend,
And the wife called a handmaid,
Steady in virtue, long restrained,
With the body's breakup go to heaven.

"These, Sujātā, are the seven kinds of wives. Now which of these are you?"
"Beginning today, Lord, you should consider me a wife who is like a handmaid."

(7:59)

111. Mental Development

Monks, although a monk who does not apply himself to the meditative development of his mind[11] may wish, "Oh, that my mind might be freed from the taints by non-clinging!," yet his mind will not be freed. For what reason? "Because he has not developed his mind," one has to say. Not developed it in what? In the four foundations of mindfulness, the four right kinds of striving, the four bases of success, the five spiritual faculties, the five spiritual powers, the seven factors of enlightenment and the Noble Eightfold Path.[12]

Suppose, monks, a hen has eight, ten or twelve eggs, but she does not sit on them sufficiently long and they are not well warmed, not developed enough for hatching. Alhough that hen may wish, "Oh, that my chicks might break the egg shells with their claws and beaks and emerge safely!," yet these chicks will not be able to do so. For what reason? Because the hen did not sit on the eggs sufficiently long, so that they are not well warmed and developed enough for hatching. Similarly is it with a monk who has not applied himself to the meditative development of his mind.

If, however, a monk has applied himself to the meditative development of his mind, even if he should not wish, "Oh, that my mind might be freed from the taints by non-clinging!," still his mind will be freed. For what reason? "Because he has developed his mind," one has to say. Developed it in what? In the four foundations of mindfulness, the four right efforts, the four bases of success, the five spiritual faculties, the five spiritual powers, the seven factors of enlightenment and the Noble Eightfold Path.

Suppose, monks, a hen has eight, ten or twelve eggs, and she has sat on them sufficiently long, so that they are well warmed and developed enough for hatching. Even if that hen did not wish, "Oh, that my chickens might break the egg shells with their claws and beaks and emerge safely!," still the chicks will break through the shells and emerge safely. For what reason? Because the hen sat on the eggs sufficiently long, so that they are well warmed and developed enough for hatching. Similarly is it with a monk who has applied himself to the meditative development of his mind.

Suppose, monks, a carpenter has an axe and its handle shows the marks of his fingers and thumb. He will not know that so much of the handle has worn away today, so much yesterday and so much at other times; but he will just know of what is wasted that it has worn away. It is similar with a monk who applies himself to the meditative development of his mind: though he has no knowledge that so much of the taints has worn away today, so much yesterday and so much at other times, yet he knows of what is wasted that it is worn away.

Or suppose, monks, an ocean-going boat rigged with ropes, having been exposed to the water for six months, has been dragged to the shore for the winter. Then the ropes that had been affected by wind and sun, when soaked by the monsoon rains, will easily go to waste and rot away. It is similar with a monk who applies himself to the meditative development of his mind: his fetters will easily be loosened and rot away.

(7:67)

112. Life's Brevity

Long ago, O monks, there lived a religious teacher named Araka, who was free of sensual lust. He had many hundreds of disciples, and this was the doctrine he taught to them:

"Short is the life of human beings, O brahmins, limited and brief; it is full of suffering, full of tribulation. This one should wisely understand. One should do good and live a pure life; for none who is born can escape death.

"Just as a dew drop on the tip of a blade of grass will quickly vanish at sunrise and will not last long; even so, brahmins, is human life like a dew drop. It is short, limited, and brief; it is full of suffering, full of tribulation. This one should wisely understand. One should do good and live a pure life; for none who is born can escape death.

"Just as, when rain falls from the sky in thick drops, a bubble appearing on the water will quickly vanish and will not last long; even so, brahmins, is human life like a water bubble. It is short ... for none who is born can escape death.

"Just as a line drawn on water with a stick will quickly vanish and will not last long; even so, brahmins, is human life like a line drawn on water. It is short ... for none who is born can escape death.

"Just as a mountain stream, coming from afar, swiftly flowing, carrying along much flotsam, will not stand still for a moment, an instant, a second, but will rush on, swirl and flow forward; even so, brahmins, is human life like a mountain stream. It is short ... for none who is born can escape death.

"Just as a strong man might form a lump of spittle at the tip of his tongue and spit it out with ease; even so, brahmins, is human life like a lump of spittle. It is short … for none who is born can escape death.

"Just as a piece of meat thrown into an iron pan heated all day will quickly burn up and will not last long; even so, brahmins, is human life like this piece of meat. It is short … for none who is born can escape death.

"Just as, when a cow to be slaughtered is led to the shambles, whenever she lifts a leg she will be closer to slaughter, closer to death; even so, brahmins, is human life like cattle doomed to slaughter; it is short, limited and brief. It is full of suffering, full of tribulation. This one should wisely understand. One should do good and live a pure life; for none who is born can escape death."

But at that time, O monks, the human lifespan was 60,000 years, and at 500 years girls were marriageable. In those days people had but six afflictions: cold, heat, hunger, thirst, excrement and urine. Though people lived so long and had so few afflictions, that teacher Araka gave to his disciples such a teaching: "Short is the life of human beings …."

But nowadays, O monks, one could rightly say, "Short is the life of human beings …"; for today one who lives long lives for a hundred years or a little more. And when living for a hundred years, it is just for three hundred seasons: a hundred winters, a hundred summers, and a hundred rains. When living for three hundred seasons, it is just for twelve hundred months: four hundred winter months, four hundred summer months and four hundred months of the rains. When living for twelve hundred months, it is just for twenty-four hundred fortnights: eight hundred fortnights of winter, eight hundred of summer and eight hundred of the rains.

And when living for twenty-four hundred fortnights, it is just for 36,000 days: 12,000 days of winter, 12,000 of summer and 12,000 of the rains. And when living for 36,000 days, he eats just 72,000 meals: 24,000 meals in winter, 24,000 in summer, and 24,000 in the rains. And this includes the taking of mother's milk and the times without food. These are the times without food: when agitated or grieved or sick, when observing a fast or when not obtaining anything to eat.

Thus, O monks, I have reckoned the life of a centenarian: the limit of his lifespan, the number of seasons, of years, months, and fortnights, of days and nights, of his meals and foodless times.

Whatever should be done by a compassionate teacher who, out of compassion, seeks the welfare of his disciples, that I have done for you. These are the roots of trees, O monks; these are empty huts. Meditate, monks, do not be negligent, lest you regret it later. This is our instruction to you.

(7:70)

113. THE MASTER'S TEACHING

On one occasion the Venerable Upāli approached the Blessed One.[13] Having arrived, he paid homage to the Blessed One, sat down to one side, and said:

"It would be good, Lord, if the Blessed One would teach me the Dhamma in brief, so that having heard the Dhamma from the Blessed One, I might dwell alone, withdrawn, diligent, ardent and resolute."

"When, Upāli, you know of certain things: 'These things do not lead to complete revulsion, to dispassion, cessation, and peace, to direct knowledge, enlightenment, and Nibbāna'—of such teachings you may be certain: 'This is not the Dhamma; this is not the Discipline; this is not the Master's Teaching.'

"But, Upāli, when you know of certain things: 'These things lead to complete revulsion, to dispassion, cessation, and peace, to direct knowledge, enlightenment, and Nibbāna'—of such things you may be certain: 'This is the Dhamma; this is the Discipline; this is the Master's Teaching.'"

(7:79)

VIII. The Chapter of the Eights

114. Vicissitudes of Life

"These eight worldly conditions, O monks, keep the world turning around, and the world turns around these eight worldly conditions. What eight? Gain and loss, fame and disrepute, praise and blame, pleasure and pain.

"These eight worldly conditions, monks, are encountered by an uninstructed worldling, and they are also encountered by an instructed noble disciple. What now is the distinction, the disparity, the difference between an instructed noble disciple and an uninstructed worldling?"

"Lord, our knowledge of these things has its roots in the Blessed One; it has the Blessed One as guide and resort. It would be good indeed, Lord, if the meaning of that statement would be explained by the Blessed One. Having heard it from him, the monks will bear it in mind."

"Listen then, monks, and attend carefully. I shall speak."

"Yes, Lord," the monks replied. The Blessed One then spoke thus:

"When an uninstructed worldling, O monks, comes upon gain, he does not reflect on it thus: 'This gain that has come to me is impermanent, bound up with suffering, subject to change.' He does not know it as it really is. And when he comes upon loss, fame and disrepute, praise and blame, he does not reflect on them thus: 'All these are impermanent, bound up with suffering, subject to change.' He does not know them as they really are. With such a person, gain and loss ... pleasure and pain keep his mind engrossed. When gain comes he is elated and when he meets with loss he is dejected. When fame comes he is elated and when he meets with disrepute he is dejected. When praise comes he is elated and when he meets with blame he is dejected. When he experiences pleasure he is elated and when he experiences pain he is dejected. Being thus involved in likes and dislikes, he will not be freed from birth, ageing and death, from sorrow, lamentation, pain, grief, and despair; he will not be freed from suffering, I declare.

"But, O monks, when an instructed noble disciple comes upon gain, he reflects on it thus: 'This gain that has come to me is impermanent, bound up with suffering, subject to change.' And so he will reflect when loss and so forth come upon him. He understands all these things as they really are, and they do not engross his mind. Thus he will not be elated by gain or dejected by loss; elated by fame or dejected by disrepute; elated by praise or dejected by blame; elated by pleasure or dejected by pain. Having thus given up likes and dislikes, he will be freed from birth, ageing and death, from sorrow, lamentation, from pain, grief, and despair; he will be freed from suffering, I declare.

"This, monks, is the distinction, the disparity, the difference between an instructed noble disciple and an uninstructed worldling."

Loss and gain, disrepute and fame,
Praise and blame, pleasure and pain —
These things are transient in human life,
Inconstant and bound to change.
The mindful wise one discerns them well,
Observant of their alterations.
Pleasant things do not stir his mind
And those unpleasant do not annoy him.
All likes and dislikes are dispelled by him,
Eliminated and abolished.
Aware now of the stainless, griefless state,[1]
He fully knows, having gone beyond."

(8:6)

115. Nanda

When speaking of Nanda, O monks, one may rightly say that he is of good family, that he is strong and handsome and very passionate.[2]

How else could Nanda live the perfect and pure holy life except by guarding the sense doors, by being moderate in eating, by cultivating wakefulness and by setting up mindfulness and clear comprehension?

This, monks, is how Nanda guards his sense doors. If Nanda has to look to the east, he does so only after having considered everything well in his mind: "While I am looking to the east, I will not let covetousness and grief, or other evil, unwholesome states, enter my mind." Thus he has clear comprehension.

If he has to look to the west, south, or north, he does so only after having considered everything well in his mind: "While I am looking to the west, south, or north, I will not let covetousness and grief, or other evil, unwholesome states, enter my mind." Thus he has clear comprehension.

This, monks, is Nanda's moderation in eating. Here, monks, Nanda takes his food wisely reflecting that it is neither for enjoyment, nor for indulgence, nor for physical beauty and attractiveness, but only for the upkeep and sustenance of this body, for avoiding harm to it and for supporting the holy life, thinking: 'Thus I shall put a stop to old feelings (of hunger) and shall not arouse new feelings, and I shall be healthy and blameless and live in comfort.' This, monks, is Nanda's moderation in eating.

This, monks, is how Nanda cultivates wakefulness. Here, monks, Nanda purifies his mind from obstructive thoughts during the day while walking back and forth or sitting; and so during the first watch of the night, (likewise) while walking and sitting; during the middle watch he lies down, lion-like, on his right side, placing one foot on the other, keeping in mind the thought of rising; rising in the last watch of the night, he again purifies his mind from obstructive thoughts while walking back and forth and sitting. This is Nanda's cultivation of wakefulness.

This, monks, is Nanda's mindfulness and clear comprehension. Here, monks, for Nanda feelings are understood as they arise, as they remain present, as they pass away; perceptions are understood as they arise, as they remain present, as they pass away; thoughts are understood as they arise, as they remain present, as they pass away. This, monks, is Nanda's mindfulness and clear comprehension.

How else, O monks, could Nanda live the perfect and pure holy life, except by guarding the sense doors, by being moderate in eating, by cultivating wakefulness and by setting up mindfulness and clear comprehension?

(8:9)

116. SĪHA THE GENERAL

One day, Sīha the general approached the Blessed One and said to him:

"I have heard it said, venerable sir, that the ascetic Gotama is a teacher of inaction, that he teaches his doctrine for inculcating a life of inaction, and in that he trains his disciples. Do those who say so, venerable sir, truly report the Blessed One's words without misrepresenting him? Is their assertion in accordance with his doctrine, so that their statement will not give cause for reproach? We certainly do not wish to misrepresent the Blessed One."

"There is indeed a way, Sīha, in which one can rightly say of me that I am a teacher of inaction; and there is also a way in which one can say that I am a teacher of action.

I do teach people to be inactive in regard to evil conduct in deeds, words, and thoughts; I teach inaction in regard to the multitude of evil, unwholesome qualities. But I also teach people to be active by way of good conduct in deeds, words, and thoughts; I teach action in regard to the multitude of wholesome qualities.

There is also a way in which one can rightly say that I am an annihilationist. For I teach the annihilation of greed, hatred, and delusion; I teach the annihilation of the multitude of evil, unwholesome qualities."

(8:12; extract)

117. THE SIMILE OF THE OCEAN

On one occasion the Blessed One was dwelling at Verañjā, at the foot of Naḷeru's nimba tree.[3] There Pahārāda, a chief of the asuras, approached the Blessed One, and having paid homage to him, he stood to one side. The Blessed One then spoke to Pahārāda thus:

"I suppose, Pahārāda, the asuras find delight in the great ocean."

"They do, Lord."

"Now, Pahārāda, how many wonderful and marvellous qualities do the asuras again and again perceive in the great ocean so that they take delight in it?"

"There are, Lord, eight wonderful and marvellous qualities which the asuras again and again perceive in the great ocean by reason of which they take delight in it. These are the eight:

(1) The great ocean, Lord, slopes away gradually, falls gradually, inclines gradually, not in an abrupt way like a precipice. This is the first wonderful and marvellous quality that the asuras perceive in the great ocean by reason of which they take delight in it.

(2) The great ocean is stable and does not overflow its boundaries. This is the second wonderful and marvellous quality....

(3) The great ocean does not tolerate a dead body, a corpse; if there is a dead body in it, the great ocean will quickly carry it to the shore and cast it on to the land. This is the third wonderful and marvellous quality....

(4) When those mighty rivers—the Ganges, the Yamunā, the Aciravatī, the Sarabhū and the Mahī—reach the great ocean, they lose their former names and designations and are reckoned just as the great ocean. This is the fourth wonderful and marvellous quality....

(5) Though all the streams of the world flow into the great ocean and rain falls into it from the sky, yet there appears neither a decrease nor an increase in the great ocean. This is the fifth wonderful and marvellous quality....

(6) The great ocean has but one taste, the taste of salt. This is the sixth wonderful and marvellous quality....

(7) In the great ocean, there are many and variegated precious substances: pearls, gems, lapis lazuli, shells, quartz, corals, silver, gold, rubies, and cats-eyes. This is the seventh wonderful and marvellous quality....

(8) The great ocean is the abode of vast creatures: the timi, the timiṅgala, the timirapiṅgala, asuras, nāgas, and gandhabbas.[4] There are in the great ocean beings one hundred yojanas long, or two, three, four and five hundred yojanas long. This is the eighth wonderful and marvellous quality that the asuras perceive in the great ocean by reason of which they take delight in it.

"These, Lord, are the eight wonderful and marvellous qualities which the asuras again and again perceive in the great ocean by reason of which they take delight in it. I suppose, Lord, the monks take delight in this Dhamma and Discipline?"

"They do, Pahārāda."

"But, Lord, how many wonderful and marvellous qualities do the monks again and again perceive in this Dhamma and Discipline by reason of which they take delight in it?"

"There are, Pahārāda, eight wonderful and marvellous qualities in this Dhamma and Discipline, which the monks again and again perceive by reason of which they take delight in it. These are the eight:

(1) Just as the great ocean slopes away gradually, falls gradually, inclines gradually, not in an abrupt way like a precipice; even so, Pahārāda, is this Dhamma and Discipline: there is a gradual training, gradual practice, gradual progress; there is no penetration to final knowledge in an abrupt way.[5] This is the first wonderful and marvellous quality in this Dhamma and Discipline, which the monks perceive by reason of which they take delight in it.

(2) Just as the great ocean is stable and does not overflow its boundaries; even so when I have made known a rule of training to my disciples, they will not transgress it even for life's sake.[6] This is the second wonderful and marvellous quality in this Dhamma and Discipline....

(3) Just as the great ocean will not tolerate a dead body, a corpse, but quickly carries it to the shore and casts it on to the land; even so the Sangha will not tolerate within its ranks a person who is immoral, of bad character, of impure and suspicious conduct, secretive in his actions, not a true ascetic but rather a sham-ascetic, not chaste but pretending to be chaste, rotten to the core, lustful and of vile behaviour. In such a case, the Sangha quickly assembles and expels such a person. Even if seated in the midst of the monks' assembly, yet he is far from the Sangha and the Sangha is far from him. This is the third wonderful and marvellous quality in this Dhamma and Discipline....

(4) Just as the mighty rivers on reaching the great ocean lose their former names and designations and are just reckoned as the great ocean; even so, when members of the four castes—nobles, brahmins, commoners and menials—go forth from home into the homeless life in this Dhamma and Discipline proclaimed by the Tathāgata, they lose their former names and lineage and are reckoned only as ascetics following the Son of the Sakyans. This is the fourth wonderful and marvellous quality in this Dhamma and Discipline....

(5) Just as in the great ocean neither a decrease nor an increase will appear though all the streams of the world flow into it and rain falls into it from the sky; even so, even if many monks attain final Nibbāna in the Nibbāna element that is without residue left, there is no decrease or increase in the Nibbāna element that is without residue left.[7] This is the fifth wonderful and marvellous quality in this Dhamma and Discipline....

(6) Just as the great ocean has but one taste, the taste of salt; even so this Dhamma and Discipline has but one taste, the taste of liberation. This is the sixth wonderful and marvellous quality in this Dhamma and Discipline....

(7) Just as in the great ocean there are many and variegated precious substances such as pearls, gems, etc.; even so in this Dhamma and Discipline there is much that is precious. These are the precious things in it: the four

foundations of mindfulness, the four right efforts, the four bases of success, the five spiritual faculties, the five spiritual powers, the seven factors of enlightenment, the Noble Eightfold Path.[8] This is the seventh wonderful and marvellous quality in this Dhamma and Discipline....

(8) Just as the great ocean is the abode of vast creatures; even so is this Dhamma and Discipline the domain of great beings: the stream-enterer and one practising for the realization of the fruit of stream-entry; the once-returner and one practising for the realization of the fruit of once-returning; the non-returner and one practising for the realization of the fruit of non-returning; the arahant and one practising for arahantship. This is the eighth wonderful and marvellous quality in this Dhamma and Discipline, which the monks perceive again and again by reason of which they take delight in it.

"These, Pahārāda, are the eight wonderful and marvellous qualities in this Dhamma and Discipline, which the monks perceive again and again by reason of which they take delight in it."

(8:19)

118. THE HOUSEHOLDER UGGA

On one occasion the Blessed One was dwelling at Vesālī in the Great Wood in the Hall with the Peaked Roof. There the Blessed One addressed the monks thus:

"Monks, you should know that Ugga the householder has eight wonderful and marvellous qualities."[9]

Having said this, the Blessed One rose from his seat and entered his dwelling.

Now one of the monks, having dressed in the morning and taken robe and bowl, went to the house of Ugga the householder. Having arrived there, he sat down on the seat prepared for him. And Ugga the householder came and, after saluting the monk, sat down to one side.

When Ugga was seated, the monk said to him: "The Blessed One has declared that eight wonderful and marvellous qualities can be found in you, householder. What are those eight qualities?"

"I do not know, venerable sir, the eight wonderful and marvellous qualities ascribed to me by the Blessed One. But as to those wonderful and marvellous qualities that can be found in me, listen and attend carefully, and I shall tell you."

"Yes, householder," replied the monk. Ugga the householder then said:

(1) "When, venerable sir, I first saw the Blessed One at a distance, at the very sight my heart had trust in him. This is the first wonderful and marvellous quality found in me.

(2) "With trusting heart I then waited upon the Blessed One. And the Blessed One gave me a gradual instruction, namely, a talk on giving, on virtue, on the heavens, on the danger, vanity and impurity of sensual pleasures and on the advantages of renunciation. When the Blessed One saw that my mind was prepared, susceptible, free of hindrances, elevated and lucid, he then revealed to me that Dhamma instruction particular to the Buddhas, namely, suffering, its origin, its cessation, and the path. Just as a clean cloth, free of stain, would take the dye perfectly, even so while I was seated at that place, there arose in me the spotless, stainless vision of the Dhamma: 'Whatever is subject to origination is all subject to cessation.' And having thus seen the Dhamma, attained to the Dhamma, understood the Dhamma, penetrated the Dhamma, having overcome doubt, cast off uncertainty and obtained assurance without depending on others in the Master's Teaching[10]—on that very occasion I went for refuge to the Buddha, the Dhamma and the Sangha, and I took upon myself the (five) precepts of training with celibacy as the fifth.[11] This is the second wonderful and marvellous quality found in me.

(3) "I had, venerable sir, four young wives, and I went and said to them: 'Sisters, I have taken upon myself the precepts of training with celibacy as the fifth. If you wish you may continue to enjoy even here the wealth (of this place) and do good deeds; or if you wish, you may go back to your own family and relatives; or if you wish to marry another man, tell

me to whom I should give you.' After I had spoken, the eldest wife said: 'Sir, give me to a man of such and such a name.' Then, venerable sir, I sent for that man, and taking my wife's hand with my left hand and the waterpot with the right,[12] I handed her over to that man. And while thus giving up my youthful wife I did not know of any change in the composure of my heart. This is the third wonderful and marvellous quality found in me.

(4) "There are, venerable sir, riches in my family, and these I distribute impartially among those who are virtuous and of good character. This is the fourth wonderful and marvellous quality found in me.

(5) "When, venerable sir, I attend upon a monk, I do it respectfully and not with disrespect. This is the fifth wonderful and marvellous quality found in me.

(6) "If, venerable sir, that venerable monk preaches the Dhamma to me, I listen respectfully and not with disrespect. But if he does not preach, then I preach the Dhamma to him. This is the sixth wonderful and marvellous quality found in me.

(7) "It is not unusual, venerable sir, that devas come to me and declare, 'Well proclaimed by the Blessed One is the Dhamma, householder!' When they speak thus, I reply to those deities: 'Well, whether you deities say so or not, the Dhamma is indeed well proclaimed by the Blessed One.' But, venerable sir, I am not aware of any proud elation of mind in me because devas visit me or because I converse with them. This is the seventh wonderful and marvellous quality found in me.

(8) "There are, venerable sir, five lower fetters declared by the Blessed One, yet I am not aware of even a single one among these which I have still not abandoned.[13] This is the eighth wonderful and marvellous quality found in me.

"These eight wonderful and marvellous qualities are found in me, venerable sir. I do not know, however, which eight qualities the Blessed One may have ascribed to me."

Then that monk, after receiving alms at Ugga's house, rose from his seat and left. Having returned from the alms round, after his meal he went to see the Blessed One and he reported to the Blessed One his conversation with the householder Ugga of Vesālī. (The Blessed One then said:)

"Well said, monk, well said! Just as the householder Ugga of Vesālī has rightly explained it, even so have I declared him to be endowed with these very same eight wonderful and marvellous qualities. And you may remember him, monk, as thus endowed with these eight qualities."

(8:21)

119. THE LAY FOLLOWER

On one occasion the Blessed One was dwelling at Kapilavatthu, in the Banyan-tree Monastery. There Mahānāma the Sakyan approached the Blessed One and, after paying homage to him, sat down at one side. So seated, he addressed the Blessed One and asked:

"How, Lord, is one a lay follower?"

"If, Mahānāma, one has gone for refuge to the Buddha, the Dhamma, and the Sangha, one is a lay follower."

"But how, Lord, is a lay follower virtuous?"

"If, Mahānāma, a lay follower abstains from the destruction of life, from taking what is not given, from sexual misconduct, from false speech and from wines, liquor and intoxicants which are a basis for negligence, the lay follower is virtuous."

"And how, Lord, does a lay follower live for his own welfare but not for the welfare of others?"

"If, Mahānāma, a lay follower has faith, virtue and generosity himself, but does not encourage others in gaining faith, virtue and generosity; if he himself likes to visit monks and to listen to the good Dhamma, but does not encourage others to do so; if he himself retains in mind the teachings heard and carefully examines the meaning of those teachings, but does not encourage others to do so; if, having understood both the letter and the meaning, he himself lives in conformity with the Dhamma, but does not encourage others to do so—in such a case, Mahānāma, a lay follower lives for his own welfare but not for the welfare of others."

"And how, Lord, does a lay follower live for the welfare of both himself and others?"

"If, Mahānāma, a lay follower himself has faith, virtue and generosity, and also encourages others in gaining them; if he himself likes to visit monks and to listen to the good Dhamma, and he also encourages others to do so; if he himself retains in mind the teachings heard and carefully examines their meaning, and he also encourages others to do so; if, having understood both the letter and the meaning, he himself practises in accordance with the Dhamma and also encourages others to do so—in such a case, Mahānāma, a lay follower lives for the welfare of both himself and others."

(8:25)

120. THE EIGHT THOUGHTS OF A GREAT MAN

On one occasion the Blessed One was dwelling among the Bhagga people, near Suṃsumāragiri, in the Deer Park of the Bhesakalā Grove. At that time the Venerable Anuruddha dwelt among the Cetis in the Eastern Bamboo Grove.[14] While living there alone and secluded, these reflections occurred to him:

"This Dhamma is for one of few wishes, not for one with many wishes. This Dhamma is for the contented, not for the discontented. This Dhamma is for the secluded, not for one who loves company. This Dhamma is for the energetic, not for the indolent. This Dhamma is for one of vigilant mindfulness, not for one of lax mindfulness. This Dhamma is for one with a concentrated mind, not for one who is unconcentrated. This Dhamma is for the wise, not for one without wisdom."

Now the Blessed One became aware of the Venerable Anuruddha's reflections and, as speedily as a strong man might stretch his bent arm or bend his stretched arm, he disappeared from the Deer Park at the Bhesakalā Grove and appeared before the Venerable Anuruddha in the Eastern Bamboo Grove.

When the Blessed One had sat down on the seat prepared for him, the Venerable Anuruddha paid homage to him and sat down to one side. Then the Blessed One addressed him thus:

"Good, Anuruddha, good! You have reflected well on the seven thoughts of a great man, namely: 'This Dhamma is for one of few wishes ... This Dhamma is for the wise, not for one without wisdom.' But, Anuruddha, you may further reflect on this eighth thought of a great man, namely: 'This Dhamma is for one who delights in the Unworldly, who rejoices in the Unworldly, not for one who delights and rejoices in worldliness.'[15]

"When reflecting on those eight thoughts of a great man, Anuruddha, you may—while secluded from sensual pleasures, secluded from unwholesome states—whenever you wish, enter and dwell in the first jhāna, which is accompanied by thought and examination, with rapture and happiness born of seclusion.

"With the subsiding of thought and examination, you may, whenever you wish, enter and dwell in the second jhāna, which has internal confidence and unification of mind, is without thought and examination, and has rapture and happiness born of concentration.

"With the fading away as well of rapture, you may, whenever you wish, dwell equanimous and, mindful and clearly comprehending, experiencing happiness with the body, you may enter and dwell in the third jhāna, of which the noble ones declare: 'He is equanimous, mindful, one who dwells happily.'

"With the abandoning of pleasure and pain, and with the previous passing away of joy and sadness, you may, whenever you wish, enter and dwell in the fourth jhāna, which is neither painful nor pleasant and includes the purification of mindfulness by equanimity.

"When you reflect upon those eight thoughts of a great man and attain whenever you wish, without difficulty and trouble, those four jhānas which pertain to the higher mind, pleasant dwellings in this very life—then, Anuruddha, your rag-robe will seem to you as his chest full of coloured garments seems to a householder or his son; and for you who live contentedly, your rag-robe will serve for your joy, for your unperturbed life, for your well-being and as an aid for entering Nibbāna.

"Then, Anuruddha, your scraps of alms-food will seem to you as his dish of rice, cleaned of black grains and served with many gravies and curries, seems to a householder or his son; and for you who live contentedly, your alms-food scraps will serve for your joy, for your unperturbed life, for your well-being and as an aid for entering Nibbāna.

"Then, Anuruddha, your abode under a tree will seem to you as his gabled mansion, plastered inside and out, draught-free, with bolts fastened and shutters closed, seems to a householder or his son; and for you who live contentedly, your tree-abode will serve for your joy, for your unperturbed life, for your well-being and as an aid for entering Nibbāna.

"Then, Anuruddha, your bed and seat made of straw will seem to you as to a householder or his son seems his couch covered with a long-fleeced and black-woollen rug or a bedspread of white wool, a coverlet decorated with flowers, spread over with an exquisite antelope skin, having a canopy overhead and scarlet cushions at both ends; and for you who live contentedly, your straw spread will serve for your joy, for your unperturbed life, for your well-being and as an aid for entering Nibbāna.

"Then, Anuruddha, your medicine of fermented cow's urine[16] will seem to you as to a householder or his son seem his various remedies of butter, ghee, oil, honey and cane sugar; and for you who live contentedly, your medicine of cow's urine will serve for your joy, for your unperturbed life, for your well-being and as an aid for entering Nibbāna.

"Therefore, Anuruddha, you may also spend the coming rainy season here in this Eastern Bamboo Grove among the Cetis."

"Yes, Lord," replied the Venerable Anuruddha.

And the Blessed One, having admonished the Venerable Anuruddha with this exhortation, as speedily as a strong man might stretch his bent arm or bend his stretched arm, then disappeared from the Eastern Bamboo Grove and re-appeared at Suṃsumāragiri, in the Deer Park of the Bhesakalā Grove.

There the Blessed One sat down on a seat prepared for him and addressed the monks as follows:

"I will declare to you, O monks, the eight thoughts of a great man. Listen to them and attend carefully, I shall speak. What are these eight thoughts of a great man?

"This Dhamma is for one of few wishes, not for one with many wishes. This Dhamma is for the contented, not for the discontented. This Dhamma is for the secluded, not for one who loves company. This Dhamma is for the energetic, not for the indolent. This Dhamma is for one of vigilant mindfulness, not for one of lax mindfulness. This Dhamma is for one with a concentrated mind, not for one who is unconcentrated. This Dhamma is for the wise, not for one without wisdom. This Dhamma is for one who delights in the Unworldly, who rejoices in the Unworldly, not for one who delights and rejoices in worldliness.

"But why, monks, was it said: 'This Dhamma is for one of few wishes, not for one with many wishes'? Here, monks, though a monk may be of few wishes, he does not wish to be known as one of few wishes. Though contented, he does not wish to be known as being contented. Though secluded, he does not wish to be known as being secluded. Though energetic, he does not wish to be known as being energetic. Though mindful, he does not wish to be known as being mindful. Though of concentrated mind, he does not wish to be known as one of concentrated mind. Though wise, he does not wish to be known as wise. Though delighting and rejoicing in the Unworldly, he does not wish to be known as one who delights and rejoices in the Unworldly. When it was said, 'This Dhamma is for one of few wishes, not for one with many wishes,' it is for this reason that this was said.

"And why was it said: 'This Dhamma is for the contented, not for the discontented'? Here, monks, a monk is contented with any kind of robe, alms-food, lodging and medicinal requisites. It is for this reason that this was said.

"And why was it said: 'This Dhamma is for the secluded, not for one who loves company'? Here, monks, while a monk lives secluded visitors come: monks and nuns, male and female lay followers, kings and their ministers, sectarians and their disciples. Then the monk, with his mind bent on seclusion, leaning towards seclusion, inclined towards seclusion, abiding in seclusion and delighting in renunciation, speaks to them only in a way tending to dismiss them. It is for this reason that this was said.

"And why was it said: 'This Dhamma is for the energetic, not for the indolent'? Here, monks, a monk lives with energy set upon the abandoning of everything unwholesome and the acquiring of everything wholesome; he is steadfast and strong in his effort, not shirking his task in regard to wholesome qualities. It is for this reason that this was said.

"And why was it said: 'This Dhamma is for one of vigilant mindfulness, not for one of lax mindfulness'? Here, monks, a monk is mindful, equipped with the keenest mindfulness and circumspection; he remembers well and keeps in mind what has been said and done long ago. It is for this reason that this was said.

"And why was it said: 'This Dhamma is for one with a concentrated mind, not for one unconcentrated'? Here, monks, a monk enters and dwells in the first jhāna ... the second ... the third ... the fourth jhāna.' It is for this reason that this was said.

And why was it said: 'This Dhamma is for the wise, not for one without wisdom'? Here, monks, a monk is wise in this way: he is equipped with that wisdom which sees into the rise and fall of phenomena, which is noble and penetrative, leading to the complete destruction of suffering. It is for this reason that this was said.

And why was it said: 'This Dhamma is for one who delights and rejoices in the Unworldly, not for one who delights and rejoices in worldliness'? Here, monks, a monk's mind urges him on towards the cessation of the world's diffuseness, he is pleased by it, confirmed in it and liberated.[17] It is for this reason that this was said."

And in the coming rainy season, too, the Venerable Anuruddha lived among the Cetis in the Eastern Bamboo Grove. And the Venerable Anuruddha, living alone and secluded, diligent, ardent and resolute, soon realized here and now, by his own direct knowledge, that unsurpassed goal of the holy life for the sake of which sons of good family rightly go forth from home to the homeless life, and entering upon it he dwelt therein. And he knew: "Destroyed is birth, the holy life has been lived, what had to be done has been done, there is no more for this world." And the Venerable Anuruddha had become one of the arahants.

At the time of reaching arahantship the Venerable Anuruddha spoke these verses:

"The Master, peerless in this world,
Knew my thoughts and came to me;
With a body made by mind,
He came to me by psychic power.
He taught me more than I knew,
More than my thoughts contained:
The Buddha, cherishing the Unworldly,
Taught me about the Unworldly state.
And having learned his Dhamma thus,
I lived delighted in his teaching.
I have gained the threefold knowledge;[18]
I have done the Master's bidding."

(8:30)

121. WAYS OF GIVING

There are, O monks, eight ways of giving. What eight? One gives spontaneously; or one gives out of fear; or because of thinking, "He too has given me a gift"; or because of thinking, "He will give me a present, too"; or because of thinking that it is good to give; or because of thinking, "I cook, but they (being ascetics) do not; since I cook, it would not be proper for me to refuse giving a meal to those who do not cook"; or because of thinking, "By giving such a gift, I shall earn a good reputation"; or one gives because it ennobles the mind, adorns the mind.[19]

(8:31)

122. Reasons for Giving

There are, O monks, eight reasons for giving. What eight? People may give out of affection; or in an angry mood; or out of stupidity; or out of fear; or because of thinking: "Such gifts have been given before by my father and grandfather and it was done by them before; hence it would be unworthy of me to give up this old family tradition"; or because of thinking, "By giving this gift, I shall be reborn in a good destination, in a heavenly world, after death"; or because of thinking, "When giving this gift, my heart will be glad, and happiness and joy will arise in me"; or one gives because it ennobles and adorns the mind.

(8:33)

123. Rebirth on account of Giving

There are, O monks, eight kinds of rebirth on account of giving. What eight?

Here, monks, a certain person makes a gift to an ascetic or a brahmin, offering him food, drink, food, drink, clothing and vehicles; garlands, scents and unguents; bedding, housing and lighting. In making the gift, he hopes for a reward. He now notices affluent nobles, affluent brahmins or affluent householders, enjoying themselves provided and furnished with the five cords of sensual pleasure, and he thinks: "Oh, with the breakup of the body, after death, may I be reborn among them!" And he sets his mind on that thought, keeps to it firmly, and fosters it. This thought of his aims at what is low, and if not developed to what is higher it will lead him to just such a rebirth.[20] With the breakup of the body, after death, he will be reborn among affluent nobles, affluent brahmins or affluent householders. This, however, I declare only for the virtuous, not for the unvirtuous; for it is due to his purity, monks, that the heart's desire of the virtuous succeeds.[21]

Then again, a certain person makes a gift to a ascetic or a brahmin, offering him food … or lighting. In making the gift, he hopes for a reward. He now hears of the long life, the beauty and the great happiness of devas in the realm of the Four Great Kings ... the Tāvatiṃsa devas ... the Yāma devas ... the Tusita devas ... the Nimmāṇaratī devas,[22] ... the Paranimmitavasavattī devas,[23] and he wishes to be reborn among them. He sets his mind on that thought, keeps to it firmly, and fosters it. This thought of his aims at what is low, and if not developed to what is higher, it will lead him to just such a rebirth. After his death, when his body breaks up, he will be reborn among the devas in the realm of the Four Great Kings ... or among the Paranimmitavasavattī devas. This, however, I declare only for the virtuous, not for the unvirtuous; for it is due to his purity, monks, that the heart's desire of the virtuous succeeds.

Then again, a certain person makes a gift to an ascetic or to a brahmin, offering him food ... or lighting. He now hears of the long life, the beauty and the great happiness of the devas of Brahmā's Company, and he wishes to be reborn among them. He sets his mind on that thought, keeps to it firmly, and fosters it. This thought of his aims at what is low, and if not developed to what is higher, it will lead him to just such a rebirth. After his death, when his body breaks up, he will be reborn among the devas of Brahmā's Company. This, however, I declare only for the virtuous, not for the unvirtuous; only for one free of lust, not for one who is lustful.[24] Because he is without lust, monks, the heart's desire of the virtuous succeeds.

These, monks, are the eight kinds of rebirth on account of giving.

(8:35)

124. WAYS OF MERITORIOUS ACTION

There are, O monks, three ways of making merit. What three? There are ways of making merit by giving, by virtue and by the development of meditation.

There is a person who has practised the making of merit by giving only to a limited degree; and, likewise to a limited degree, he has practised the making of merit by virtue; but the making of merit by meditation he has not undertaken. This one, with the breakup of the body, after death, will be reborn among humans in an unfavourable condition.[25]

Another person has practised to a high degree the making of merit by giving as well as by virtue; but the making of merit by meditation he has not undertaken. Such a one, with the breakup of the body, after death, will be reborn among humans in a favourable condition.

Or he will be reborn in the company of the devas of the Four Great Kings. And there, the Four Great Kings, who had practised to a very high degree the making of merit by giving and by virtue, surpass the devas of their realm in ten respects: in divine lifespan, divine beauty, divine happiness, divine fame, divine power, divine sights, sounds, smells, tastes and touches.

Or he will be reborn in the company of the Tāvatiṃsa devas. And there, Sakka, king of the devas, who had practised to a very high degree the making of merit by giving and by virtue, surpasses the devas of their realm in ten respects: in divine lifespan, divine beauty, divine happiness, divine fame, divine power, divine sights, sounds, smells, tastes and touches.

(The same statements are made for rebirth among the Yāma devas, Tusita devas, the Nimmāṇaratī devas, the Paranimmitavasavattī devas, and for the respective rulers of these realms.)

These, monks, are the three ways of making merit.

(8:36)

125. Streams of Merit

There are, O monks, eight streams of merit, streams of the wholesome, nourishments of happiness, which are heavenly, ripening in happiness, conducive to heaven, and which lead to whatever is wished for, loved and agreeable, to one's welfare and happiness.[26] What are the eight?

Here, monks, a noble disciple has gone for refuge to the Buddha. This is the first stream of merit, stream of the wholesome, nourishment of happiness, which is heavenly, ripening in happiness, conducive to heaven, and which leads to whatever is wished for, loved and agreeable, to one's welfare and happiness.

Further, a noble disciple has gone for refuge to the Dhamma ... to the Sangha. This is the second stream ... the third stream ...

There are further, monks, these five gifts—pristine, of long standing, traditional, ancient, unadulterated, and never before adulterated, which are not being adulterated and which will not be adulterated, not despised by wise ascetics and brahmins. What are these five gifts?

Here, monks, a noble disciple gives up the destruction of life and abstains from it. By abstaining from the destruction of life, the noble disciple gives to immeasurable beings freedom from fear, gives to them freedom from hostility, gives to them freedom from oppression. By giving to immeasurable beings freedom from fear, hostility, and oppression, he himself will enjoy immeasurable freedom from fear, hostility, and oppression. This is the first of those great gifts and the fourth flood of merit.

Further, monks, a noble disciple gives up the taking of what is not given and abstains from it. By abstaining from taking what is not given, the noble disciple gives to immeasurable beings freedom from fear ... This is the second of those great gifts and the fifth flood of merit.

Further, monks, a noble disciple gives up sexual misconduct and abstains from it. By abstaining from sexual misconduct, the noble disciple gives to immeasurable beings freedom from fear ... This is the third of those great gifts and the sixth flood of merit.

Further, monks, a noble disciple gives up false speech and abstains from it. By abstaining from false speech, the noble disciple gives to immeasurable beings freedom from fear ... This is the fourth of those great gifts and the seventh flood of merit.

Further, monks, a noble disciple gives up wines, liquors, and intoxicants which are the basis for negligence, and abstains from them. By abstaining from wines, liquors, and intoxicants, the noble disciple gives to immeasurable beings freedom from fear, freedom from hostility, and freedom from oppression. By giving to immeasurable beings freedom from fear, hostility, and oppression, he himself will enjoy immeasurable freedom from fear, freedom from hostility, and freedom from oppression. This is the fifth of those great gifts and the eighth flood of merit.

These, monks, are the eight streams of merit, streams of the wholesome, nourishments of happiness, which are heavenly, ripening in happiness, conducive to heaven, and which lead to whatever is wished for, loved and agreeable, to one's welfare and happiness.

(8:39)

126. MINDFULNESS OF DEATH-1

On one occasion the Blessed One was dwelling at Nādikā in the Brick Hall. There he addressed the monks as follows:

"Mindfulness of death, O monks, if developed and cultivated, brings great fruit and benefit; it merges in the Deathless, ends in the Deathless. Therefore, monks, you should develop mindfulness of death."

After the Blessed One had spoken, a certain monk said:

"Lord, I develop mindfulness of death."

"And how do you develop it?"

"I think in this way, Lord: 'Oh, were I to live just for one day and a night, I would direct my mind on the Blessed One's teaching. Much, indeed, could then be done by me!' Thus, Lord, do I cultivate mindfulness of death."

(Other monks in that assembly likewise said that they developed mindfulness of death and, being asked how they did so, they answered:)

"I think in this way, Lord: 'Oh, were I to live but for a single day ... for half a day ... just for the time I need to eat one meal ... half a meal ... just for the time I need to chew and swallow four or five morsels of food ... to chew and swallow one morsel of food ... just for the time I breathe in after the out-breath or breathe out after the in-breath, I would direct my mind on the Blessed One's teaching. Much, indeed, could then be done by me!' Thus, Lord, do I develop mindfulness of death."

After the monks had thus spoken, the Blessed One said:

"The monks who said that they develop mindfulness of death with the thought, 'Oh, were I to live just for one day and a night ... for the time needed to chew and swallow four or five morsels of food ...'—of these monks it must be said that they live indolently and that they develop mindfulness of death in a slack way for the destruction of the taints.[27]

"But, monks, those who develop mindfulness of death with the thought, 'Oh, were I to live for the time I need to chew and swallow one morsel of food; or for the time of breathing in after the out-breath, or breathing out after the in-breath, I would direct my mind on the Blessed One's teaching. Much, indeed, could then be done by me!'-of these monks it can be said that they live diligently, and that they develop mindfulness of death ardently for the destruction of the taints.

"Therefore, monks, you should train yourselves thus, 'We will dwell diligently and we will develop mindfulness of death ardently for the destruction of the taints!' Thus indeed, monks, you should train yourselves."

(8:73)

127. Mindfulness of Death-II

On one occasion the Blessed One was dwelling at Nādikā in the Brick Hall. There he addressed the monks as follows:

"Mindfulness of death, O monks, if developed and cultivated, brings great fruit and benefit; it merges in the Deathless, ends in the Deathless. And how, monks, is mindfulness of death developed in such a way?

"When the day fades and night sets in ... or when the night is spent and day breaks, a monk should reflect thus: 'Many things might be the cause of my death: a snake or a scorpion or a centipede may sting me, and on that account I may die. This would be a hindrance to me.[28] Or I may stumble and fall; or the food I ate may cause illness; or bile, phlegm, or piercing winds may upset my health; or humans or non-humans may assault me, and on that account I may die. This would be a hindrance to me.'

"Then that monk should further reflect thus: 'Do I harbour in myself any evil, unwholesome qualities, which are still unabandoned and which would be a hindrance to me if I were to die tonight or during the day?'

"If, on reflection, that monk realizes that those evil, unwholesome qualities still remain within him, then he should, with strong resolve, apply all his effort, vigour and exertion, (together with) mindfulness and clear comprehension, to abandon them.

"Just as a man whose turban or hair is on fire would resolutely apply all his effort, vigour, and exertion, (together with) mindfulness and clear comprehension, to extinguish the fire; even so should that monk resolutely apply all his effort … to abandon those evil, unwholesome qualities.

"But if, on reflection, that monk realizes that no such evil, unwholesome qualities still remain within him, then he may well experience gladness and joy. By day and night he should train himself in everything that is wholesome.

"If, monks, mindfulness of death is developed and cultivated in such a way, it will be of great fruit and benefit; it will merge in the Deathless, end in the Deathless."

(8:74)

IX. The Chapter of the Nines

128. Meghiya

On one occasion the Blessed One was dwelling at Cālikā, on the Cālikā hill. There the Venerable Meghiya, who was at that time the Blessed One's attendant,[1] approached the Blessed One, paid homage to him, and said to him while standing at one side:

"Lord, I wish to go to Jantugāma for alms."

"You may do as you think fit, Meghiya."

Then the Venerable Meghiya, dressing himself in the morning and taking robe and bowl, entered Jantugāma for alms. Having made the alms round and taken his meal, he went to the bank of the Kimikālā River.

There, while walking around to stretch his legs, he saw a pleasant and beautiful mango grove. Seeing it, he thought: "Pleasant, indeed, is this mango grove; it is beautiful. Truly, it is fit for a clansman who wishes to strive in meditation. If the Blessed One allows it, I shall return to this mango grove to strive in meditation."

Then the Venerable Meghiya approached the Blessed One … and said to him: "Lord, after my alms round in Jantugāma, when I had taken my meal, I went to the bank of the Kimikālā River. While walking there I saw a pleasant and beautiful mango grove which I thought to be fit for a clansman who wishes to strive in meditation. If the Blessed One permits me, I shall go there and strive."

"Wait a while, Meghiya. We are now alone here. First let another monk come."

But the Venerable Meghiya repeated his request, saying: "Lord, for the Blessed One there is nothing further to achieve and no need to consolidate what he has achieved. But as for me, Lord, there is still more to achieve and the need to consolidate what I have achieved. If the Blessed One permits me, I shall go to that mango grove and strive."

Again the Blessed One asked him to wait and again the

Venerable Meghiya made his request for a third time. (Then the Blessed One said:)

"As you speak of striving, Meghiya, what can we say? You may do now as you think fit."

The Venerable Meghiya then rose from his seat, saluted the Blessed One, and keeping him to his right, left for the mango grove. Having arrived, he went deeper into the grove and sat down under a tree to spend the day there. But while staying in that mango grove, three kinds of evil, unwholesome thoughts constantly assailed him: sensual thoughts, thoughts of ill will and thoughts of violence.

Then he thought: "Truly, it is strange, it is amazing! I have gone forth from home into the homeless life out of faith, and yet I am harassed by these three kinds of evil, unwholesome thoughts: sensual thoughts, thoughts of ill will, and thoughts of violence."[2]

Then the Venerable Meghiya went back to the Blessed One, and having saluted him, he told him what had occurred and exclaimed: "Truly it is strange, it is amazing! I have gone forth from home into the homeless life out of faith, and yet I am harassed by those three kinds of evil, unwholesome thoughts."

"If, Meghiya, the mind still lacks maturity for liberation, there are five conditions conducive to making it mature. What five?

"The first thing, Meghiya, for making the immature mind mature for liberation is to have a noble friend, a noble companion, a noble associate.[3]

"Further, Meghiya, a monk should be virtuous, restrained by the restraint of the Pātimokkha, perfect in conduct and resort, seeing danger in the slightest faults. Having undertaken the training rules, he should train himself in them. This is the second thing that makes the immature mind mature for liberation.

"Further, Meghiya, the talk in which a monk engages should befit an austere life and be helpful to mental clarity; that is to say, it should be talk on fewness of wishes, on contentment, on solitude, on seclusion, on application of energy, on virtue, concentration, wisdom, liberation, and on the knowledge and vision of liberation. If a monk finds opportunities for such talk easily and without difficulty, this is the third thing that makes the immature mind mature for liberation.

"Further, Meghiya, a monk lives with his energy set upon the abandoning of everything unwholesome and the acquiring of everything wholesome; he is steadfast and strong in his effort, not shirking his task in regard to wholesome qualities. This is the fourth thing that makes the immature mind mature for liberation.

"Further, Meghiya, a monk possesses wisdom; he is equipped with that wisdom which sees into the rise and fall of phenomena, which is noble and penetrative, leading to the complete destruction of suffering. This is the fifth thing that makes the immature mind mature for liberation.

"When, Meghiya, a monk has a noble friend, a noble companion and associate, it can be expected the he will be virtuous ... that he will engage in talk befitting the austere life and helpful to mental clarity ... that his energy will be set upon the abandoning of everything unwholesome and the acquiring of everything wholesome ... that he will be equipped with the wisdom that leads to the complete destruction of suffering.

"Then, Meghiya, when the monk is firmly grounded in these five things, he should cultivate four other things: he should cultivate the meditation on the foulness (of the body) for abandoning lust; he should cultivate loving-kindness for abandoning ill will; he should cultivate mindfulness of breathing for cutting off distracting thoughts; he should cultivate the perception of impermanence for eliminating the conceit 'I am'. In one who perceives impermanence, the perception of non-self becomes firmly established; and one who perceives non-self achieves the elimination of the conceit 'I am' and attains Nibbāna in this very life."[4]

(9:3)

129. FREED OF FIVEFOLD FEAR

There are, O monks, four powers. What four? The power of wisdom, the power of energy, the power of an unblemished life and the power of beneficence.

And what, monks, is the power of wisdom? As to those things which are unwholesome and are held to be unwholesome, those things which are wholesome and are held to be wholesome; blameless and blameworthy, and held to be so; dark and bright, and held to be so; fit or unfit to be practised, and held to be so; worthy and unworthy of noble ones, and held to be so—to see all these things clearly and to consider them well, this is called the power of wisdom.

And what, monks, is the power of energy? As to those things that are unwholesome, blameworthy, dark, unfit to be practised, unworthy of noble ones, and which are held to be so—to generate desire, to make an effort and stir up one's energy for abandoning all these things; and as to those things that are wholesome, blameless, bright, fit to be practised, worthy of noble ones, and which are held to be so—to generate desire, to make an effort and stir up one's energy for gaining all these things, this is called the power of energy.

And what, monks, is the power of an unblemished life? Here, monks, a noble disciple is unblemished in his deeds, unblemished in his words, unblemished in his thoughts. This is called the power of an unblemished life.

And what, monks, is the power of beneficence? There are four bases of beneficence:[5] by gifts, by friendly speech, by helpful acts and by bestowal of equity. This is the best of gifts: the gift of Dhamma. And this is the best of friendly speech: to teach the Dhamma again and again to those who wish for it and who listen attentively. And this is the best of helpful acts: to arouse, instil and strengthen faith in the unbeliever; to arouse, instil, and strengthen virtue in the immoral; to arouse, instil and strengthen generosity in the miser; to arouse, instil, and strengthen wisdom in the ignorant. And this is the best bestowal of equity: if a stream-enterer becomes equal to a stream-enterer; a once-returner equal to a once-returner; a non-returner equal to a non-returner; and an arahant equal to an arahant. This, monks, is called the power of beneficence.

And this concludes the four powers.

Now, monks, a noble disciple endowed with these four powers has left behind five fears: the fear for his livelihood, the fear of disrepute, the fear of embarrassment in assemblies, the fear of death and the fear of an unhappy future destiny.

A noble disciple thus endowed will think: "No fear do I have for my livelihood. Why should I have fear about it? Have I not the four powers of wisdom, energy, unblemished life and beneficence? It is one who is foolish and lazy, of blameworthy conduct in deeds, words, and thoughts, and who has no beneficence—such a one might have fear for his livelihood.

"No fear do I have about disrepute or about embarrassment in assemblies; nor have I fear of death or of an unhappy future destiny. Why should I have these fears? Have I not the four powers of wisdom, energy, unblemished life, and beneficence? It is one who is foolish and lazy, of blameworthy conduct in deeds, words, and thoughts, and who has no beneficence—such a one might have all these fears."

Thus it should be understood, monks, that a noble disciple endowed with the four powers has left behind five fears.

(9:5)

130. Sāriputta's Lion's Roar

On one occasion the Blessed One was dwelling at Sāvatthī in Jeta's Grove, Anāthapiṇḍika's monastery. At that time the Venerable Sāriputta approached the Blessed One. Having paid homage to the Blessed One, he sat down to one side and said to him:

"Lord, I have now completed the rains retreat at Sāvatthī and wish to leave for a country journey."

"Sāriputta, you may go whenever you are ready." The Venerable Sāriputta rose from his seat, saluted the Blessed One, and keeping him to his right, departed.

Soon after the Venerable Sāriputtā had left, one monk said to the Blessed One: "The Venerable Sāriputta has hit me and has left on his journey without an apology."[6]

Then the Blessed One called another monk and said: "Go, monk, and call the Venerable Sāriputta, saying, 'The Master calls you, Sāriputta.'"[7]The monk did as he was bidden, and the Venerable Sāriputta responded, saying, "Yes, friend."

Then the Venerable Mahāmoggallāna and the Venerable Ānanda, taking the keys, went around the monks' lodgings and said: "Come, revered sirs, come! For today the Venerable Sāriputta will utter his lion's roar in the presence of the Blessed One."

The Venerable Sāriputta approached the Blessed One, and after saluting him, sat down to one side. When he was seated, the Blessed One said: "One of your fellow monks here has complained that you hit him and left on your journey without an apology."

"Lord, one in whom mindfulness directed to the body[8] is not present in regard to the body may well hit a fellow monk and leave without an apology.

"Just as, Lord, people throw upon the earth things clean and unclean, dung, urine, spittle, pus and blood, yet for all that the earth has no revulsion, loathing or disgust towards it;[9] even so, Lord, do I dwell with a heart that is like the earth, vast, exalted and measureless, without hostility, and without ill will. However, one in whom mindfulness directed on the body in regard to the body is not present may well hit a fellow monk and leave without an apology.

"Just as, Lord, people use water to wash things clean and unclean, things soiled with dung, urine, spittle, pus and blood, yet for all that the water has no revulsion, loathing or disgust towards it; even so, Lord, do I dwell with a heart that is like water, vast, exalted and measureless, without hostility, and without ill will. However, one in whom ... and leave without an apology

"Just as, Lord, fire burns things clean and unclean, things soiled with dung, urine, spittle, pus and blood, yet for all that the fire has no revulsion, loathing or disgust towards it; even so, Lord, do I dwell with a heart that is like fire, vast, exalted and measureless, without hostility, and without ill will. However, he in whom ... and leave without an apology.

"Just as, Lord, the wind blows over things clean and unclean, over dung, urine, spittle, pus and blood, yet for all that the wind has no revulsion, loathing or disgust towards it; even so, Lord, do I dwell with a heart that is like the wind, vast, exalted and measureless, without hostility, and without ill will. However, he in whom ... and leave without an apology.

"Lord, just as a duster wipes over things clean and unclean, things soiled with dung, urine, spittle, pus and blood, yet for all that the duster has no revulsion, loathing or disgust towards it; even so, Lord, do I dwell with a heart that is like a duster, vast, exalted and measureless, without hostility, and without ill will. However, he in whom ... and leave without an apology.

"Lord, just as an outcast boy or girl, begging-vessel in hand and clad in rags, enters a village or town with a humble heart; even so, Lord, do I dwell with a heart like that of an outcast youth, a heart that is vast, exalted and measureless, without hostility, and without ill will. However, he in whom ... and leave without an apology.

"Lord, just as a bull with his horns cut, gentle, well tamed and well trained, when roaming from street to street, from square to square, will not hurt anyone with feet or horns; even so, Lord, do I dwell like a bull with horns cut, with a heart that is vast, exalted and measureless, without hostility, and without ill will. However, he in whom ... and leave without an apology.

"Lord, just as a woman or a man, young, youthful and fond of ornaments, who has just washed the head, would be filled with revulsion, loathing and disgust if the carcass of a snake, a dog or a man were to be slung around the neck; even so, Lord, am I filled with revulsion, loathing and disgust for this foul body of mine. However, one in whom mindfulness directed to the body in regard to the body is not present may well hit a fellow monk and leave without an apology.

"Lord, just if one were to carry around a bowl of liquid fat that is full of holes and crevices, oozing and dripping; even so, Lord, do I carry around this body that is full of holes and crevices, oozing and dripping. However, one in whom mindfulness directed on the body in regard to the body is not present may well hit a fellow monk and leave without an apology."

Then that accusing monk rose from his seat, arranged his upper robe over one shoulder, and with his head on the ground bowed at the feet of the Blessed One, saying: "Lord, I committed an offence when I was so foolish, stupid and unskilful that I accused the Venerable Sāriputta falsely, wrongly and untruthfully. Let the Blessed One accept my admission of the offence and pardon me, and I shall practise restraint in the future."

"Truly, monk, you committed an offence when you were so foolish, stupid and unskilful that you accused Sāriputta falsely, wrongly and untruthfully. But as you have recognized your offence as such and make amends for it according to the rule, we pardon you. For it is a sign of growth in the Discipline of the Noble One that one recognizes one's offence, makes amends for it according to the rule, and in future practises restraint."

The Blessed One then turned to the Venerable Sāriputta and said: "Forgive this foolish man, Sāriputta, before his head splits into seven pieces on this very spot."

"I shall forgive him, Lord, if this revered monk asks for my pardon. And he, too, may forgive me."

(9:11)

131. SAMIDDHI

(Once the Venerable Samiddhi went to see the Venerable Sāriputta and the latter questioned him as follows:)

"What, Samiddhi, is the conditioning basis of the purposive thoughts that arise in a person?"—"Name-and-form, venerable sir."[10]

"From what does their variety derive? —"From the elements."

"What is their origin?" —"Contact."

"On what do they converge?"—"Feeling."

"What is their head?"—"Concentration."

"What is their master?"—"Mindfulness."

"What is their climax?"—"Wisdom."

"What is their essence?"—"Liberation."

"Where do they merge?"—"In the Deathless."[11]

(In the original text, the Venerable Sāriputta repeats these questions and answers, and concludes:)

"Well spoken, Samiddhi, well spoken! You have answered well the various questions put to you. But do not be proud of yourself on that account!"

(9:14)

132. ROOTED IN CRAVING

Monks, I shall teach you nine things rooted in craving. Listen and attend carefully, I shall speak.

What are the nine things rooted in craving? Because of craving there is pursuit; because of pursuit, there is acquisition; because of acquisition, there is decision; because of decision there is desire and lust; because of desire and lust there is selfish tenacity; because of selfish tenacity there is possessiveness; because of possessiveness there is avarice; because of avarice there is concern for protection; and for the sake of protection there is the seizing of cudgels and weapons, and various evil, unwholesome things such as quarrels, strife, dissension and offensive talk, slander and lies.[12]

These are the nine things rooted in craving.

(9:23)

X. The Chapter of the Tens

133. The Benefits of Virtue

On one occasion the Blessed One was dwelling at Sāvatthī in Jeta's Grove, Anāthapiṇḍika's monastery. At that time the Venerable Ānanda approached the Blessed One, paid homage to him, and asked:[1]

"What, Lord, is the benefit of virtuous ways of conduct, what is their reward?"

"Non-remorse, Ānanda, is the benefit and reward of virtuous ways of conduct."

"And what, Lord, is the benefit and reward of non-remorse?"

"Gladness, Ānanda."

"And what, Lord, is the benefit and reward of gladness?"

"Joy."

"And what, Lord, is the benefit and reward of joy?"

"Serenity."

"And what, Lord, is the benefit and reward of serenity?"

"Happiness."

"And what, Lord, is the benefit and reward of happiness?"

"Concentration of the mind."

"And what, Lord, is the benefit and reward of concentration?"

"Knowledge and vision of things as they really are."

"And what, Lord, is the benefit and reward of knowledge and vision of things as they really are?"

"Revulsion and dispassion."

"And what, Lord, is the benefit and reward of revulsion and dispassion?"

"The knowledge and vision of liberation.

"Hence, Ānanda, virtuous ways of conduct have non-remorse as their benefit and reward; non-remorse has gladness as its benefit and reward; gladness has joy as its benefit and reward; joy has serenity as its benefit and reward; serenity has happiness as its benefit and reward; happiness has concentration as its benefit and reward; concentration has knowledge and vision of things as they really are as its benefit and reward; knowledge and vision of things as they really are has revulsion and dispassion as its benefit and reward; revulsion and dispassion have the knowledge and vision of liberation as their benefit and reward. In this way, Ānanda, virtuous ways of conduct lead step by step to the highest."

(10:1)

134. LAWFULNESS OF PROGRESS

For one who is virtuous and endowed with virtue, there is no need for an act of will: "May non-remorse arise in me!" It is a natural law, monks, that non-remorse will arise in one who is virtuous.

For one free of remorse, there is no need for an act of will: "May gladness arise in me!" It is a natural law that gladness will arise in one who is free from remorse.

For one who is glad at heart, there is no need for an act of will: "May joy arise in me!" It is a natural law that joy will arise in one who is glad at heart .

For one who is joyful, there is no need for an act of will: "May my body be serene!" It is a natural law that the body will be serene for one who is joyful.

For one of serene body, there is no need for an act of will: "May I feel happiness!" It is a natural law that one who is serene will feel happiness.

For one who is happy, there is no need for an act of will: "May my mind be concentrated!" It is a natural law for one who is happy that the mind will be concentrated.

For one who is concentrated, there is no need for an act of will: "May I know and see things as they really are!" It is a natural law for one with a concentrated mind to know and see things as they really are.

For one who knows and see things as they really are, there is no need for an act of will: "May I experience revulsion and dispassion!" It is a natural law for one who knows and sees things as they really are to experience revulsion and dispassion.

For one who experiences revulsion and dispassion, there is no need for an act of will: "May I realize the knowledge and vision of liberation!" It is a natural law for one who experiences revulsion and dispassion to realize the knowledge and vision of liberation.

Thus, monks, revulsion and dispassion have knowledge and vision of liberation as their benefit and reward ... (continued in conformity with the above, back to) ... virtuous ways of conduct have non-remorse as their benefit and reward.

Thus, monks, the preceding qualities flow into the succeeding qualities; the succeeding qualities bring the preceding qualities to perfection, for going from the near shore to the far shore.[2]

(10:2)

135. THE MEDITATIVE EXPERIENCE OF NIBBĀNA-1

Once the Venerable Ānanda approached the Blessed One and asked:

"Can it be, Lord, that a monk attains to such a concentration of mind that in earth he is not percipient of earth, nor in water is he percipient of water, nor in fire ... air ... the base of the infinity of space ... the base of the infinity of consciousness ... the base of nothingness ... the base of neither-perception-nor-non-perception is he percipient of all these; nor is he percipient of this world or a world beyond—but yet he is percipient?"[3]

"Yes, Ānanda, there can be such a concentration of mind that in earth he is not percipient of earth ... nor is he percipient of this world or a world beyond—but yet he is percipient."

"But how, Lord, can a monk attain to such a concentration of mind?"

"Here, Ānanda, the monk is percipient thus: 'This is the peaceful, this is the sublime, namely, the stilling of all formations, the relinquishment of all acquisitions, the destruction of craving, dispassion, cessation, Nibbāna.' It is in this way, Ānanda, that a monk may attain to such a concentration of mind."[4]

(10:6)

136. THE MEDITATIVE EXPERIENCE OF NIBBĀNA-II

Once the Venerable Ānanda approached the Venerable Sāriputta and asked:

"Can it be, friend Sāriputta, that a monk attains to such a concentration of mind that in earth he is not percipient of earth ... (as above) ... nor is he percipient of this world or a world beyond—but yet he is percipient?"

"Yes, friend Ānanda, he can attain to such a concentration of mind."

"But how, friend Sāriputta, can a monk attain to such a concentration of mind?"

"Once, friend Ānanda, I lived here in Sāvatthī, in the Dark Forest. There I attained to such a concentration of mind that in earth I was not percipient of earth ... (as above) ... nor was I percipient of this world or a world beyond—and yet I was percipient."

"But what was the Venerable Sāriputta percipient of on that occasion?"

"'Nibbāna is cessation of becoming, Nibbāna is cessation of becoming'[5]—one such perception arose in me and another such perception ceased. Just as, friend Ānanda, from a fire of faggots one flame arises and another flame ceases, even so, 'Nibbāna is cessation of becoming, Nibbāna is cessation of becoming'—one such perception arose in me and another such perception ceased. On that occasion, friend, I perceived that Nibbāna is the cessation of becoming."

(10:7)

137. THE BUDDHA'S LION'S ROAR

Monks, the lion, the king of beasts, comes forth from his lair in the evening. Then he stretches himself, surveys the four directions all around, and roars three times his lion's roar.[6] And why? (He does so with the thought:) "May I not cause the death of small creatures that have gone astray!"

"The lion"—this, monks, is a name for the Tathāgata, the Arahant, the Fully Enlightened One. When, monks, the Tathāgata expounds the Dhamma in an assembly, that is his lion's roar.

There are, monks, these ten Tathāgata powers[7] of a Tathāgata, endowed with which the Tathāgata claims the foremost rank, utters his lion's roar in the assemblies and sets rolling the supreme Wheel of the Dhamma.[8] What are these ten Tathāgata powers?

(1) Here, the Tathāgata understands, as it really is, cause as cause and non-cause as non-cause.[9] This is a Tathāgata power of the Tathāgata, by reason of which he claims the foremost rank, utters his lion's roar in the assemblies and sets rolling the supreme Wheel of the Dhamma.

(2) Again, the Tathāgata understands, as it really is, by way of cause and root condition,[10] the result of past, future, and present actions that are performed. This too is a Tathāgata power of the Tathāgata....

(3) Again, the Tathāgata understands, as it really is, the way leading to all destinies.[11] This too is a Tathāgata power of the Tathāgata ....

(4) Again, the Tathāgata understands, as it really is, the world with its many and different elements.[12] This too is a Tathāgata power of the Tathāgata....

(5) Again, the Tathāgata understands, as it really is, the different dispositions of beings.[13] This too is a Tathāgata power of the Tathāgata....

(6) Again, the Tathāgata understands, as it really is, the inferior and superior condition of the faculties of other beings, of other persons.[14] This too is a Tathāgata power of the Tathāgata....

(7) Again, the Tathāgata understands, as it really is, with regard to the jhānas, the liberations, the concentrations and the meditative attainments, their defects and purity and the emergence from them.[15] This too is a Tathāgata power of the Tathāgata....

(8) Again, the Tathāgata recollects his manifold past lives, that is to say, one birth, two births, three births, four births, five

births, ten births, twenty births, thirty births, forty births, fifty births, a hundred births, a thousand births, a hundred thousand births, many aeons of world-contraction, many aeons of world-expansion, many aeons of world-contraction and expansion ... (as in Text 34) ... Thus with their aspects and particulars he recollects his manifold past lives. This too is a Tathāgata power of the Tathāgata....

(9) Again, with the divine eye, which is purified and surpasses the human, the Tathāgata sees beings passing away and reappearing, inferior and superior, fair and ugly, of good or bad destination. He understands beings as faring according to their deeds ... (as in Text 34) ...This too is a Tathāgata power of the Tathāgata....

(10) Again, the Tathāgata, by the destruction of the taints, in this very life enters and dwells in the taintless liberation of mind, liberation by wisdom, having realized it for himself by direct knowledge. This too is a Tathāgata power of the Tathāgata, by reason of which he claims the foremost rank, roars his lion's roar in the assemblies and sets rolling the supreme Wheel of the Dhamma.

These, monks, are the ten Tathāgata powers of the Tathāgata, endowed with which the Tathāgata claims the foremost rank, roars his lion's roar in the assemblies and sets rolling the supreme Wheel of the Dhamma.

(10:21)

138. DOCTRINAL TERMS

Once the Venerable Ānanda approached the Blessed One and, after paying homage to him, sat down to one side. The Blessed One then addressed the Venerable Ānanda thus:

"Here, Ānanda, I am confident about those things that lead to the realization by direct knowledge of the various doctrinal terms,[16] and I claim to teach the Dhamma about these matters in such a way that a person who acts accordingly will know the real as being real and the unreal as being unreal; he will know the inferior as being inferior and the excellent as being excellent; he will know what can be surpassed as being surpassable and the unsurpassable as being unsurpassable; and there is the possibility that he will know, understand and realize it just as it ought to be known, understood and realized.

"But that, Ānanda, is the highest knowledge, namely, the knowledge of these things as they really are. And I say, Ānanda, there is no knowledge higher and more excellent than this."

(Here follows a full repetition of the text on the ten Tathāgata powers, as in the preceding sutta).

(10:22; extract)

139. Universal Impermanence

(1) Monks, as far as there are Kāsi[17] and Kosala people, as far as the realm of King Pasenadi of Kosala extends, King Pasenadi of Kosala ranks as the highest. But even for King Pasenadi change[18] takes place, transformation takes place. When seeing this, monks, an instructed noble disciple is repelled by it; being repelled, he becomes dispassionate towards the highest,[19] not to speak of what is low.

(2) Monks, as far as sun and moon revolve and illuminate all directions by their radiance, so far does the thousandfold world system extend. And in that thousandfold world system there are a thousand moons, a thousand suns, a thousand Mount Sinerus the king of mountains, a thousand Jambudīpa continents, a thousand Western Goyana continents, a thousand Northern Kuru continents, a thousand Eastern Videha continents, a thousand four great oceans, a thousand Four Divine Kings and their heavens, a thousand each of the heavens of the Tāvatiṃsa devas, of the Yāma devas, of the Tusita devas, of the Nimmāṇarati devas, of the Paranimmitavasavattī devas, and there are a thousand Brahma-worlds. As far, monks, as this thousandfold world system extends, Mahābrahmā ranks there as the highest. But even for Mahābrahmā change takes place, transformation takes place. When seeing this, monks, an instructed noble disciple is repelled by it; being repelled, he becomes dispassionate towards the highest, not to speak of what is low.

(3) There will be a time, monks, when this world comes to an end. And at that time, beings are generally reborn among the devas of Streaming Radiance.[20] There they live, made of mind, feeding on joy, radiating light from themselves, traversing the skies, living in glory, and thus they remain for a very long time. When the world comes to an end, monks, these devas of Streaming Radiance rank as the highest. But even for these devas change takes place, transformation takes place. When seeing this, monks, an instructed noble disciple is repelled by it; being repelled, he becomes dispassionate towards the highest, not to speak of what is low.

(4) Monks, there are the ten kasiṇa devices.[21] What are the ten? Someone perceives the earth kasiṇa, above, below, on all sides, undivided, unbounded; another person perceives the water kasiṇa … the fire kasiṇa … the wind kasiṇa … the blue … yellow … red … white kasiṇa … the space kasiṇa … the consciousness kasiṇa, above, below, on all sides, undivided, unbounded. These are the ten kasiṇa devices. Among these ten, this is the highest: when one perceives the consciousness kasiṇa above, below, on all sides, undivided, unbounded. There are indeed, monks, persons who perceive in such a way. But even for them change takes place, transformation takes place. When seeing this, monks, an instructed noble disciple is repelled by it; being repelled, he becomes dispassionate towards the highest, not to speak of what is low.

(5) Monks, there are eight stages of mastery.[22] What are the eight?

(i) Perceiving forms internally, one sees forms externally, small ones, beautiful or ugly; and in mastering them, one understands: "I know, I see!" This is the first stage of mastery…. (viii) Not perceiving forms internally, one sees forms externally, white forms, of white colour, white appearance, white lustre, and mastering these, one understands: "I know, I see!" This is the eighth stage of mastery.

Among these eight, the last is the highest. There are indeed, monks, persons who perceive in such a way. But even for them change takes place, transformation takes place. When seeing this, monks, an instructed noble disciple is repelled by it; being repelled, he becomes dispassionate towards the highest, not to speak of what is low.

(6) Monks, there are four modes of progress: The mode of progress that is painful, with sluggish direct knowledge; the mode of progress that is painful, with quick direct knowledge; the mode of progress that is pleasant, with sluggish direct knowledge; and the mode of progress that is pleasant, with quick direct knowledge.[23] Among these four, the highest is the mode of progress that is pleasant, with quick direct knowledge. There are indeed, monks those who make progress in such a way. But even for them change takes place, transformation takes place. When seeing this, monks, an instructed noble disciple is repelled by it; being repelled, he becomes dispassionate towards the highest, not to speak of what is low.

(7) Monks, there are four modes of perception: one person perceives what is limited; another perceives what is exalted; another perceives what is measureless; and still another, aware that "There is nothing," perceives the base of nothingness.[24]

Among these four modes of perception, the highest is when, aware that "There is nothing," one perceives the base of nothingness. There are indeed, monks, those who perceive in such a way. But even for them change takes place, transformation takes place. When seeing this, monks, an instructed noble disciple is repelled by it; being repelled, he becomes dispassionate towards the highest, not to speak of what is low.

(8) Monks, among the views of outsiders, this is the highest: "I might not be and it might not be mine; I shall not be and it will not be mine."[25]

For one, monks, who has such a view, it can be expected that he will not feel attracted to becoming and will have no aversion against the cessation of becoming.[26] There are indeed, monks, those who have such a view. But even for them change takes place, transformation takes place. When seeing this, monks, an instructed noble disciple is repelled by it; being repelled, he becomes dispassionate towards the highest, not to speak of what is low.

(9) Monks, there are some ascetics and brahmins who teach an "ultimate purification."[27] Those who teach an "ultimate purification" regard it as the highest if, after transcending the base of nothingness, one enters into and dwells in the base of neither-perception-nor-non-perception. They teach their doctrine for the direct knowledge and realization of that. There are indeed, monks, those who teach thus. But even for them change takes place, transformation takes place. When seeing this, monks, an instructed noble disciple is repelled by it; being repelled, he becomes dispassionate towards the highest, not to speak of what is low.

(10) Monks, there are some ascetics and brahmins who teach the supreme Nibbāna in this very life.[28] To those who teach the supreme Nibbāna in this very life, the highest is the liberation-without-clinging attained after seeing the six bases of contact as they really are, namely, their arising and passing away, the gratification and danger in them, and the escape from them.

And though I teach and proclaim thus, some ascetics and brahmins wrongly, baselessly, falsely and incorrectly misrepresent me thus: "The ascetic Gotama does not teach the full understanding of sensual pleasures, nor of forms, nor of feelings." But, monks, I do teach the full understanding of sensual pleasures, and of forms, and of feelings.[29] And being stilled, quenched and cooled even in this very life, I proclaim the supreme Nibbāna that is free from clinging.[30]

(10:29)

140. KING PASENADI'S HOMAGE TO THE BUDDHA

On one occasion the Blessed One was dwelling at Sāvatthī in Jeta's Grove, Anāthapiṇḍika's monastery. At that time King Pasenadi of Kosala had returned from a sham battle,[31] having been victorious and having achieved his purpose. The king then set out in the direction of the monastery. He rode by chariot as far as the road went; then he alighted from his chariot and entered the monastery on foot.

At that time, a number of monks were walking up and down in the open. The king approached them and asked: "Where, venerable sirs, is the Blessed One staying now?"

"He is staying in the lodging there, great king, where the door is shut. You may go there quietly and without haste. Then enter the verandah, clear your throat, and knock with the door bar. The Blessed One will open the door for you."

The king did as he was told and the Blessed One opened the door for the king. Having entered the dwelling, King Pasenadi bent low before the Blessed One with his head on the ground and kissed the Blessed One's feet, embracing them with his hands. Then he announced his name: "I am Pasenadi, Lord, the king of Kosala. I am Pasenadi, Lord, the king of Kosala."

"But, great king, what reason do you see for showing to this body such profound humility and for offering it such loving devotion?"

"To express my grateful thanks, Lord; for that reason do I show to the Blessed One such profound humility and offer him my loving devotion.

"The Blessed One, Lord, lives for the welfare of the multitude, for the happiness of the multitude, he has established many people in the noble way, in good and wholesome principles. It is for this reason, Lord, that I show to the Blessed One such profound humility and offer him my loving devotion.

"Again, Lord, the Blessed One is virtuous, of mature virtue, of noble virtue, of wholesome virtue; he is endowed with wholesome virtue. It is for this reason ....

"Again, Lord, the Blessed One has been a forest dweller for a long time; he resorts to remote forest lands, to secluded dwellings. It is for this reason ....

"Again, Lord, the Blessed One is content with whatever robes, alms-food, lodging, and medicinal requisites he receives. It is for this reason ....

"Again, Lord, the Blessed One is worthy of gifts, worthy of hospitality, worthy of offerings, worthy of reverential salutation, being the unsurpassed field of merit for the world. It is for this reason ....

"Again, Lord, the Blessed One obtains at will, without trouble or difficulty, (the opportunity for) talk that befits an austere life and is helpful to mental clarity; that is to say, talk on fewness of wishes, on contentment, on solitude, on seclusion, on application of energy, on virtue, concentration, wisdom, liberation and the knowledge and vision of liberation. It is for this reason ....

"Again, Lord, the Blessed One attains at will, without trouble or difficulty, the four jhānas, which pertain to the higher mind and are pleasant dwellings in this very life. It is for this reason ....

"Again, Lord, the Blessed One recollects his manifold past lives, that is to say, one birth ... (as in Text 137) ... It is for this reason ....

"Again, Lord, with the divine eye, which is purified and surpasses the human, the Blessed One sees beings passing away and reappearing ... (as in Text 137) ... It is for this reason ....

"And again, Lord, the Blessed One, by the destruction of the taints, in this very life enters and dwells in the taintless liberation of mind, liberation by wisdom, having realized it for himself by direct knowledge. It is for this reason, Lord, that I show to the Blessed One such profound humility and offer him my loving devotion.

"But now, Lord, we must go. We have much work and many duties."

"Do as you think fit, great king."

And King Pasenadi of Kosala rose from his seat, paid homage to the Blessed One, and respectfully and keeping him to his right, he departed.

(10:30)

141. SELF-EXAMINATION

If, O monks, a monk is not skilled in knowing the ways of others' minds, he should resolve, "I must become skilled in knowing the ways of my own mind." Thus, monks, should you train yourselves.

And how is a monk skilled in knowing the ways of his own mind? It is just as if a woman or a man, young, youthful and fond of ornaments, would look at their face in a clean, bright mirror or in a bowl of clear water. If they then see any dust or dirt, they will make all effort to remove it. But if no dust or dirt is seen, they will be glad about it, and their wish satisfied, they will think, "How good! I am clean!"

Similarly, monks, for a monk self-examination is very helpful for the growth of wholesome qualities: "Am I often covetous or often not covetous? Do I often have ill will in my heart or am I often free of it? Am I often immersed in sloth and torpor or am I often free of it? Am I excited or often free of excitement? Am I often in doubt or often free of doubt? Am I often angry or often free of anger? Is my mind often defiled by unwholesome thoughts or often free of defilements? Is my body often restless or often free of restlessness? Am I often lazy or often energetic? Am I often unconcentrated or often concentrated?"

When, by such self-examination, a monk finds that he is often covetous, full of ill will, slothful, excited, doubtful, angry, mentally defiled, bodily restless, lazy and unconcentrated, then he should apply his utmost zeal and energy, effort and exertion, as well as unremitting mindfulness and clear comprehension, to the abandoning of all those evil, unwholesome qualities.

Just as a man whose clothes or turban are on fire would apply his utmost zeal and energy, effort and exertion, as well as mindfulness and clear comprehension, so that he may extinguish the fire; even so, the monk should apply his utmost zeal and energy ... for the abandoning of those evil, unwholesome qualities.

But if, on examining himself, that monk finds that he is more often without covetousness and ill will, more often free from sloth and torpor, free from excitement and doubt; more often free from anger; and finds that his mind is more often undefiled and his body free of restlessness; that he is more often energetic and well concentrated—then grounding himself firmly in all these wholesome qualities, he should make a further effort for the destruction of the taints.

(10:51)

142. DO NOT STAGNATE!

I do not approve, monks, of stagnation in things wholesome, not to speak of a decline. It is growth in things unwholesome that I praise, and not stagnation, not decline in them.

(10:53, extract)

143. THE ROOTS OF EVERYTHING

It may be, O monks, that wandering ascetics of another persuasion might ask you:[32] "In what are all things rooted? How do they come to actual existence? Where do they arise? Where do they converge? What is the foremost in all things? What is their master? What is the highest of all things? What is the essence in all things? Where do all things merge? Where do they end?"

If you are thus questioned, monks, you should reply as follows: "All things are rooted in desire.[33] They come to actual existence through attention,[34] originate from contact, and converge on feelings. The foremost of all things is concentration. All things are mastered by mindfulness. Their peak is wisdom, their essence liberation. All things merge in the Deathless, and Nibbāna is their culmination."[35]

(10:58)

144. THE SPIRIT OF MONKHOOD

O monks, you should train yourselves thus: "In the spirit of our going forth should our mind be strengthened![36] No evil, unwholesome thoughts should persist obsessing our minds! In the perception of impermanence shall our mind be strengthened! In the perception of non-self shall our mind be strengthened! In the perception of foulness shall our mind be strengthened! In the perception of danger shall our mind be strengthened! In knowing the even and uneven ways of the world shall our mind be strengthened! In knowing growth and decline in the world shall our mind be strengthened![37] In knowing the origination and the passing away of the world shall our mind be strengthened![38] In the perception of abandoning shall our mind be strengthened! In the perception of dispassion shall our mind be strengthened! In the perception of cessation shall our mind be strengthened!"[39] In such a way, monks, should you train yourselves.

When a monk's mind is strengthened in all these ways, one of two fruits may be expected: either final knowledge in this present life, or else, if there is a residue of clinging, the stage of non-returning.

(10:59)

145. IGNORANCE AND CRAVING

(AN 10:61) A first beginning of ignorance, O monks, cannot be discerned,[40] of which it can be said, "Before that, there was no ignorance and it came to be after that." Though this is so, monks, yet a specific condition of ignorance is discerned. Ignorance, too, has its nutriment, I declare; and it is not without a nutriment. And what is the nutriment of ignorance? "The five hindrances" should be the answer.[41]

(AN 10:62) A first beginning of the craving for becoming, O monks, cannot be discerned, of which it can be said, "Before that, there was no craving for becoming and it came to be after that." Though this is so, monks, yet a specific condition for the craving for becoming is discerned. The craving for becoming, too, has its nutriment, I declare; and it is not without a nutriment. And what is the nutriment of the craving for becoming? "Ignorance," should be the answer. But ignorance, too, has its nutriment; it is not without a nutriment. And what is the nutriment of ignorance? "The five hindrances" should be the answer.

(AN 10:61 & 62) But the five hindrances, too, have their nutriment, monks; they are not without a nutriment. And what is the nutriment of the five hindrances? "The three ways of wrong conduct" should be the answer.[42]

The three ways of wrong conduct, too, have their nutriment; they are not without a nutriment. And what is their nutriment? "Lack of sense restraint" should be the answer.

Lack of sense restraint, too, has its nutriment; it is not without a nutriment. And what is its nutriment? "Lack of mindfulness and clear comprehension" should be the answer.

Lack of mindfulness and clear comprehension, too, has its nutriment; it is not without a nutriment. And what is the nutriment of the lack of mindfulness and clear comprehension? "Improper attention" should be the answer.

Improper attention, too, has its nutriment; it is not without a nutriment. And what is the nutriment of improper attention? "Lack of faith" should be the answer.

Lack of faith, too, has its nutriment; it is not without a nutriment. And what is the nutriment of the lack of faith? "Listening to wrong teachings" should be the answer.

Listening to wrong teachings, too, has its nutriment; it is not without a nutriment. And what is the nutriment of listening to wrong teachings? "Association with bad people" should be the answer.

Hence, when association with bad people prevails, listening to wrong teachings will prevail.[43] When listening to wrong teachings prevails, it will make lack of faith prevail. When lack of faith prevails, it will make improper attention prevail. When improper attention prevails, it will make lack of mindfulness and clear comprehension prevail. When lack of mindfulness and clear comprehension prevails, it will make lack of sense restraint prevail. When lack of sense restraint prevails, it will make the three ways of wrong conduct prevail. When the three ways of wrong conduct prevail, they will make the five hindrances prevail. When the five hindrances prevail, they will make ignorance prevail. (AN 10:62 adds: When ignorance prevails, it will make the craving for becoming prevail.) Such is the nutriment of that ignorance (AN 10:62: of that craving for becoming), and so it prevails.

Just as, when there is heavy rain high up in the mountains and the sky is rumbling, the water, flowing downwards, will fill up the clefts, crevices and fissures in the mountains, and when these are full, they will fill up the little pools; the full little pools will fill up the lakes; the full lakes will fill up the small rivers; the full small rivers will fill up the big rivers; and the full big rivers will fill up the great ocean. Such is the nutriment of the great ocean, and so it becomes full.

In the same way, monks, when association with bad people prevails, listening to wrong teachings will prevail ... when the five hindrances prevail, ignorance (and the craving for becoming) will prevail. Such is the nutriment of ignorance (and of the craving for becoming), and so it prevails.

Liberation by supreme knowledge too, O monks, has its nutriment, I declare; it is not without a nutriment. And what is the nutriment of liberation by supreme knowledge? "The seven factors of enlightenment" should be the answer.

The seven factors of enlightenment, too, have their nutriment, I declare; they are not without a nutriment? And what is the nutriment of the seven factors of enlightenment? "The four foundations of mindfulness" should be the answer.

The four foundation of mindfulness, too, have their nutriment; they are not without a nutriment. And what is the nutriment of the four foundations of mindfulness? "The three ways of good conduct" should be the answer.

The three ways of good conduct, too, have their nutriment; they are not without a nutriment. And what is the nutriment of the three ways of good conduct? "Restraint of the senses" should be the answer.

Restraint of the senses, too, has its nutriment; it is not without a nutriment. And what is the nutriment of restraint of the senses? "Mindfulness and clear comprehension" should be the answer.

Mindfulness and clear comprehension, too, have their nutriment; they are not without a nutriment. And what is the nutriment of mindfulness and clear comprehension? "Proper attention" should be the answer.

Proper attention, too, has its nutriment; it is not without a nutriment. And what is the nutriment of proper attention? "Faith" should be the answer.

Faith, too, has its nutriment; it is not without a nutriment. And what is the nutriment of faith? "Listening to the true Dhamma" should be the answer.

Listening to the true Dhamma, too, has its nutriment; it is not without a nutriment. And what is the nutriment of listening to the true Dhamma? "Association with superior people" should be the answer.

Hence, when association with superior people prevails, it will make prevail the listening to the true Dhamma ... When the seven factors of enlightenment prevail, they will make prevail liberation by supreme knowledge. Such is the nutriment of that liberation by supreme knowledge, and so it prevails.

Just as, when there is heavy rain high up in the mountains and the sky is rumbling, the water, flowing downwards, will fill up the clefts, crevices and fissures in the mountains, and when these are full, they will fill up the little pools; the full little pools will fill up the lakes; the full lakes will fill up the small rivers; the full small rivers will fill up the big rivers; and the full big rivers will fill up the great ocean. Such is the nutriment of the great ocean, and so it becomes full.

In the same way, monks, when association with superior people prevails, listening to the true Dhamma will prevail. When listening to the true Dhamma prevails, faith will prevail. When faith prevails, proper attention will prevail. When proper attention prevails, mindfulness and clear comprehension will prevail. When mindfulness and clear comprehension prevail, restraint of the senses will prevail. When restraint of the senses prevails, the three ways of good conduct will prevail. When the three ways of good conduct prevail, the four foundations of mindfulness will prevail. When the four foundations of mindfulness prevail, the seven factors of enlightenment will prevail. When the seven factors of enlightenment prevail, liberation by supreme knowledge will prevail. Such is the nutriment of that liberation by supreme knowledge, and so it prevails.

(10:61 & 62; combined)

146. Happiness and Suffering

On one occasion the Venerable Sāriputta was dwelling in Magadha, in the village Nālaka.[44] On that occasion, Sāmaṇḍakāni, a wandering ascetic, approached him and asked:

"What, friend Sāriputta, is happiness, and what is suffering?"

"To be reborn, friend, is suffering; not to be reborn is happiness."

(10:65; extract)

147. Birth, Old age, and death

If, O monks, three things were not to be found in the world, the Tathāgata, the Arahant, the Fully Enlightened One, would not appear in the world, nor would the Dhamma and Discipline proclaimed by him shed its light over the world. What are these three things? Birth, old age, and death. But since these three things are to be found in the world, the Tathāgata appears in the world, the Arahant, the Fully Enlightened One, and the Dhamma and Discipline proclaimed by him sheds its light over the world.

Without abandoning three things, one is unable to abandon birth, old age, and death. What are these three? Greed, hatred, and delusion: without abandoning these three things one is unable to abandon birth, old age, and death.

Without abandoning three things, one is unable to abandon greed, hatred, and delusion. They are: personality view, sceptical doubt, and clinging to rules and vows.[45]

Without abandoning three things, one is unable to abandon personality view, sceptical doubt, and clinging to rules and vows. They are: improper attention, pursuing wrong ways, and mental lassitude.

Without abandoning three things, one is unable to abandon improper attention, the pursuing of wrong ways and mental lassitude. They are: unmindfulness, lack of clear comprehension, and mental distraction.

Without abandoning three things, one is unable to abandon unmindfulness, lack of clear comprehension and mental distraction. They are: disinterest in seeing noble ones, disinterest in listening to their teachings, and a fault-finding mentality.

Without abandoning three things, one is unable to abandon lack of interest in seeing noble ones, disinterest in listening to their teachings, and a fault-finding mentality. They are: restlessness, lack of restraint, and immorality.

Without abandoning three things, one is unable to abandon restlessness, lack of self-control, and immorality. They are: lack of faith, unfriendliness, and laziness.

Without abandoning three things, one is unable to abandon lack of faith, unfriendliness, and laziness. They are: disrespect, stubbornness, and bad friendships.

Without abandoning three things, one is unable to abandon disrespect, stubbornness, and bad friendships. They are: shamelessness, lack of moral dread and negligence.

There is a person, monks, who is shameless, morally reckless, and negligent. Being negligent, he cannot abandon disrespect, stubbornness, and bad friendships. Having bad friends, he cannot abandon lack of faith, unfriendliness, and laziness. Being lazy, he cannot abandon restlessness, lack of restraint and immorality. Being immoral, he cannot abandon disinterest in seeing noble ones, disinterest in listening to their teachings, and a fault-finding mentality. Being a fault-finder, he cannot abandon unmindfulness, lack of clear comprehension, and mental distraction. Having a distracted mind, he cannot abandon improper attention, the pursuit of wrong ways and mental lassitude. With mental lassitude, he cannot abandon personality view, sceptical doubt, and clinging to rules and vows. Troubled by sceptical doubt, he cannot abandon greed, hatred, and delusion. And without giving up greed, hatred, and delusion, he cannot abandon birth, old age, and death.

But by abandoning three things, one is able to abandon birth, old age, and death. What are these three? They are: greed, hatred, and delusion. By abandoning them, one is able to abandon birth, old age, and death.

By abandoning three things, one is able to abandon greed, hatred, and delusion. They are: personality view, sceptical doubt, and clinging to rules and vows.

(To be continued with the same sequence of terms as above, up to:)

By abandoning three things, one is able to abandon disrespect, stubbornness, and bad friendships. They are: shamelessness, lack of moral dread, and negligence.

There is a person, monks, who is conscientious, scrupulous, and diligent. Being diligent, he can abandon disrespect, stubbornness, and bad friendships. Having noble friends, he can abandon lack of faith, unfriendliness, and laziness. Being energetic, he can abandon restlessness, lack of restraint, and immorality. Being virtuous, he can abandon disinterest in seeing noble ones, disinterest in listening to their teachings, and a fault-finding mentality. Not being a fault-finder, he can abandon unmindfulness, lack of clear comprehension, and mental distraction. Having an undistracted mind, he can abandon improper attention, pursuit of wrong ways, and mental lassitude. Being without mental lassitude, he can abandon personality view, sceptical doubt, and clinging to rules and vows. Being free from doubt, he can abandon greed, hatred, and delusion. Having abandoned greed, hatred, and delusion, he can abandon birth, old age, and death.

(10:76)

148. A Discriminative Teaching

On one occasion the Blessed One was dwelling near Campā, on the bank of the Gaggarā lotus pond.

One day the householder Vajjiyamāhita left Campā at an early hour in order to see the Blessed One.[46] Then he thought: "It is not the right time to visit the Blessed One, who will now be in seclusion. Nor is it the proper time to visit the venerable monks; they, too, will be in seclusion. Let me now go to the park where the wandering ascetics of another persuasion stay."

When Vajjiyamāhita the householder arrived at the park, those wanderers were gathered there in company and were sitting together shouting and speaking loudly, engaged in diverse kinds of low talk. But when they saw Vajjiyamāhita the householder approaching in the distance, they admonished each other to be quiet, saying: "Make less noise, your reverences, and be quiet! Here the householder Vajjiyamāhita is coming, a disciple of the ascetic Gotama. He is one of the white clad lay disciples of the ascetic Gotama who stays now at Campā. These worthy ones do not like much noise, they are used to being noiseless and they praise noiselessness. Perhaps if Vajjiyamāhita sees our group to be quiet, he may think of coming here."

These wandering ascetics now kept silent. When the householder Vajjiyamāhita arrived there, he exchanged polite greetings and cordial talk with them and sat down at one side. When he was seated, the wanderers asked him:

"Is it true, householder, what they say—that the ascetic Gotama blames all asceticism and that he unreservedly condemns and reproves all ascetics who live a harsh and austere life?"

"No, venerable sirs, the Blessed One does not blame all asceticism, nor does he unreservedly condemn and reprove all ascetics living a harsh and austere life. What is blameworthy, the Blessed One blames; what is praiseworthy, he praises. By blaming what is blameworthy and praising what is praiseworthy, the Blessed One teaches with discrimination, he does not teach here in a one-sided way."[47]

At these words, a certain wanderer said this to the householder Vajjiyamāhita: "Wait a moment, householder! That ascetic Gotama, whom you praise so much, is a nihilist, and he is one who refrains from making any definite declarations."[48]

"About that, too, venerable sir, I shall speak to your reverences according to the Dhamma. The Blessed One, venerable sir, declares that some things are wholesome and other things unwholesome. The Blessed One, having thus declared what is wholesome and what is unwholesome, is in fact one who makes definite declarations. He is not a nihilist, nor one who refrains from making definite declarations."

At these words the wanderers kept silent, embarrassed, sitting there with slumping shoulders and heads lowered, brooding and unable to utter a word. When Vajjiyamāhita saw them in that condition, he rose from his seat and left to see the Blessed One. Having arrived, after saluting the Blessed One, he told him of his conversation with these wanderers of another persuasion. And the Blessed One said:

"Good, householder, good! In that way, householder, should such foolish persons, when occasion offers, be well refuted by you according to the Dhamma.

"I do not say, householder, that all asceticism should be practised; nor do I say of all asceticism that it should not be practised. I do not say that all undertakings should be performed; nor do I say of all undertakings that they should not be performed. I do not say that every spiritual effort should be done or every act renunciation be carried out; nor do I say of every spiritual effort that it should not be done nor of every act of renunciation that it should not be carried out. I do not say that one should free oneself by every kind of freedom; nor do I say of every kind of freedom that one should not free oneself by it.

"What I declare, householder, is that such an asceticism should not be practised which makes unwholesome states grow and wholesome states wane. But, I declare, an asceticism which makes unwholesome states wane and wholesome states grow should be practised.

"If in performing undertakings, making spiritual efforts, carrying out acts of renunciation, freeing oneself by certain kinds of freedom, unwholesome states grow, then, I declare, all these practices should not be carried out."

"But if in performing undertakings, making spiritual efforts, carrying out acts of renunciation, freeing oneself by certain kinds of freedom, unwholesome states wane and wholesome states grow, then, I declare, all these practices should be carried out."

Then Vajjiyamāhita the householder, thus instructed by the Blessed One's Dhamma talk, roused by it, inspired and gladdened, rose from his seat, saluted the Blessed One respectfully, and keeping him to his right, departed.

Soon after he had left, the Blessed One addressed the monks thus: "Monks, even a monk who has had for a long time clear vision as to this Dhamma and Discipline would well refute those wanderers of another persuasion in the very same way that the householder Vajjiyamāhita has done."

(10:94)

149. WILL ALL BEINGS ATTAIN LIBERATION?

On one occasion a wandering ascetic named Uttiya approached the Blessed One. After exchanging greetings and cordial talk, he sat down to one side and asked the Blessed One:

"How is it, Master Gotama: is the world eternal—is only this true and everything else false?"

"This, Uttiya, I have not declared: that the world is eternal; and that only this is true and everything else false."

"How then, Master Gotama: is the world non-eternal—is only this true and everything else false?"

"That, too, Uttiya, I have not declared: that the world is non-eternal; and that only this is true and everything else false."

"How is it, Master Gotama: is the world finite or infinite? Are the life principle and the body the same or different? Does the Tathāgata exist after death or does he not exist after death? Does he exist as well as not exist or neither exist nor not exist after death? Is any one of these statements the only one that is true and everything else false?"

"All that, Uttiya, I have not declared: that the world is finite ... that the Tathāgata neither exists nor does not exist after death; nor do I declare that any one of these statements is the only true one and everything else false."

"But how is it, Master Gotama? To all my questions you have replied that you have not so declared. What, after all, does Master Gotama actually declare?"

"Having directly known it, Uttiya, I have taught the Dhamma to my disciples for the purification of beings, for getting beyond sorrow and lamentation, for the ending of pain and grief, for attaining to the method of liberation and for realizing Nibbāna."

"But if Master Gotama, from direct knowledge, teaches the Dhamma to his disciples for the purification of beings, for getting beyond sorrow and lamentation, for the ending of pain and grief, for attaining to the method of liberation and for realizing Nibbāna, will the whole world thereby be emancipated,[49] or half of it or a third part of it?"

At these words, the Blessed One kept silent.[50]

Then this thought occurred to the Venerable Ānanda: "May Uttiya the wanderer not conceive a harmful opinion, by thinking, 'When I asked the ascetic Gotama a question on an ultimate issue, he foundered and did not reply. Probably he was unable to do so.' For such a view would bring harm and suffering to Uttiya for a long time."

Then the Venerable Ānanda turned to Uttiya, saying: "I shall give you a simile, friend Uttiya, for with the help of a simile intelligent people may come to understand the meaning of what was said.

"Suppose, friend Uttiya, there is a king's border town, with strong ramparts and turrets on sound foundations, and with a single gate. There is also a gate-keeper, intelligent, experienced and prudent, who keeps out people unknown and admits only those who are known. That gate-keeper walks along the path that girdles the town all round, and while doing so he does not notice in the ramparts any hole or opening, not even one big enough for a cat to slip through. Though he does not have the knowledge of how many creatures enter the town or leave it, yet he does know this: 'Any larger creatures that enter or leave this town can do so only by this gate.'

"Similarly, friend Uttiya, the Tathāgata is not concerned with whether the entire world will be emancipated by his teaching or half of it or a third part. But the Tathāgata is aware that whosoever has been emancipated, is now emancipated or will be emancipated from the world, all these will do so by removing the five hindrances that defile the mind and weaken understanding, by firmly establishing their minds in the four foundations of mindfulness, and by cultivating the seven factors of enlightenment in their true nature. That same question, friend Uttiya, which you had asked the Blessed One before, you have asked him again in another way."[51]

(10:95)

150. NOT OUTSIDE THE BUDDHA'S DISCIPLINE

Ten things, monks, do not have purity and clarity outside the Discipline of the Sublime Master. What are the ten?

(AN 10:123) Right view, right intention, right speech, right action, right livelihood, right effort, right mindfulness, right concentration, right knowledge, and right liberation.[52]

(AN 10:124) And if these ten things have not arisen, they will not arise outside the Discipline of the Sublime Master.

(AN 10:125) Outside the Discipline of the Sublime Master, these ten things will not be of great fruit and benefit.

(AN 10:126) Outside the Discipline of the Sublime Master, these ten things will not end in the elimination of greed, hatred, and delusion.

(AN 10:127) Outside the Discipline of the Sublime Master, these ten things will not conduce to complete disenchantment, dispassion, cessation, peace, direct knowledge, enlightenment, and Nibbāna.

(10:123–27)

151. THE CONCATENATION OF KAMMA

The destruction of life, monks, I declare to be threefold: as caused by greed, caused by hatred, caused by delusion. So too, taking what is not given, sexual misconduct, false speech, divisive speech, harsh speech, frivolous chatter, covetousness, ill will and wrong view, I declare to be threefold: as caused by greed, caused by hatred and caused by delusion.[53]

Hence, monks, greed is a producer of kammic concatenation, hatred is a producer of kammic concatenation, delusion is a producer of kammic concatenation. But by the destruction of greed, hatred, and delusion, there is the exhaustion of kammic concatenation.

(10:174)

152. The Extinction of Kamma

I declare, monks, that actions willed, performed and accumulated will not become extinct as long as their results have not been experienced, be it in this life, in the next life or in subsequent future lives. And as long as these results of actions willed, performed, and accumulated have not been experienced, there will be no making an end to suffering, I declare.[54]

There are, monks, tainted failures in living caused by unwholesome volition, issuing in suffering, resulting in suffering. These tainted failures are threefold in bodily acts, fourfold in verbal acts and threefold in mental acts.

How are these tainted failures in living caused by unwholesome volition threefold in bodily acts?

There is a person who destroys life; he is cruel and his hands are blood-stained; he is bent on slaying and murdering, having no compassion for any living being.

He takes what is not given to him, appropriates with thievish intent the property of others, be it in the village or the forest.

He conducts himself wrongly in matters of sex: he has intercourse with those under the protection of father, mother, brother, sister, relatives, or clan, or of their religious community; or with those promised to a husband, protected by law, and even with those betrothed with a garland.[55]

In this way tainted failure in living is threefold in bodily acts.

And how is tainted failure in living fourfold in verbal acts?

There is one who is a liar. When he is in the council of his community or in another assembly, or among his relatives, his guild, in the royal court, or when he has been summoned as a witness and is asked to tell what he knows, then, though he does not know, he will say, "I know"; though he does know, he will say, "I do not know"; though he has not seen, he will say, "I have seen"; and though he has seen, he will say, "I have not seen." In that way he utters deliberate lies, be it for his own sake, for the sake of others, or for some material advantage.

He utters divisive speech: what he hears here he reports elsewhere to foment conflict there; and what he hears elsewhere he reports here to foment conflict here. Thus he creates discord among those united, and he incites still more those who are in discord. He is fond of dissension, he delights and rejoices in it, and he utters words that cause dissension.

He speaks harshly, using speech that is coarse, rough, bitter, and abusive, that makes others angry and causes distraction of mind. It is such speech that he utters.

He indulges in frivolous chatter: he speaks what is untimely, unreasonable, and unbeneficial, having no connection with the Dhamma or the Discipline. His talk is not worth treasuring, it is inopportune, inadvisable, unrestrained, and harmful.

In this way, tainted failure in living is fourfold in verbal acts.

And how is tainted failure in living threefold in mental acts?

There is a person who is covetous; he covets the wealth and property of others, thinking: "Oh, that what he owns might belong to me!"

There is also one who has ill will in his heart. He has depraved thoughts, such as these: "Let these beings be slain! Let them be killed and destroyed! May they perish and cease to exist!"

He has wrong views and perverted ideas, such as these: "There is no moral value in a gift, offering or sacrifice; there is no fruit or recompense from deeds good or evil; there is neither this world nor another world;[56] there are no duties towards mother and father; there are no spontaneously reborn beings; and there are no ascetics and brahmins in this world, living and conducting themselves rightly, who can explain this world and the world beyond, having realized them by their own direct knowledge."

In this way tainted failure in living, which is caused by unwholesome volition, issuing in suffering and resulting in suffering, is threefold in mental acts.

As to that tainted failure in living, which is threefold in bodily acts, fourfold in verbal acts and threefold in mental acts, and which, having been caused by unwholesome volition, issues in suffering, results in suffering—it is due to that very failure in living that with the breakup of the body, after death, beings are reborn in the plane of misery, in a bad destination, in the lower world, in hell.

Just as a perfect throw of dice, when thrown upwards, will come to rest firmly wherever it falls, similarly, due to those tainted failures in living caused by unwholesome volition, beings will be reborn in the plane of misery ... in hell.

I declare, monks, that actions willed, performed and accumulated will not become extinct as long as their results have not been experienced, be it in this life, in the next life or in subsequent future lives. And as long as these results of actions willed, performed, and accumulated have not been experienced, there will be no end to suffering, I declare.

There are, monks, successes in living caused by wholesome volition, issuing in happiness, resulting in happiness. They are threefold in bodily acts, fourfold in verbal acts and threefold in mental acts.

How are these successes in living caused by wholesome volition threefold in bodily acts?

There is a person who abstains from the destruction life; with the rod and weapon laid aside, he is conscientious and kindly and dwells compassionate towards all living beings.

He does not take what is not given to him and does not appropriate with thievish intention the property of others, be it in the village or the forest.

He gives up sexual misconduct and abstains from it. He does not have intercourse with those under the protection of father, mother ... nor with those betrothed with a garland.

In this way, success in living is threefold in bodily acts.

And how is success in living fourfold in verbal acts?

There is a person who has given up false speech and abstains from it. When he is in the council of his community or in another assembly, or among his relatives, his guild, in the royal court, or has been summoned as a witness and is asked to tell what he knows, then, when he knows, he will say, "I know"; and when he does not know he will say, "I do not know"; when he has seen, he will say, "I have seen"; and when he has not seen, he will say, "I have not seen." He will not utter any deliberate lie, be it for his own sake, for the sake of others or for some material advantage.

He has given up divisive speech and abstains from it. What he has heard here he will not report elsewhere to foment conflict there; and what he has heard elsewhere he will not report here to foment conflict here. In that way he unites those who are divided and encourages those who are in harmony. Concord gladdens him, he delights and rejoices in concord, and he utters words that foster concord.

He has given up harsh speech and abstains from it. His words are gentle, pleasant to hear, endearing, heartwarming, courteous, agreeable to many folk, pleasing to many folk.

He has given up vain talk and abstains from it. He speaks at the right time, in accordance with facts and of matters that are beneficial. He speaks on the Dhamma and the Discipline and talks in a way that is worth treasuring. His talk is opportune, helpful, moderate, and meaningful.

In this way success in living is fourfold in verbal acts.

And how is success in living threefold in mental acts?

Here a person is free from covetousness; he does not covet the wealth and property of others, thinking, "Oh, that what he owns might belong to me!"

He has no ill will in his heart. He has pure thoughts and intentions, such as these: "May these beings be free from enmity, free from anxiety! May they be untroubled and live happily!"

He has right view and a correct perspective, such as this: "There is moral value in gifts, offerings and sacrifice; there is fruit and recompense from deeds good or evil; there is both this world and another world; there are duties towards mother and father; there exist beings who have been spontaneously reborn; and there exist in this world ascetics and brahmins living and conducting themselves rightly, who can explain this world and the world beyond, having realized them by their own direct knowledge."

In this way, success in living, which is caused by wholesome volition, is threefold in mental acts.

As to that success in living which is threefold in bodily acts, fourfold in verbal acts and threefold in mental acts, and which, having been caused by wholesome volition, issues in happiness, results in happiness—it is due to that very success in living that with the breakup of the body, after death, beings are reborn in a good destination, in a heavenly world.

Just as a perfect throw of dice, when thrown upwards, will come to rest firmly wherever it falls, similarly, due to success in living caused by wholesome volition, beings will be reborn in a good destination, in a heavenly world.

I declare, monks, that actions willed, performed, and accumulated will not become extinct as long as their results have not been experienced, be it in this life, in the next life or in subsequent future lives. And as long as these results of actions willed, performed, and accumulated have not been experienced, there will be no making an end to suffering, I declare.

(10:206)

153. THE FOUR BOUNDLESS STATES

"I declare, monks, that actions willed ... *(as at the end of the preceding text).*

"But a noble disciple—devoid of covetousness, devoid of ill will, unconfused, clearly comprehending, ever mindful—dwells pervading one quarter with a mind imbued with loving-kindness, likewise the second quarter, the third and the fourth. Thus above, below, across and everywhere, and to all as to himself, he dwells pervading the entire world with a mind imbued with loving-kindness, vast, exalted, measureless, without hostility, and without ill will.

"He knows: 'Formerly my mind was narrow and undeveloped; but now my mind is measureless and well developed. No measurable kamma will remain in it, none will persist there.'[57]

"What do you think, monks: if a young man, from his boyhood onwards, were to develop the liberation of the mind by loving-kindness, would he then do an evil deed?"

"He would not, Lord."

"And not doing any evil deed, will suffering afflict him?"[58]

"It will not, Lord. How could suffering afflict one who does no evil deeds?"

"Indeed, monks, the liberation of the mind by loving-kindness should be developed by a man or a woman. A man or a woman cannot take their body with them and depart; mortals have consciousness as the connecting link.[59]

"But the noble disciple knows: 'Whatever evil deeds I did before with this physical body, their results will be experienced here and they will not follow me along.'[60]

"Loving-kindness, if developed in such a way, will lead to the state of non-returning, in the case of a monk who is established in the wisdom found here in this teaching, but who has not penetrated to a higher liberation.[61]

"He dwells pervading one quarter with a mind imbued with compassion ... with altruistic joy ... with equanimity, likewise the second quarter, the third, and the fourth. Thus above, below, across and everywhere, and to all as to himself, he dwells pervading the entire world with a mind imbued with compassion, altruistic joy, and equanimity, vast, exalted, measureless, without hostility, and without ill will.

"He knows: 'Formerly my mind was narrow and undeveloped; but now my mind is measureless and well developed. No measurable kamma will remain in it, none will persist there.'

"What do you think, monks: if a young man, from his boyhood onwards, were to develop compassion, altruistic joy, and equanimity, would he then do an evil deed?"

"He would not, Lord."

"And not doing any evil deed, will suffering afflict him?"

"It will not, Lord. How could suffering afflict one who does no evil deeds?"

"Indeed, monks, the liberation of the mind by compassion ... by altruistic joy ... by equanimity should be developed by a man or a woman. A man or a woman cannot take their body with them and depart; mortals have consciousness as the connecting link.

"But the noble disciple knows: 'Whatever evil deeds I did before with this physical body, their results will be experienced here and they will not follow me along.'

"Compassion, altruistic joy, and equanimity, if developed in such a way, will lead to the state of non-returning, in the case of a monk who is established in the wisdom found here in this teaching, but who has not penetrated to a higher liberation."

(10:208)

XI. The Chapter of the Elevens

154. The Blessings of Loving-kindness

If, O monks, the liberation of the mind by loving-kindness is developed and cultivated, frequently practised, made one's vehicle and foundation, firmly established, consolidated, and properly undertaken, eleven blessings may be expected. What eleven?

One sleeps peacefully; one awakens peacefully; one sees no bad dreams; one is dear to human beings; one is dear to non-human beings; one will be protected by devas; fire, poison and weapons cannot injure one; one's mind becomes easily concentrated; one's facial complexion will be serene; one will die unconfused; and if one does not penetrate higher, one will be reborn in the Brahma-world.[1]

(11:16)

NOTES

I. THE CHAPTER OF THE ONES

1. Undeveloped (*abhāvitaṃ*). A-a: A mind not grown, not progressing in mental development (*bhāvanā*).
2. A-a explains this as meaning that the mind (i.e. a moment of consciousness) arises and vanishes very rapidly, but the same expression is used elsewhere in the canon in a context that suggests the intended meaning is the mind's vulnerability to quick changes in intentions and preferences. See e.g. Vin I 150, where the Buddha permits a monk to break his rains residence prematurely when he is being lured by a seductive woman "because the mind is said to be quickly changing."
3. *Luminous (pabhassaraṃ)*. A-a states that here "the mind" (*citta*) refers to the *bhavaṅga-citta,* the "life-continuum" or underlying stream of consciousness which supervenes whenever active consciousness lapses, most notably in deep sleep. The *adventitious defilements* are greed, hatred, and delusion, which appear at a stage of the cognitive process which, in later Buddhist literature, is called *javana,* "impulsion." A-a says that the defilements do not arise simultaneously with the *bhavaṅga,* but they "arrive" later, at the phase of *javana.* The fact that this expression "luminous mind" does not signify any "eternal and pure mind-essence" is evident from the preceding text, in which the mind is said to be extremely fleeting and transitory. The "uninstructed worldling" (*assutavā puthujjana*) is one who lacks adequate knowledge of the Dhamma and training in its practice.
4. Since monks and nuns depend for sustenance upon the generosity of householders, they must make themselves worthy of their offerings by devoting their efforts to the development of the mind. A-a distinguishes four modes in which monks might use the offerings they receive: (i) an immoral monk uses them as a thief; (ii) a virtuous worldling who does not reflect uses them as a debtor; (iii) a trainee (one at the lower three stages of awakening) uses them as an inheritance; and (iv) the arahant uses them as a proper owner.
5. *Manopubbaṅgamā*. This phrase also occurs at Dhp 1, 2. Unwholesome states (*akusalā dhammā*) are mental states born of greed, hatred and delusion. The wholesome states (*kusalā dhammā*) mentioned just below are mental states arisen from non-greed, non-hatred, and non-delusion. Mind (*mano*) here refers to the intention. While mind does not actually precede the wholesome and unwholesome states in a temporal sense, it is said to arise first because it is the volition or intention that determines the ethical quality of the deeds that issue from the mind.

6. *Pamāda* is moral laxity, heedlessness, lack of constancy and persistence in the pursuit of self-purification. It is often explained as lack of mindfulness and energy in the development of wholesome qualities. For a formal definition, see Vibh 350 (§846). Its opposite is *appamāda*, diligence, heedfulness, or earnestness, sometimes defined as constancy of mindfulness. For the contrast of the two, see Dhp 21–32, and for a eulogy of diligence, AN 10:15.
7. *Tathāgata* is the designation by which the Buddha usually speaks of himself. The commentaries offer a number of explanations, e.g. "one who has come thus" (*tathā āgata*), i.e. through the same path of practice that the Buddhas of the past came; "one who has gone thus" (*tathā gata*), i.e. gone to enlightenment along the same path that all Enlightened Ones have gone, etc. See Text 46 and Bodhi, *All Embracing Net of Views*, BPS, 2007, Part V.
8. On the *six things unsurpassed* (*anuttariyā*) see Text 89. The *four analytical knowledges* (*paṭisambhidā*) are four special types of knowledge concerning the meaning, doctrines, and linguistic formulations of the Dhamma, and the way to utilize this knowledge in expounding the Dhamma to others. By *elements* (*dhātu*) are meant here in particular the eighteen elements (the six sense faculties, six sense objects and the corresponding six kinds of consciousness). For other groups of elements see MN 115, MN 140 and SN Ch. 14. The four fruits of stream-entry, etc., are the four stages of awakening, on which see Bodhi, *Middle Length Discourses of the Buddha*, Boston 2006, p. 41.
9. A person possessed of right view (*diṭṭhi-sampanna*) is a stream-enterer or one at a higher stage of awakening. *Saṅkhārā*—"formations" or formations—include everything produced by conditions.
10. In this passage *saṅkhārā* is replaced by *dhammā*, which includes all phenomena whatever, whether conditioned or unconditioned. This passage is commonly held to be applicable to the unconditioned element (*asaṅkhata-dhātu*), Nibbāna. Thus, even though Nibbāna, being imperishable and the highest bliss, is not impermanent or suffering, it still cannot be identified as a self. See Dhp 277–79.
11. "Mindfulness directed to the body" (*kāyagatā-sati*) comprises all fourteen exercises described under contemplation of the body in the Kāyagatā-sati Sutta (MN 119) and the Satipaṭṭhāna Sutta (DN 22, MN 10): mindfulness of breathing, attention to the postures, clear comprehension of activities, reflection on foulness (on the thirty-one parts of the body), analysis into the four elements, and the nine cemetery contemplations (on decaying corpses). The great stress laid on contemplation of the body derives from the fact that meditative comprehension of the impermanent, painful, and selfless nature of bodily processes

forms the indispensable basis for a corresponding comprehension of mental processes; and it is only the comprehension of both that will lead to liberating insight and the noble path.

12. The three fetters (*saṃyojana*) eliminated by the stream-enterer are: personality view, i.e. the view of a self in relation to the five aggregates; doubt about the Buddha, his Teaching and the path of training; and clinging to rules and vows, i.e. penitential and ritualistic practices adopted in the belief that they are conducive to liberation.
13. The non-returner breaks all five lower fetters (*orambhāgiyāni saṃyojanāni*)—the first three fetters (see preceding paragraph) as well as the next two fetters, sensual desire and ill will. Since these fetters bind beings to the sensual realm of becoming (see Text 33), the non-returner can never again be reborn in the sense sphere but takes rebirth in the form realm (generally in one of the Pure Abodes), where he attains final Nibbāna.
14. The arahant destroys the five "higher fetters" (*uddhambhāgiyāni saṃyojanāni*): desire for the form realm, desire for the formless realm, conceit, restlessness, and ignorance. The fetters partly overlap with the taints (*āsava*): the first two are included under the taint of desire for becoming; the last is identical with the taint of ignorance.
15. The underlying tendencies (*anusaya*) are seven mental defilements deeply engrained in the mind through past habituation: sensual desire, aversion, conceit, views, doubt, attachment to becoming and ignorance. Views and doubt are eliminated at the stage of stream-entry; sensual desire and aversion, at the stage of non-returning; conceit, attachment to becoming and ignorance only at the stage of arahantship.

II. THE CHAPTER OF THE TWOS

1. Here the Buddha refers to the time when he was still a bodhisatta striving for enlightenment. A-a mentions, as "good states achieved," the jhānas and the "inner light" seen in meditative vision.
2. This text proclaims, in simple and memorable words, the human potential for achieving the good, thus invalidating the common charge that Buddhism is pessimistic. But since human beings have, as we know only too well, also a strong potential for evil, there is as little ground for unreserved optimism. Which of our potentialities, that for good or for evil, becomes *actual*, depends on our own choice. What *makes* a human being, *is* to have choices and to make use of them. The range of our choices and our prior awareness of them will expand with the growth of mindfulness and wisdom. And along with the growth of these two qualities, those forces that seem to "condition" and even compel our

choices into the wrong direction will become weakened. It is, indeed, a bold and heartening assurance of the Buddha—a veritable "lion's roar"—when he said, in such a wide and deep sense, that the good can be attained and the evil can be conquered.

3. *Vijjābhāgiyā*; that is, they are constituents of supreme knowledge (*vijjā*). This may refer either to the three true knowledges (*tevijjā*), often mentioned in the discourses: (1) the knowledge of recollection of former births; (2) the knowledge of the passing away and rebirth of beings; and (3) the knowledge of the destruction of the taints, i.e. the attainment of arahantship; or it may refer to an eightfold division: (1) insight knowledge (*vipassanā-ñāṇa*), (2) the power of creating a mind-made body (*manomayā iddhi)*; (3)–(8) the six direct knowledges (*abhiññā*). For the latter (which include the three true knowledges) see Text 34.
4. *Tranquillity* (*samatha*) is concentration culminating in the jhānas, being supremely tranquil and peaceful states; *insight* (*vipassanā*), according to A-a, is "the knowledge comprehending the formations" (*saṅkhāra-pariggāhaka-ñāṇa*) as impermanent, suffering and non-self.
5. When tranquillity is developed independently of insight, it brings about the suppression of the five hindrances, the first of which is sensual lust, and issues in the "higher mind" of the jhānas, characterized by the absence of lust. But it is only when tranquillity is developed in conjunction with insight that it can give rise to the noble path, which eradicates the underlying tendency to sensual lust (by the path of non-returning) and attachment to becoming (by the path of arahantship). A-a interprets tranquillity here in this second sense—presumably on account of the last sentence of the sutta—and explains: "The mind becomes developed into the path-consciousness (*magga-citta*). Lust (*rāga*) becomes abandoned because it is opposed to (incompatible with) path-consciousness, and the path is incompatible with lust. At a moment of lust there is no path-consciousness; and at the path-moment there is no lust. When lust arises, it obstructs the arising of the path-moment, cutting off its basis; but when the path arises it uproots and eradicates lust."
6. A-a: "It is path-wisdom (*magga-paññā*) that becomes developed, i.e. it is expanded and augmented. The "ignorance abandoned' is the great ignorance at the root of the cycle of existence. Ignorance is incompatible with path-wisdom, and path-wisdom is incompatible with ignorance. At a moment of ignorance there is no path-wisdom, and at a moment of path-wisdom there cannot be ignorance. When ignorance arises, it obstructs the arising of

path-wisdom and cuts off its basis; but when path-wisdom arises it uproots and eradicates ignorance. In this way, two coexistent phenomena have been dealt with here: path-consciousness (*magga-citta*) and path-wisdom (*magga-paññā*)."

7. Arahantship is often described as "taintless liberation of mind, liberation by wisdom" (*anāsava-cetovimutti-paññāvimutti*); see Text 18, etc. A-a explains "liberation of mind" as the concentration connected with the fruit (of arahantship; *phala-samādhi*), "liberation by wisdom" (*paññāvimutti*) as the wisdom connected with the fruit.
8. *Sāsavañca sukhaṃ anāsavañca sukhaṃ*. This refers to the three taints: sensual desire, craving for existence and ignorance. See Text 99. One whose taints are destroyed (*khīṇāsava*) is an arahant.

III. THE CHAPTER OF THE THREES

1. The *rājā cakkavatti* is the ideal ruler of Buddhist legend. He conquers the world by righteousness (*dhamma*) rather than by force and establishes a reign of universal virtue and prosperity. The epithet means literally "wheel-turning king," because the symbol of his stature as universal monarch is the mystical "gem of the wheel" (*cakkaratana*) which becomes manifest before him through the power of his virtue as testimony to his right to rule the world. For details see in particular DN 17 and 26, and MN 129.
2. In connection with the world ruler, Dhamma does not signify the Buddha's Teaching (as in the following section) but the moral law of justice and righteousness applied to governing a country.
3. In Indian iconography the wheel (*cakka*) is the symbol of sovereignty in both temporal and spiritual domains. The world ruler, as explained above, rules under the standard of his "gem of the wheel," which represents his entitlement to universal sovereignty. The Dhamma too is symbolized by a wheel, which according to the commentaries represents the Buddha's perfect realization of truth and his entitlement to serve as a world teacher. See too Ch. X, n.8.

   Māra is the Tempter or Evil One, depicted as an evil deity who tries to divert aspirants from the path to liberation. Unlike Satan he is not particularly concerned with inducing people to commit deeds that will lead them to hell, but remains content with keeping them trapped in the snare of sensuality and thereby preventing them from escaping the round of rebirths. Brahmā is the old brahmanical creator God, who appears in Buddhism as the temporal governor of the world system, powerful and long-lived but still a transient being enveloped in ignorance and bound to the wheel of becoming (see Text 139).

4. A-a: "The first type of patient, who is incurable, should nevertheless receive nursing because he might think that, with proper care, he may yet recover. If he is neglected, he will feel resentment and harbour thoughts of ill will, which may bring him an unhappy rebirth. But if he is looked after well, he will see that everything needful and possible has been done for him, and he will ascribe his affliction to the unavoidable results of his own kamma. He will be friendly towards those who nurse him and because of these thoughts of friendliness he will have a happy rebirth. The second type—one who is sure to recover—and one only slightly ill should also be nursed, so that their recovery may be quickened."
5. "Enter the path of assurance" (*okkamati niyāmaṃ*), i.e. the assurance of final liberation, by entering upon the path of stream-entry, or one of the higher stages of awakening.
6. According to A-a, the first of the three is called *pada-paramo,* i.e. "one for whom the mere words (of the Teaching) are the most he can achieve"; he will not attain the stages of awakening in his present life. The second is called *ugghaṭitaññu,* i.e. one who penetrates the truth at once when a brief instruction is given. The third type is called *vipacitaññu,* i.e. one who will penetrate the truth after receiving detailed and repeated instruction; this category also includes the type called *neyya,* who can penetrate the truth after a period of training. These types are explained at Pug 41. A-a says further that the instruction given to the first type may help him in a future existence. If the second type is instructed, it will quicken his progress towards final attainment. But the third type is definitely in need of repeated instruction and guidance.
7. The person with "a mind like lightning" (*vijjūpamacitto*) is a trainee (*sekha*), one who has penetrated the truth of the Teaching but not yet fully realized the truth. The one with "a mind like a diamond" (*vajirūpamacitto*) is the arahant, who has destroyed all taints.
8. Sāriputta was the chief disciple of the Buddha and the disciple most distinguished in wisdom. See Text 130, where he sounds his "lion's roar."
9. A-a explains "I-making" (*ahaṅkāra*) as wrong view, and "mine-making" (*mamaṅkāra*) as craving; "conceit" (*māna*) includes all deluded imaginings based on the notion of a real "I." The term "this conscious body" (*saviññāṇake kāye*) comprises both one's own conscious body and those of others. "All external objects" (*bahiddhā sabbanimittesu*): all sense objects, persons and phenomena.
10. Sn 1106–7. The *Pārāyana,* "The Way to the Far Shore," is the last chapter of Sn, containing sixteen sub-sections in each of which a different brahmin inquirer asks profound questions of the Buddha. "The Questions of Udaya" is the fourteenth (vv.1105–11).

The fact that this work is quoted several times in the Nikāyas testifies to its antiquity. See too AN 4:59.

11. The first four lines of the stanza allude to four of the five hindrances: sensual desire, ill will, sloth and torpor, and restlessness and worry. In line 5 "purified mindfulness and equipoise" (*upekkhā-sati-saṃsuddhaṃ*) is an allusion to the fourth jhāna (see the standard formula for the jhānas, Text 33). According to A-a "preceded by thinking on the Dhamma" (*dhammatakka-purejavaṃ*) refers to right intention (*sammā-saṅkappa*), the second factor of the Noble Eightfold Path, which comprises thoughts free from sensuality, ill will and violence. The breaking apart of ignorance is the fruit of arahantship, which arises when ignorance has been broken apart by the path of arahantship.
12. *Lobha, dosa, moha.* These three are generally called "roots of the unwholesome" (*akusala-mūla*). The term "greed" comprises all degrees of attraction, from the slightest trace of attachment up to the crassest form of greed and egotism; "hatred," all degrees of aversion, from the slightest touch of ill-humour up to the extreme forms of violent wrath and vengefulness; "delusion" is identical with ignorance (*avijjā*), but with an emphasis on its psychological and ethical implications. For a fuller treatment, see Nyanaponika Thera, *The Roots of Good and Evil*, in *Vision of Dhamma*, BPS.
13. The Buddha refers here to a threefold division in the ripening of kamma. A kamma can bring results either in the present life (*diṭṭhadhamma-vedanīya*), or in the immediately following life (*upapajja-vedanīya*), or in any life subsequent to the next one (*aparapariyāya-vedanīya*). See Vism XIX,14.
14. The positive aspects of the three wholesome roots are: dispassion (renunciation, detachment), loving-kindness, and wisdom. Here the action arisen from non-greed, non-hatred, and non-delusion should be understood, not as an ordinary wholesome action, but as the "kamma that is neither dark nor bright, with neither dark nor bright results, which leads to the destruction of kamma" (AN 4:232), that is, the volition in the development of the Noble Eightfold Path. Mundane actions arising from the three wholesome roots could not be described as "no more subject to arise in the future." Such actions, rather, being "bright kamma with bright result" (AN 4:232), will bring agreeable fruits and generate a fortunate rebirth.
15. A-a explains the simile thus: The seeds here represent the wholesome and unwholesome kammas. The man who burns them with fire represents the meditator. The fire represents the knowledge of the noble path. The time when the man burns up the seeds is like the time when the meditator burns up the

defilements with path-knowledge. Like the time when the seeds have been reduced to ashes is the time when the five aggregates stand cut off at the root (i.e. during the arahant's life, when they are no longer sustained by craving). Like the time when the ashes have been winnowed in the wind or carried away by a stream and can no longer grow is the time when the five aggregates utterly cease (with the arahant's parinibbāna) and never again become manifest in the round of becoming.

16. Hatthaka was a son of the king of Āḷavi and became a non-returner (*anāgāmi*). He was praised by the Buddha as a model for lay followers and declared the foremost lay disciple among those who win a following through the four bases of beneficence (*saṅgaha-vatthu*; see Text 129).
17. *Devadūta*. In the traditional account of the Buddha's early life it was the shocking initial encounter with an old man, a sick man, and a corpse that destroyed his worldly complacency and set him searching for a path to enlightenment. According to the traditional story these beings were actually *devadūta*, gods in disguise who had descended to earth in order to awaken him from his slumber of delusion.
18. This section of the text, describing the torments, has been abridged. In Buddhism, life in hell is not eternal. Such a painful form of existence is the lawful consequence of evil deeds and will come to an end when the causal force conditioning it is exhausted. Good causes of the past may then have a chance to operate and bring about a happier rebirth.
19. The following passage describes, in psychologically realistic terms, the same experience represented symbolically in the traditional legend of the future Buddha's encounter with the three divine messengers. See n.17 above.
20. The three types of pride (*mada*) described here, which are more akin to intoxication than to arrogance, are: (1) pride in one's youthfulness (*yobbana-mada*); (2) pride in one's health (*ārogya-mada*); (3) pride in life (*jīvita-mada*); cp. Text 79. Pride in the sense of conceit appears in Buddhist texts under the name *māna*. On the three modes of *māna*, see Text 95.
21. The present sutta draws a fundamental ontological distinction between conditioned reality and the unconditioned. Conditioned reality includes everything arisen through causes and conditions, i.e. the entire world of physical and mental phenomena, extending through all the three realms of becoming. The "conditioned marks of the conditioned" (*saṅkhatassa saṅkhata-lakkhaṇāni*) are, according to A-a, the grounds for being perceived or recognized as conditioned.

The Pāli terms for these three marks are: *uppādo, vayo, ṭhitassa aññathattaṃ*. This passage is the source of the later Abhidhamma division of a single moment of experience into the three sub-moments of arising, subsistence and dissolution (*uppāda, thiti, bhaṅga*). A-a identifies "change while persisting" with decay (*jarā*), which A-ṭ here takes to be the sub-moment of subsistence, when for a fleeting instant the arisen phenomenon "faces its own dissolution" (*bhaṅgābhimukha*) before actually dissolving.

22. *Asaṅkhatassa asaṅkhata-lakkhaṇāni*. The Unconditioned is Nibbāna, which does not exhibit any arising, change or disappearance.
23. *Akatabhīruttāṇā*. That is, by doing meritorious deeds which give protection in the next life.
24. This brahmin was a chaplain of King Pasenadi; he frequently asked questions of the Buddha, as in Text 67, 97, and AN 7:47.
25. This refers to the "Nibbāna element with residue left" (*sa-upādisesanibbāna-dhātu*). See It 44: "Here a monk is an arahant, one whose taints are destroyed.... His five sense faculties remain unimpaired, by which he still experiences what is agreeable and disagreeable and feels pleasure and pain. It is the extinction in him of lust, hatred, and delusion that is called the Nibbāna-element with residue left." See too Ch. IV, n.10.
26. The wanderer Vacchagotta often appears in the Suttas engaging the Buddha in anxious queries about points of speculative metaphysics, which the Buddha refuses to answer; see MN 72, SN Ch. 33, SN 44:7–11. According to MN 73 he eventually became a monk under the Buddha and attained arahantship.
27. This refers to the kammic merit acquired by making offerings to brahmins and ascetics. According to the Buddha the "fruitfulness" of an act of giving, i.e. its capacity to bring desired benefits to the donor, depends upon the interaction of two factors: the intention of the donor and the moral purity of the recipient. A gift given with faith, humility and respect by a wise and virtuous donor is more fruitful than one given casually by an immoral person; and a gift given to a virtuous and upright ascetic is more fruitful than one given to a spiritually undeveloped person. Gifts to the arahants, the supreme field of merit, are the most meritorious, as the Buddha will explain. For a more detailed treatment of this theme see MN 142.

    The qualities abandoned are the five hindrances. The qualities possessed are the five "dhamma-aggregates" of "one perfect in training" (*asekha*), an arahant.
28. The brahmin Saṅgārava also appears in AN 5:193. His criticism of the Buddha succinctly expresses the differences in perspective that separated the brahmins from the non-brahmanical ascetics,

the *samaṇa*. While the brahmins led settled household lives as priests, dedicated to earning merits through ritual and sacrifice, the ascetics stressed the importance of renunciation and self-mastery through meditation. The brahmins aimed at rebirth in the heavens or in the Brahma-world, while the ascetics sought liberation from the entire cycle of repeated birth and death. Generally the ascetics did not recognize the authority of the Vedas (see Text 30), and the Buddha specifically criticized the brahmanical practice of animal sacrifice, which he declared a source of demerit rather than of merit.

29. Ānanda was the Buddha's personal attendant. He had memorized virtually all the Buddha's discourses and was responsible for the codification of the Sutta Piṭaka at the council held after the Buddha's parinibbāna.
30. *Nimitta*. As explained in A-a, this refers to external indications, which are interpreted as referring to the state of mind of the person concerned.
31. This passage has been abridged. A-a explains the first of these to mean revelations from deities who have supernormal knowledge of others' minds. The second indication are subtle sounds produced by thoughts themselves, to be penetrated by the divine-ear faculty. The third refers to a person in a thought-free meditative absorption; in this case the thought-reader cannot read the meditator's thoughts but predicts, on the basis of his mental dispositions, the thoughts he will think on emerging from absorption.
32. *Anusāsanīpāṭihāriya*. A-a gives as examples of such instruction: "You should think thoughts of renunciation, not thoughts of sensuality. You should contemplate the idea of impermanence, not the idea of permanence. You should give up lust for the five cords of sensual pleasure and acquire the supramundane Dhamma of the four paths and fruits." For examples of the Buddha's miraculous pedagogical powers see Text 61.
33. The expression *titthāyatana* is a figurative term for the speculative views of non-Buddhists thinkers. The doctrine of inaction (*akiriyavāda*) teaches the moral inefficacy of actions and involves a denial of kamma, which undermines the motivation for purposeful moral action.
34. The first view, that all experience is the result of past kamma, is ascribed by the Buddhists to the Jains. The third view, which denies the role of human effort, was taught by Makkhali Gosāla, a contemporary of the Buddha, who held that all events were governed by fate (see DN 2; MN 76). This doctrine, as well as that of inaction, belongs to the "wrong views with fixed destiny" (*niyata-micchā-diṭṭhi*), i.e. views leading to a bad rebirth.

35. These are the ten courses of unwholesome action. In the Devadaha Sutta (MN 101), the Buddha confronts the Jains with other arguments against their theory that everything we experience is caused by past action.
36. A-a: "Having shown that these three views, as leading to inaction (in the moral sense), are empty, unsubstantiated and not conducive to liberation, the Blessed One now begins to expound his own teaching, which is well substantiated and leads to liberation. As there is no end of what unintelligent people may say without proper understanding, the intelligent ones only are specified here."
37. A-a: "Hereby reference is made to the meditation subject of the elements (*dhātu-kammaṭṭhāna*). Taking it by way of the six elements, a brief explanation as follows: The elements of earth, water, fire and air are the four primary material elements (*mahā-bhūta*). The element of space represents "derived' or secondary form (*upādā-rūpa*). When this single item of derived form is mentioned, the other types of derived form (i.e. the sense faculties and their objects, etc.) are thereby implied. The element of consciousness (*viññāṇa-dhātu*) is mind (*citta*) or the aggregate of consciousness (*viññāṇa-khandha*). The coexistent feeling is the aggregate of feeling; the coexistent perception, the aggregate of perception; the coexistent contact and volition, the aggregate of volitional formations. These are the four mental aggregates; the four primaries and the form derived from them are the aggregate of form. The four mental aggregates are "name" (or "mentality," *nāma*) and the aggregate of form is "form" (or matter, *rūpa*). Thus there are only these two things: name and form (*nāmarūpa*). Beyond that, there is neither a substantial being (*satta*) nor a soul (*jīva*). In this way one should understand in brief the meditation subject of the six elements that leads up to arahantship." In a similar way, the other classifications given in the sutta are elaborated in A-a, as a preparation for the practice of analytical insight.
38. The technical term used here, *manopavicāra*; denotes intentional mental activity, as capable of engendering particular types of affective experience.
39. *Gabbhassāvakkanti*. The figurative term *avakkanti* (or *okkanti;* descent) stands, according to A-a, for origination or manifestation. What is being designated by this expression is the process of rebirth, or more precisely, "reconception." The four material elements (and space) are the material foundation for rebirth, supplied by the fertilized ovum. However, for rebirth to occur, a non-material component is necessary, namely, the stream of consciousness contributed by a being who had expired in a

previous life. This stream of consciousness is the sixth element, the "element of consciousness." In MN 38 the consciousness component is referred to as the *gandhabba*, and it is there said that for conception to take place three factors are necessary: the sexual union of the parents, the fertility of the woman, and the *gandhabba* or consciousness of the being to be reborn.

40. *Okkantiyā sati nāmarūpaṃ.* This is a variant of the link of "dependent origination" (see n.43) usually expressed thus: "with consciousness as condition, name-and-form comes to be." The link "consciousness" is here replaced by "descent into the womb" (i.e. the descending of consciousness into the womb, where it infuses life into the fertilized ovum, thus activating the sentient organism, referred to as "name-and-form"). This is one of the canonical sources justifying the commentarial explanation of the link "consciousness" as rebirth-consciousness (*paṭisandhi-viññāṇa*). At this point the formula of dependent origination is given only as far as the link "feeling," but just below the formula is stated in its entirety.
41. *Vediyamānassa kho pan'āhaṃ bhikkhave 'idaṃ dukkhan' ... ti paññāpemi.* A-a says that by feeling is meant here not mere sensation (*anubhavanto*), but a feeling linked with understanding (*jānanto*), for which it quotes the contemplation of feeling of the Satipaṭṭhāna Sutta as an example. That is to say, the Four Noble Truths are chiefly addressed to those who comprehend the true nature of feeling as it reveals itself in actual experience and to mindful observation.
42. The "five aggregates subject to clinging" (*pañc'upādānakkhandhā*) is the principal classification scheme the Buddha used for analysing the nature of experience. Between them, these five factors constitute experience in its entirety: material form, feeling, perception, volitional formations, and consciousness. They are also the "fuel" or sustenance for clinging (*upādāna*), the sustenance taken up at the commencement of each existence. According to the Buddha's teachings, there is no substantial self above and beyond these five aggregates to serve as the nucleus of personal identity. The five aggregates are included in the truth of suffering because they are all impermanent and the basis of pain and suffering.
43. The usual analysis of the Four Truths mentions only craving (*taṇhā*) as the origin of suffering, but here the entire formula of dependent origination (*paṭicca-samuppāda*) is brought in to provide a fuller explanation. Similarly just below, instead of explaining the cessation of suffering simply as a consequence of the cessation of craving, here the full formula for the reversal of dependent origination is given.

44. According to A-a, this town was situated at the edge of a forest and thus served as a way station for various groups of wanderers and ascetics. Their visits gave the townsfolk exposure to a wide range of philosophical theories, but the conflicting systems of thought to which they were exposed caused doubt and confusion. This sutta is often described as "the Buddha's charter of free inquiry," but while it certainly discourages blind belief it does not quite advocate the supremacy of personal opinion in the spiritual domain. One important criterion for sound judgement the Buddha will propose is, as we shall see, the opinion of the wise, and to apply this criterion implies that one is prepared to recognize others as wiser than oneself and to accept their recommendations in the confidence they will lead to one's long-range benefit.
45. These ten inadequate criteria of truth may be grouped into three categories: (1) The *first* are propositions based on tradition, which includes the first four criteria. Of these "oral tradition" (*anussava*) is generally understood to refer to the Vedic tradition, which, according to the Brahmins, had originated with the Primal Deity and had been handed down orally through successive generations. "Lineage" (*paramarā*) signifies tradition in general, an unbroken succession of teachings or teachers. "Hearsay" (or "report"; *itikarā*) may mean popular opinion or general consensus. And "a collection of scriptures" (*piṭaka-sampadā*) signifies any collection of religious texts regarded as infallible. (2) The *second* set, which comprises the next four terms, refers to four types of reasoning recognized by thinkers in the Buddha's age; their differences need not detain us here. (3) The *third* set, consisting of the last two items, comprises two of personal authority: the first is the personal charisma of the speaker (perhaps including too his external qualifications, e.g. that he is highly educated, has a large following, is respected by the king, etc.); the second is the authority stemming from the speaker's relationship to oneself, i.e. that he is one's own personal teacher (the Pāli word *garu* used here is identical with the Sanskrit *guru*). For a detailed analysis, see Jayatilleke, *Early Buddhist Theory of Knowledge*, London, 1963, pp. 175–202, 271–75.
46. These, according to the Buddha, are the three unwholesome roots, which underlie all immoral conduct and all defiled states of mind; see Texts 20, 31. As the aim of the Buddha's Teaching is the destruction of greed, hatred and delusion, the Buddha has subtly led the Kālāmas to affirm his teaching simply by reflecting on their own experience, without any need for him to impose his authority on them.
47. At this point the Buddha introduces the practice of the four "divine abidings" (*brahmavihāra*), the development of universal

loving-kindness, compassion, altruistic joy and equanimity. Loving-kindness (*mettā*) is formally defined as the wish for the welfare and happiness of all beings; compassion (*karuṇā*), as empathy with those afflicted by suffering; altruistic joy (*muditā*), as rejoicing in the success and good fortune of others; and equanimity (*upekkhā*), as an attitude of neutrality or impartiality towards beings. For a detailed discussion of these qualities, both as general virtues and as meditation objects, see Vism Ch. IX.

48. A-a: "'In both respects' (*ubhayen'eva*): because he does no evil and because no evil will befall him."

49. Lust (*rāga*). Often the synonymous term greed (*lobha*) is used where, as here, the three roots of unwholesome action (*akusala-mūla*) are treated.

50. To show that lust is "less blamable," A-a offers as an example that no social stigma attaches to marriage, though it is rooted in sexual desire; and if, in such a case, lust remains within the limits of the basic moral law, such lust will not by itself lead to an unhappy rebirth in lower states. Hence it is less blamable in regard to its kammic consequences. But as lust has very deep roots in human nature, it is "as hard to remove as oily soot, and a particular attachment might follow a person even through two or three lives." *Hatred* and *delusion* are both regarded as blamable in society and have dire kammic consequences, because both may lead to rebirth in states of misery. Hatred, however, is an unpleasant state of mind, and as beings naturally wish for happiness they will generally wish to be rid of it. Also by asking pardon from those whom one has wronged through anger, it is easier to nullify the effects of anger in oneself and in others. Delusive ideas, however, if deeply rooted in craving, wrong views or conceit, will be as hard to remove as lust.

51. The present passage corresponds to AN 1:2.1–10, with "ill will" represented here by "hatred," of which it is a synonym, and "doubt" replaced by "delusion," its underlying root. For clarification of the technical terms, see the following notes.

    On improper attention: AA quotes the definition of improper attention (*ayoniso manasikāra*) from the Abhidhamma Vibh 373, § 936): "Therein, what is 'improper attention'? There is improper attention thus, 'In the impermanent there is permanence' ... 'In pain there is pleasure' ... 'In what is non-self there is self' ... 'In what is foul there is beauty'; or, turning of the mind, repeated turning, cognition, advertence, attention to what is contrary to truth. This is called improper attention" (trans. Ashin Thittila, slightly modified). Although improper attention is mentioned at AN 1:2.1–10 as the main cause for doubt, it is elsewhere said to contribute to the arising of all five hindrances. See SN 46:2, 46:51.

On proper attention: Proper attention (*yoniso manasikāra*) is attention to the impermanent as impermanent to what is suffering as suffering, to what is non-self as non-self, and to what is foul as foul. In AN 3:53–54 it is mentioned as the main cause for the non-arising of unarisen delusion and for the abandoning of arisen delusion. In. MN 2.10 it is mentioned as the cause for non-arising of unarisen taints (*āsavas*) and for the abandoning of arisen taints.

On foul object: A foul object (*asubhanimitta*) is a theme for meditation which reveals the inherent unattractiveness of the body. The commentaries mention ten types of corpses, in different stages of decay (see Vism Ch. IV), but in the Nikāyas the chief object of foulness meditation is the thirty-one parts of the body (increased to thirty-two in the later literature by the addition of the brain). See the treatment of "the perception of foulness" in Texts AN 4:49, AN 5:30, AN 9:30 and AN 7:46, AN 10:60 (see *Wheel Publication* 177), and MN 10.10. To be fully effective as an antidote against lust, AA holds, the contemplation of foulness should be developed to the level of the first jhāna

On the liberation of the mind by loving-kindness: *Mettācetovimutti.* Loving-kindness (*mettā*) is the wish for the welfare and happiness of all living being. It is called a "liberation of the mind" when it is developed to the level of the jhānas, since it then effectively liberates the mind from such oppressive states as ill will, anger and aversion.

52. *Bhava*: personal existence, which is always conceived by Buddhism as a dynamic process of becoming. The commentaries distinguish between two constantly oscillating phases of becoming—*kammabhava*, "kammically active becoming," the occasions when we engage in volitional activity (= kamma), which sows the "seeds" of rebirth and future experience; and *upapattibhava,* "rebirth becoming," the occasions of experience that result from the maturation of past kamma and within which kamma bears its fruits. The present sutta offers an explanation of how *kammabhava* generates *upapattibhava.*
53. *Kāmabhava*: "sense-sphere becoming" is existence in the sense-sphere realm, the lowest of the three realms of existence, comprising the hells, the animal realm, the sphere of ghosts, the human world and the six lower heavens. (See Sunthorn Na-Rangsi, *The Four Planes of Existence,* BPS, *Wheel Publication* No. 462.)
54. Just as a seed has the potential to develop into the kind of plant that corresponds to its nature, so the consciousness with which one performs a volitional action functions as a seed with the potential to generate a new form of existence corresponding to the ethical quality of the action. The statement is a capsule summary of the

principle of dependent origination: consciousness accompanied by ignorance and craving is driven by kamma (= "volitional formations") into a new existence (= consciousness and name-and-form) bounded by birth at one end and death at the other.

55. *Rūpabhava*: the realm of subtle form, the intermediate realm of the Buddhist cosmos; here the grosser levels of sensory experience are absent and the beings pass most of their time in meditative bliss. Rebirth into this realm comes about through mastery over the jhānas (see AN 4:123). Within this realm are the five Pure Abodes into which non-returners are reborn.
56. *Arūpabhava*: the highest cosmological realm, where matter has completely disappeared and only mind exists. This realm consists of four extremely subtle planes, into which rebirth is gained by mastery over the four formless or non-material meditations (*Āruppa*; see AN 4:190).
57. This is said with reference to the Pātimokha, the code of monastic rules, which in its Pāli version actually contains 227 rules. Perhaps at this time the Pātimokha had not yet reached its final shape.
58. *Adhisila-sikkhā, adhicitta-sikkhā, adhipaññā-sikkhā*. These three divisions of the Buddhist training are often correlated with the eight factors of the Noble Eightfold Path.
59. This, of course, is the penetration of the Four Noble Truths. The full penetration of the Four Truths comes with the attainment of the supramundane path, but the higher wisdom can also include the wisdom of insight which leads up to the supramundane path.
60. The editions of the Pāli text show here various and uncertain readings, but as the meaning is clear enough a simplified, free rendering has been given.
61. *Kāmavitakka, byāpādavitakka, vihiṃsāvitakka*. These are identical with the three wrong thoughts or wrong intentions, to be overcome by right intention, the second factor of the Noble Eightfold Path. See too Texts 43, 128, AN 10:20.
62. *Dhammavitakka*. This translation is based on the explanation of A-a, which takes this expression to refer to the ten corruptions of insight meditation (*dasa vipassanūpakkilesā*); see Vism XX, 105–28. A similar explanation is given of *dhammuddhacca*, "agitation about higher states," in Text 64. It may, however, be possible to understand *dhammavitakka* simply as reflections about the Teaching.
63. *Sati sati āyatane*. This refers to the preliminary conditions required for the attainments to follow, namely, the six "super-knowledges" (*abhiññā*). Five of these are mundane; the sixth is the supramundane attainment of arahantship, here called the destruction of the taints (*āsavakkhaya*). The necessary condition for the five super-knowledges is mastery over the fourth jhāna; the

foundation for arahantship is the development of insight based on concentration. For a detailed explanation of the five mundane super-knowledges, see Vism Ch. XII and XIII.

64. In Ee this discourse is included in Sutta No. 100, i.e. linked to our preceding Text 34. There is, however, little doubt that it is a separate sutta, and it appears as such in Be as well as in A-a.
65. *Upekkhānimitta*. This refers to the detached observation and examination of the meditative state of mind. A-a: He examines the speed or velocity of knowledge (*ñāṇajavaṃ upekkheyya*), i.e. the penetrative intensity of insight.
66. *Ajjhupekkhati*. This refers to the third item, *upekkhā*, equanimity, which literally means "onlooking," i.e. detached observation or examination.
67. These three terms, which often appear together in the texts, are in Pāli: *assāda, ādīnava, nissaraṇa*. The commentaries relate them to the Four Noble Truths thus: "danger" indicates the truth of suffering; "gratification," the truth of the origin (for pleasure is the stimulus for craving, the true origin of suffering); and "escape," the truth of the cessation of suffering, or Nibbāna. Although the fourth truth, the truth of the path, is not explicitly mentioned in the triad, it is implied as the means of escape.
68. According to A-a, these monks were the same as those to whom the Buddha had earlier taught the Mūlapariyāya Sutta (MN 1). They had been proud and arrogant, but the Buddha had humbled them with the Mūla Sutta and later preached the present sutta to them when he knew that their attitude had changed and that their understanding had matured. This time the monks gave their approval and, while seated, attained to arahantship together with the four analytical knowledges (*paṭisambhidā*—see Ch. I, n.8). If we consider that it was this Gotamaka Sutta which brought the impact of the great Mūlapariyāya Sutta to fulfilment, we shall better understand why it is said that this short text had such great power that it could cause the world system to shake.
69. *Sabbe saṅkhārā aniccā, sabbe saṅkhārā dukkhā, sabbe dhammā anattā.* On the distinction between the *saṅkhārā* or "formations" and the *dhammā*, "things" in general, see Ch. I, n.10.

IV. THE CHAPTER OF THE FOURS

1. The stream signifies the world (*saṃsāra*) and worldliness. The dry land or secure ground is Nibbāna. The word "brahmin" is used here in the sense of one foremost in purity and holiness.
2. He violates the Five Precepts.

3. According to A-a, this refers to stream-enterers and once-returners (particularly to those whose path of progress is difficult) and to virtuous persons who are still unliberated worldlings (*puthujjana*).
4. This passage refers to the non-returner (*anāgāmi*), whose character is firm because he has unshakeable faith and other steadfast qualities; and because, his mind being free from sensual desire and hatred, he is not liable to return from the celestial world to a lower plane.
5. The Buddha here identifies the true brahmin with the arahant. See in this connection Dhp 383–423.
6. These are the five hindrances.
7. *Khandhānaṃ udayabbayaṃ*. This alludes to the practice of insight meditation on the arising and passing away of the five aggregates; see AN 4:41, on "the concentration that leads to the destruction of the taints."
8. *Sammappadhāna*. These four occur frequently in the texts as the standard explanation of the 6th factor of the Noble Eightfold Path, i.e. Right Effort (*sammā-vāyāma*). These four are also called the Effort of Avoiding, of Overcoming, of Developing and Maintaining, respectively.
9. On the designation "Tathāgata," see Ch. I, n.7.
10. *Anupādisesāya nibbānadhātuyā* (missing in Ee). The "residue" is the five aggregates. This remains as long as the Buddha or the arahant lives, in which case he is said to abide in the "Nibbāna-element with residue left," i.e. the permanent destruction of all defilements headed by greed, hatred and delusion (see Text 26 and Ch. III, n.25). With his physical demise, the last residue of the five aggregates is discarded and he attains the Nibbāna-element with no residue left; see It 44.
11. *Sakkāya*, "personality," is a collective designation for the five aggregates (see Ch. III, n.42). The word is derived from *sat* in the sense of existing and *kāya* in the sense of a mass, i.e. a mass of bodily and mental processes which are impermanent and without an abiding self. Since, in the explanation of the first noble truth, the Buddha states that the five aggregates are suffering, this implies that "personality" can be used to represent the first noble truth, as is done in the present exposition.
12. A-a: Who are those excepted here (by the word "mostly")? Those devas who are noble disciples. As they have destroyed the taints, fear and terror do not arise in their minds.
13. A-a: Thus when the Fully Enlightened One teaches them the Dhamma showing the faults in the round of becoming, stamped with the three characteristics (impermanence, suffering, non-self), the "fear arisen through knowledge" (*ñāṇa-bhaya*) descends on them.

14. Those beings "with form" (*rūpino*) are those that have material bodies; those "without form" (*arūpino*) are the beings of the four formless realms, who lack material bodies. The "non-percipient" beings (*asaññino*) are a class of beings in the form realm bereft of conscious experience; those "neither-percipient-nor-non-percipient" (*nevasaññī-nāsaññino*) are the denizens of the fourth formless realm. The word *saññā*, translated as "perception," here stands for the entirety of consciousness and its concomitant mental factors.
15. *Aggo vipāko*, i.e. the fruit of wholesome kamma at its best.
16. The Eightfold Path consists of eight mental factors which arise from causes and conditions and are thus conditioned phenomena (*saṅkhata*). Though the path is the best of all conditioned states, being conditioned it is in that respect defective. It is contrasted just below with Nibbāna, which is unconditioned (*asaṅkhata*) and thus the best of everything that exists.
17. All these terms are synonyms for Nibbāna, the sole unconditioned state.
18. On the eight noble individuals:

    The Buddha often speaks of four principal stages of awakening culminating in unshakeable liberation of mind. Each of these stages is in turn divided into two phases: a phase of the path (*magga*), when the disciple is practising for the realization of a particular fruit; and a phase of the fruit (*phala*), the actual attainment of the corresponding stage. From these four pairs we obtain the eight types of persons who make up the Sangha of the Blessed One's noble disciples, "the unsurpassed field of merit for the world."

    The four stages are distinguished by their ability to eliminate particular clusters of fetters (*saṃyojana*), mental defilements that keep living beings bound to the round of existence (see Ch. I, n.12). The first stage of awakening is called *stream-entry* (*sotāpatti*). With this attainment the disciple clearly sees the Four Noble Truths for the very first time, and thereby enters irreversibly upon the "stream of the Dhamma" that leads to Nibbāna (see Text 103). Stream-entry is marked by the eradication of the coarsest three fetters: personality view; doubt in the Buddha and his Teaching; and wrong grasp of rules and vows. With the attainment of stream-entry the disciple is freed from the prospect of rebirth in the plane of misery and is certain to reach final liberation in a maximum of seven more lives passed either in the human world or in the heavens.

    The next major stage of awakening is that of the *once-returner* (*sakadāgāmī*), who will be reborn only one more time in the human realm or in the sense-sphere heavens and there reach the goal. The path of once-returning does not eradicate any additional fetters, but it attenuates greed, hatred, and delusion so that they arise only sporadically and mildly. The third path, that of the *non-returner* (*anāgāmī*), cuts off two additional fetters, sensual lust and ill will, the principal ties that keep beings bound to the sense-sphere realm. For this reason the non-returner, as the name implies, never returns to the sensuous realm but is spontaneously reborn in one of the exalted form-realm heavens called the Pure Abodes (*suddhāvāsa*), and there attains final Nibbāna. The fourth and final stage of the path is that of arahantship (*arahatta*), which is attained by the elimination of the five subtle fetters that remain unabandoned even in the non-returner: desire for existence in the form realm and formless realm, conceit, restlessness and ignorance. See also AN 3:85, AN 8:19, AN 8:59.

19. *Sabbākāraparipūrāni* . The wheel marks on the soles of the feet are one of the thirty-two marks of a great man (*mahāpurisalakkhaṇa*) attributed to the Buddha (see DN 30, MN 91).
20. The brahmin's question uses the future tense *bhavissati,* but it is difficult to tell whether he actually intended the question to refer to the Buddha's future (as A-a supposes) or used the future form simply as a polite mannerism. Possibly there is a word play going on, the brahmin using the future in the polite sense, the Buddha deliberately speaking as if the future was literally intended. A-a: "The brahmin could also have asked whether he is at present a deva, but thinking that the Buddha could in future become a powerful king of the devas, he formulated his question with reference to the future."
21. *Gandhabba*: a class of demi-gods belonging to the heaven of the Four Great Kings, said to be celestial musicians; they also dwell in trees and flowers and inhabit the ocean. The *yakkha* (mentioned just below) were demonic beings depicted as inhabiting forests and hillsides.
22. According to A-a, at the end of the discourse Doṇa reached the first three paths and fruits and composed a long poem in praise of the Buddha, called "Doṇa's Thunder" (*doṇa-gajjita*). He is said to be identical with the brahmin Doṇa who, after the passing away of the Buddha, distributed his relics, as described at the end of the Mahā Parinibbāna Sutta (DN 16.6.25).
23. *Devaputta*: a youthful celestial being.
24. No earthly travel or space travel, no peregrinations through the endless possibilities of human or divine experience, can terminate the world with its suffering, can stop the migrations and transmigrations of beings who are beckoned again and again by the illusory promises of an ever-receding horizon.

25. The Buddha explains the "origination of the world" as a constant re-creation of worldly existence through the craving arisen in response to pleasant objects at the six sense doors. Thus the cessation of the world, or liberation from the round of existence, has to be achieved by removing craving; see in this connection SN 12:44. The process of becoming itself, i.e. the round of rebirths, is without discoverable beginning, as Text 145 affirms.
26. *Vipallāsa*: distortion, or perversion, of reality. Distortion of perception (*saññā-vipallāsa*) is the most fundamental; distortion of thought (*citta-vipallāsa*) introduces a more reflective note to the distorted perception; and distortion of view (*diṭṭhi-vipallāsa*) transforms the thought into a definitive thesis. To give an analogy: A man spontaneously perceives a coiled up piece of rope in the dark as a snake (= distortion of perception); he assumes that what he has seen is a snake (= distortion of thought); he fashions the view that the coiled up object he saw in the dark was a snake (= distortion of view).
27. Nakulapitā and Nakulamātā are said to have been foremost among the Buddha's male and female lay disciples with regard to their mutual trust and harmony (*vissāsaka*). According to A-a, they had been the Buddha's parents and relatives in more than five hundred past births.
28. Suppavāsā is said to have been foremost among those female lay disciples who offer choice alms-food to monks. She was the mother of the arahant Sīvali.
29. Parents are said to be similar to the ancient teachers and ancient deities (*pubbācariyā, pubbadevatā*) because they are the first teachers and spiritual guides of their children. Those "worthy of worship" are saints and sages. Cp. Text 12.
30. *Sappurisa*; a person of good character, a worthy person. The word is sometimes, though not always, used as a near-synonym for *ariya*, noble one, in the technical sense. See AN 5:148, AN 8:38.
31. *Acinteyyāni*. Com.: not fit to be thought about; not fit subjects of speculative thoughts.
32. *Buddhavisayo*. Com.: the specific qualities of the Buddhas and their range of influence.
33. *Jhāna-visayo … kamma-vipāko … loka-cintā*
34. For more on how a lay follower practises for his own good and the good of others, see Text 119.
35. On diligence (*appamāda*), see Ch I, n.6.
36. *Madanīyesu dhammesu. Mada:* intoxication, pride. In Text 23 pride in one's youth, health and life are mentioned. Vibh 350 (§§843–44) lists twenty-seven types of infatuated pride, among them: the pride of birth, clan, beauty, success, fame, ability, skill, virtue, meditative attainments, etc. This fourth item is missing in the PTS translation.

37. A-a: The arahant is indicated here.
38. A-a says that this nun sent for the Venerable Ānanda because she was in love with him.
39. A-a: Perceiving the nun's state of mind, Ānanda spoke to her gently on the foulness of the body in order to free her from her passion.
40. *Setughāta*. This seems to be a metaphorical way of saying that a monk or nun should totally uproot sexual desire. The point of Ānanda's discourse is that even food, craving and conceit, which are normally factors of bondage, can be skilfully employed to attain arahantship; but with sexuality there is absolutely no skilful way it can be used for the goal of the holy life.
41. The formula is one of the four prescribed reflections on the monk's basic requisites—robes, food, lodging and medicine. A-a: "Based on the present intake of material food, of which he partakes wisely, he abandons that "food' which consists in previous kamma; but also the longing and craving for the present material food has to be abandoned."
42. *Taṇhaṃ nissāya taṇhaṃ pajahati*. A-a: "Based on the present craving (i.e. to become an arahant), he gives up the previous craving that was the root-cause of the cycle of rebirth." Similarly in the next case, based on his wounded conceit in learning that another monk has outdone him by becoming an arahant, he strives for arahantship and, precisely by overcoming conceit, fulfils his aim .
43. The statement of confession, and Ānanda's response, are stock formulas; see Text 130 (end).
44. *Samatha-pubbaṅgamaṃ vipassanaṃ*. This refers to a meditator who makes tranquillity the vehicle of his practice (*samatha-yānika*), i.e. one who first develops access concentration, the jhānas or the formless attainments and then takes up insight meditation (*vipassanā*).
45. "The path" (*magga*) is the first supramundane path, that of stream-entry. To "develop that path," according to A-a, means to practise for the attainment of the three higher paths. On the ten fetters and the seven underlying tendencies, see Ch. I, n.12.
46. *Vipassanā-pubbaṅgamaṃ samathaṃ*. A-a: "This refers to one who by his natural bent first attains to insight and then, based on insight, produces concentration (*samādhi*)." A-ṭ: "This is one who makes insight the vehicle (*vipassanā-yānika*)."
47. *Samatha-vipassanaṃ yuganaddhaṃ*. In this mode of practice, one enters the first jhāna and then, after emerging from it, applies insight to that experience, i.e. one sees the five aggregates within the jhāna (form, feeling, perception, etc.) as impermanent, liable to suffering, and non-self. Then one enters the second jhāna and contemplates it with insight; and applies the same pairwise

procedure to the other jhānas as well, until the path of stream-entry, etc., is realized.

48. *Dhammuddhacca-viggahitaṃ mānasaṃ hoti.* According to A-a, the "agitation" (*uddhacca*) meant here is a reaction to the arising of the ten "corruptions of insight" (*vipassanūpakkilesa*) when they are wrongly taken as indicating path-attainment. The term *dhammavitakka*, "thoughts about higher states" (see Text 34 and Ch. III, n.62) is taken to refer to the same ten corruptions. It is plausible, however, that the "agitation caused by higher states of mind" is mental distress brought on by eagerness to realize the Dhamma, a state of spiritual anxiety that sometimes can precipitate an instantaneous enlightenment experience. For an example, see the story of Bāhiya Dārucīriya at Ud 1.10.
49. A-a: "When there is the body": When there is the "door" of bodily action, or "bodily intimation" (of intention; *kāyaviññatti*). The same explanation applies to speech; in the case of mind, however, intimation does not apply. "Bodily volition" (*kāyasañcetanā*): the volition at the bodily door which accompanies and directs bodily action. Similar explanations apply to speech and mind. Pleasure arises as a kamma-result of wholesome volition, pain as a result of unwholesome volition.
50. *Avijjā-paccayā va.* A-a says that it is ignorance that is at the root of all these kammic volitions.
51. It is probable that the Abhidhamma division of wholesome and unwholesome consciousness into "unprompted" (*asaṅkhārika*) and "prompted" (*sasaṅkhārika*) was derived from the first pair of terms in this passage. The other division, into being associated with knowledge or dissociated from knowledge, may have been derived from the second pair.
52. Ignorance is a direct, simultaneous condition for unwholesome volitional activity, but also an indirect condition for wholesome activity, for it is the underlying presence of ignorance in the mind which makes wholesome action kammically productive.
53. This refers to an arahant. Though he too engages in bodily, verbal, and mental activity, the volition responsible for these activities does not produce any kamma-result.
54. For more of the same theme, fear of death, see Sāriputta's two discourses of the ailing lay disciple Anāthapiṇḍika at SN 55.26, 27.
55. The idea is that he speaks or behaves in one manner in private (when he may be frank) and differently in contact with others (when he may have ulterior motives).
56. On the eight worldly conditions, see Text 114.
57. *Yathā ummaggo,* (2) *yathā ca abhinīhāro,* (3) *yathā ca pañhā-samudāhāro.* (1) The translation of this difficult expression follows A-ṭ which, in

this context, explains it by *pañhā-gavesana*, research into a problem or a question, and adds that it refers to the capacity of knowing how to examine the subject inquired into (see n.58). (2) A-a: *pañhābhisaṅkharaṇa-vasena cittassa abhinīhāro*, "the mind's application to the forming (or formulating) of a problem." (3) A-a: *pañhā-pucchana*, "asking a question or posing a problem"; this may refer to the ability to ask pertinent questions or to see a problem.

58. *Ummajjamānaṃ, ummaggo.* The use of these words in this simile, in the sense of emerging, rising up, is probably an allusion to the earlier figurative use of the term; see the preceding note.
59. These are the four conditioning factors for the attainment of stream-entry (*sotāpattiyaṅga*).
60. In Be, this forms a separate discourse, elaborated as in the preceding. It is significant that these four conditions of stream-entry are here regarded as helpful in the preservation of a truly human status.

V. THE CHAPTER OF THE FIVES

1. *Sekhabala.* A *sekha* (a trainee, or a learner) is one who, in pursuing the three kinds of training (*sikkhā*) in virtue, concentration and wisdom, has attained to one of the four supramundane paths or one of the three lower fruits. One who has attained to the fourth fruition, the arahant, is called an *asekha*, i.e. one beyond training, one perfect in training.
2. While *shame* (*hiri*) is motivated by self-respect and is inward-looking, *moral dread* (*ottappa*) is outward-looking, being the fear of such consequences as blame, bad reputation, and punishment.
3. AN 5:12 says: "Of these five powers of one in higher training, this is the highest, this is what holds them together, namely, the power of wisdom."
4. While, in the preceding text, these five qualities have been treated as powers of the trainee, here they are shown in their general capacity for warding off the intrusion of unwholesome states of mind. This conveys the encouraging message that moral qualities of an average level carry in themselves the seed of highest development. In another text (AN 5:4), the possession of these five qualities is said to lead to rebirth in a celestial world, while the lack of them causes rebirth in the lower realms.
5. A-a: "The sickle for cutting grass, the pole for carrying it away." This is given as an example of means of livelihood.
6. According to A-a, this refers to a stream-enterer.
7. These five powers (*bala*) are an intensification of the identical five faculties (*indriya*). As powers they are said to be "unshakeable by their opposites."

8. In this passage the explanation of *sati* draws upon its original meaning of remembrance, keen memory. The two senses are connected in that mindfulness of the present is the basis for a keen memory.
9. *Sotāpattiyaṅga*. These are the four characteristic qualities of a stream-enterer, namely, unshakeable faith in the Buddha, Dhamma and Sangha, and "the virtues dear to the noble ones," i.e. perfect morality. For a different set of *sotāpattiyaṅga*, the four factors *for* attaining stream-entry, see Text 69.
10. *Sammappadhāna*. The efforts: (1) to prevent the arising of unarisen evil, unwholesome states; (2) to eliminate arisen evil, unwholesome states; (3) to develop unarisen wholesome states; and (4) to sustain and perfect arisen wholesome states.
11. *Satipaṭṭhāna*: mindfulness as to body, feelings, states of mind and mind-objects.
12. *Ariyasacca*: the truths of suffering, its origin, its cessation, and the way to its cessation; see Text 29. A-a says that in the characteristic field for each faculty or power, the respective faculty or power is dominant and at the height of its function, while the other four are concomitant and support the dominant function. But the power of wisdom is the highest in rank among the five.
13. "Liberation of mind" (*cetovimutti*) is the concentration present at the attainment of the noble paths and fruitions. "Liberation by wisdom" (*paññāvimutti*) is the wisdom pertaining to the fourth fruition, that of arahantship.
14. This fivefold help to right view is, in A-a, compared to the growing of a mango tree: right view is like the mango seed, the other supporting factors are like measures taken to ensure the growth of the tree, and the two liberations are like the fruits.
15. A-a: That is, a path of meritorious conduct by practising generosity, virtue and meditation.
16. This means that we are responsible for our good and bad actions and heirs to their kammic consequences, whether favourable or unfavourable.
17. On the threefold pride, see Text 23. The first three contemplations commended serve to replicate, in the thoughtful disciple, the same awakening to the inescapable realities of the human condition that was thrust upon the future Buddha while he was still dwelling in the palace.
18. It is significant that the Buddha ascribes to these seemingly elementary contemplations the power to engender the supramundane path. It seems that to acquire such potency the themes of contemplation must be extended universally so that they disclose the all-pervasive nature of old age, illness and death.

Cp. Text 64. On the ten fetters and the seven underlying tendencies, see Ch. I, n.12. and Ch. III, n. 61.
"The path" (*magga*) is the first supramundane path, that of stream-entry. To "develop that path", according to AA, means to practise for the attainment of the three higher paths.

19. The formulation of the verse here suggests that it was originally connected with Text 23, as it refers to a period when the Buddha was still a seeker of enlightenment. It may have become detached from that sutta and connected to this one during the period when the texts were transmitted orally.
20. *Dhammaṃ nirūpadhiṃ*. In the commentaries the technical term *upadhi* ("props," acquisitions) is explained as fourfold: the five aggregates, the defilements, the five cords of sensual pleasure and volitional activities. Here, the "props" are the five aggregates, "the state free from props" Nibbāna.
There are two readings of this last line: *nekkhamme datthu khemataṃ* (used in this translation) and *nekkhammaṃ datthu khemato* ("seeing renunciation as security").
21. The "unrepulsive" may refer to persons or things that are either attractive or indifferent. Paṭis II 212–13 explains tone five modes of perception thus: (1) In the case of an agreeable object, one either permeates it with (the meditative thought of) foulness or views it as impermanent. (2) In the case of a disagreeable object, one either pervades it with loving-kindness or views it as impersonal elements. (3) One permeates both agreeable and disagreeable objects with the thought of foulness and views them as impermanent; thus one perceives both as repulsive. (4) One pervades both disagreeable and agreeable objects with loving-kindness or views them as (impersonal) elements; thus one perceives both as unrepulsive. (5) Having seen a form with his eyes ... cognized a mind-object with the mind, one is neither glad nor sad but abides in equanimity, mindful and clearly comprehending; thus one avoids both the repulsive and the unrepulsive aspect. A-a says that this last item is "six-factored equanimity, similar to, though not identical with, that possessed by the arahant."
22. The practice here described is called *ariya-iddhi*, the "noble magic" or "the power of the noble ones." It is a kind of subtle "magic of transformation" by which habitual emotional attitudes can be changed at will or replaced by equanimity. In its perfection, this practice "is only produced in noble ones (*ariya*) who have reached mind-mastery" (Vism XII, 36). But A-a emphasizes that those of lesser attainments as well can and should practise it, if they are experienced in insight meditation and have keen intelligence. Insight meditation is helpful in this respect, as it teaches us to

distinguish between the facts of an experience and the emotive (or other) reactions to them. With keen intelligence one can become aware of the possibility of emotive responses other than the habitual ones and of the possibility of withholding any such responses.

23. That is, one should speak in a way that leads to successively deeper and more exalted topics, or one should teach the Dhamma in a manner that is suited to the mental dispositions of the listeners. See Text 118.
24. A-a: "Moved by the wish: 'I shall set free from their plight those beings who are in great distress.'"
25. A-a: "One should speak without extolling oneself and disparaging others."
26. These are the first, second and fourth of the four divine abodes (*brahma-vihāra*). According to A-a, the third abode, altruistic joy, is not mentioned here because it is difficult to practise it towards those against whom one has a grudge.
27. A-a explains "trading in living beings" (*sattavaṇijjā*) as the selling of human beings, i.e. slave trade; this may be too narrow and we should probably include in this category the raising of livestock for slaughter. A-a says that one should neither engage in these trades oneself nor should one encourage others to do so. Abstention from these wrong occupations belongs to the practice of right livelihood, the fifth factor of the Noble Eightfold Path.
28. *Pasaṭṭha-pasaṭṭho*: lit., "praised by the praised." A-a: "He is praised by his very own virtues; hence there is no need for their being praised by others." More likely, the point is that he is praised by those who are themselves praised by others.
29. *Nissaraṇīyo dhātuyo*; they offer an escape from adverse or obstructive states of mind.
30. A-a: "Having risen from jhāna produced by contemplating foulness (*asubha*), he directs his mind towards a sensual object in order to examine it, just as one who has taken an antidote examines the poison."
31. A-a explains "renunciation" here as the first jhāna arisen by contemplating bodily foulness. This offers a temporary escape, but if one uses this jhāna as a basis for insight meditation and attains the stage of non-returning (*anāgāmiphala*), then one escapes completely from sensual desire.
32. *Byāpāda*. A-a: "Examining it after rising from a jhāna produced by contemplating loving-kindness."
33. *Abyāpāda*. This negative term is synonymous with loving-kindness (*mettā*).
34. *Vihesā*; cruelty, hurt, hostility, almost synonymous with *vihiṃsā*, violence, harm. A-a: "Examining it after rising from a jhāna produced by contemplating compassion (*karuṇā*)."

35. *Rūpa*. A-a: "Examining it after rising from a formless jhāna." On the four formless attainments, see AN 4:190.
36. *Sakkāya*. See Ch. IV, n.11. A-a: "This refers to one who practises bare insight (*sukkha-vipassako*) and who, after having comprehending the bare formations, has attained to arahantship; after rising from the attainment of fruition (*phala-samāpatti*), he then directs his mind towards the five aggregates for the purpose of examining them." In the case of "form" and "personality," the final escape (*accanta-nissaraṇa*) is the fruition of arahantship (*arahatta-phala*).
37. *Niranusayo*: one without proclivities (or dormant tendencies) towards those five things (sensuality, etc.). A-a: "This statement is made to praise the arahant as he abides having reached cessation, the escape from personality."

VI. THE CHAPTER OF THE SIXES

1. *Anuttariya-dhammā*. This translation is based on a draft translation by Bhikkhu Khantipālo.
2. The elephant-treasure, etc.: these terms probably mean the chief elephant, etc., belonging to the king.
3. This same description—"for the purification of beings ... for the realization of Nibbāna"—is used by the Buddha at the opening of the Satipaṭṭhāna Sutta (DN 22, MN 10) with reference to the practice of the four foundations of mindfulness.
4. Cp. Text 20. Here, because the wholesome roots are productive of rebirth, the actions which they motivate should be understood as ordinary wholesome kamma rather than the volition of the noble path, as in Text 20, where the wholesome actions are said to be "cut off at the root."
5. The fourth heaven of the sense-sphere realm.
6. A-a takes this to refer to the "knowledge of the inferior and superior condition of the faculties of other persons" (*indriyaparopariyañāṇa*), one of the special types of knowledge possessed in full measure only by a Buddha. See Text 137.
7. *Sāmayikam pi vimuttiṃ*. This expression usually signifies the jhānas, but here A-a explains differently: "He does not occasionally experience joy and enthusiasm when listening to the Dhamma from time to time."
8. A-a: "Purāṇa (being a celibate) was superior in virtue and Isidatta was superior in wisdom. Purāṇa's morality made up for Isidatta's superior wisdom; and Isidatta's wisdom made up for Purāṇa's superior morality."
9. It increases his moral indebtedness through his wrong conduct.
10. *Dhammayogā*. A-a says that the term refers to preachers (*dhammakathikā*), but it probably refers to all those who are keen

on studies and cultivate principally the intellectual approach. The term seems to be unique to the present text and the distinction posited between meditators and "those keen on Dhamma" is suggestive of a late origin.

11. *Jhāyanti pajjhāyanti nijjhāyanti avajjhāyanti.* These synonyms, formed by prefixes to the verb "to meditate," cannot be rendered adequately into English. They are meant to indicate belittlement and ridicule.
12. If people refuse to give respect or recognition to those with talents, temperaments or pursuits different from those of their own, only mutual displeasure will result. An exclusive emphasis on one-sided development will not lead to progress and true happiness, which can be found only in an ever-renewed attempt at harmonizing what should be complementary, and not antagonistic, in the human mind and in society.
13. See Text 26.
14. In the original text there follow here sections which differ only in replacing the words greed, hate and delusion by "mental states linked with greed (*lobhadhammā*)," etc., explained by A-a as "mental states concomitant with it" (*taṃsampayutta-dhammā*).
15. These are the three modes of conceit, called the three discriminations (*tisso vidhā*), respectively, superiority conceit, equality conceit, and inferiority conceit (*seyyamāna, sadisamāna, hīnamāna*). See SN 45:162; Vibh 367 (§920). The arahant is free from all such conceits, as well as from their opposites, as the Venerable Sumana's declaration shows.
16. A-a explains "knowledge and vision of things as they really are" (*yathābhūta-ñāṇadassana*) as tender insight knowledge; "revulsion" (*nibbidā*) as powerful insight knowledge; "dispassion" (*virāga*) as the noble path (the four stages of awakening; and "knowledge and vision of liberation" (*vimutti-ñāṇa-dassana*) as reviewing knowledge. *Vimutti* (not mentioned separately here) signifies the fruit of arahantship (*arahattaphala*).
17. The *khattiya* is the warrior caste, which in ancient India represented nobility.
18. The word *paññā* here, usually rendered "wisdom," also denotes "intelligence" in a more general sense. In the case of the nobles, brahmins, and householders, it may refer to the worldly knowledge relevant to their respective status—in the sense that "knowledge is power"—though in relation to the ascetic "wisdom" would be the suitable rendering. A-a says that a nobleman's ambition is to be crowned as king or ruling sovereign.
19. In the Indian society at that time only male progeny made a wife's position secure in the family.
20. This is Soṇa Kolivīsa, who was declared by the Buddha to be

foremost among those vigorous in their energy. His verses appear at Th 632–44. Vv. 638–39 refer to our "simile of the lute"; vv. 640–44 are identical with the verses at the end of this discourse. Our text appears in an expanded form at Vin I 179–85.

21. A-a: "Keep to tranquillity combined with energy. Link tranquillity with energy. Keep to a balance of the (five) spiritual faculties. When faith is linked with wisdom and wisdom with faith; when energy is linked with concentration and concentration with energy, then the balance of the faculties is being maintained." On "there seize your object" (*tattha ca nimittaṃ gaṇhāhi*), A-a says: "When such balance exists, the object can arise clearly, just like the reflection of the face in a mirror; and you should seize this object, be it of tranquillity, insight, path or fruition."
22. *Nibbedhika-pariyāya*. A-a takes *pariyāya* here in the sense of "cause" (*kāraṇa*), that is, the means of penetrating, or piercing through, the defilements: "It is called 'penetrative' because it penetrates through the mass of greed, etc., which had never before been penetrated or cleaved."
23. *Kāma* may refer to "the defilement of sensuality" (*kilesakāma*), i.e. sensual desire; or to "objective sensuality" (*vatthukāma*), i.e. the sensually alluring objects.
24. This verse, which plays upon the double meaning of *kāma*, emphasizes that purification is to be achieved by mastering the defilement of sensuality, not by fleeing sensually enticing objects.
25. *Phassa*. A-a: "It is the (sense-) contact arisen simultaneously (with the sensual thought)." "Contact" is the coming together of consciousness and the object via the sense faculty.
26. The usual meaning of *vipāka*, "kamma-result," does not fit well all items treated in this discourse; hence "outcome" is used to suggest a wider meaning. A-a: "If one who aspires to celestial sensual pleasures and leads a good life is reborn in a celestial world, his personal existence pertains to the meritorious. If, due to evil conduct, he is reborn in a world of misery, it pertains to the demeritorious."
27. *Nibbedhikaṃ brahmacariyaṃ*. A-a: "The holy life (*brahmacariya*) signifies here the supramundane path (of stream-entry, etc.)." It should be noted that each section of this discourse is built upon the scaffolding of the Four Noble Truths, with two additional categories: diversity and outcome.
28. A-a "'Born of this or that feeling': born of the feeling that has arisen simultaneously with kammically active consciousness."
29. In MN 9, the taints (including the taint of ignorance) are said to be the cause for ignorance, and ignorance to be the cause for the taints. On how ignorance can be the cause for the "taint of

ignorance," Comy to MN 9 explains: "The ignorance that arises subsequently should be understood as "the taint of ignorance'. The previously arisen ignorance itself becomes a decisive-support condition for the subsequently arisen taint of ignorance." The same principle explains how the taint of ignorance can be the cause of (simple) ignorance. (See Bhikkhu Ñāṇamoli, *Discourse on Right View,* BPS, *Wheel Publication* 377/379, p.67.)

30. *Cetanā 'haṃ bhikkhave kammaṃ vadāmi.* A-ṭ: "This includes all (kammically) wholesome and unwholesome volition." Besides volition, there are, of course, also other mental factors arising simultaneously in a kammic thought, but volition is the factor that gives moral or immoral significance to an action.
31. See Text 20 and Ch. III, n.13.
32. *Anāgāmiphala.* The third stage of awakening. See Ch. I, n.12, Ch. IV, n.4.
33. *Ariyāyatane.* A-a: In the mid-country (of India).
34. The stream-enterer has "set a limit to suffering" by limiting the number of future existences he will have to undergo to a maximum of seven. The "uncommon knowledge" (*asādhāraṇa-ñāṇa*) is the supramundane knowledge with Nibbāna as object, which is not shared by the common worldling. The understanding of causes, and of things arisen by causes, are reckoned as two distinct blessings.
35. "Conviction that conforms" (i.e. with Dhamma; *anuloma-khanti*). Paṭis II 236 quotes our text in full, followed by a set of questions and answers. Paṭis A-a says on this passage: "The "conformity' is that of insight knowledge (*vipassanāñāṇa*) with the supramundane path (*lokuttara-magga*). The conformity refers to an acceptance (or conviction) of just that. To accept and approve that all formations are impermanent, suffering and non-self—this is the conviction (*khanti*). The "conforming conviction' is threefold: (1) as slight (*mudukā*), it extends from the (insight knowledge of) comprehension by groups to the knowledge of rise and fall; (2) as medium (*majjhimā*) it extends from contemplation of dissolution up to the knowledge of equanimity about formations; (3) as strong (*tikkha*) it is the knowledge of conformity with truth (*saccānuloma-ñāṇa*)."
36. The "certainty of rightness" (*sammatta-niyāma*) refers, according to Paṭis-a, to the supramundane path, and in particular to the path of stream-entry. Therefore, because of the certainty of path-assurance (*magga-niyāma*), it is said of the stream-enterer: "He is assured (of the final end of rebirth), bound to (attain) enlightenment" (*niyato sambodhi-parāyaṇo*). The "rightness" refers to one's assurance of having the right direction, and to the right,

i.e. undistorted, view of reality. The "certainty" (*niyāma*) is that this path will immediately yield its fruition (*phala*) and will finally result in arahantship.
The "group of six" in this text (causing inclusion in this Book of the Sixes) is constituted by the conforming conviction, the certainty of rightness, and the four fruitions of stream-entry, etc.
37. On the fetters, see Ch. I, n.12.
38. On the underlying tendencies, see Ch. I, n.12.
39. Note that the perception of non-self is to be extended to all things (*dhammā*) without qualification, rather than merely to all "formations" or conditioned phenomena (*saṅkhārā*) like the perceptions of impermanence and suffering. See Ch. I, n.10.

VII. THE CHAPTER OF THE SEVENS

1. Mahāmoggallāna was the second chief disciple of the Buddha; "*mahā*" is an honorific meaning "great." This sutta is set during his period of striving for arahantship, which he achieved after a week of intense effort immediately after entering the Sangha. According to A-a, he had been walking up and down vigorously in meditation, so when he sat down on his meditation seat drowsiness overcame him. The sutta is included among The Sevens because it enumerates seven ways of dispelling sloth, but it also includes as an eighth item taking a nap when all other methods fail.
2. In MN 37 this same question is asked by Sakka, king of the devas, and the Buddha replies in the same way as in the following passage of our text.
3. *Sabbe dhammā nālaṃ abhinivesāya*; lit., "All things are not fit to be clung to." A-a: "'To be clung to' by way of craving (*taṇhā*) or wrong views (*diṭṭhi*). 'All things' are the five aggregates, the twelve sense bases and the eighteen elements (*khandha, āyatana, dhātu*)." A-ṭ: "These are the domain of insight (*vipassanā*), which is here relevant."
4. "He directly knows everything" (*sabbaṃ dhammaṃ abhijānāti*). A-a: "This refers to the "full understanding of what is known' (*ñātapariññā*)"; that is, the knowledge of the object in terms of its characteristic, function, manifestation and conditions." In the classical Theravāda map of the path, "direct knowledge" (*abhiññā*) corresponds to "the defining of name-and-form" and "the discernment of conditions" (see Vism Chs. XVIII and XIX).
"He fully understands everything" (*sabbaṃ parijānāti*). A-a: "This refers to 'full understanding through scrutinization' (*tīraṇa-pariññā*), the examination of things by way of the three characteristics (impermanence, suffering, non-self)." This corresponds to "knowledge by comprehension in groups"; see Vism Ch. XX.

The contemplations of impermanence, etc., are also mentioned in the final tetrad of mindfulness of breathing; see AN 10:60. These four also belong to a group of seven contemplations which become prominent in the exegetical literature (see Vism XX,4; XXI,14–18). The additional three, not mentioned here, are the contemplations of suffering, non-self and revulsion.

5. A-a: "This discourse served Moggallāna as practical advice (for overcoming drowsiness) as well as an instruction on insight. After he had, by following this very discourse, strengthened insight within himself, he attained arahantship." This occurred one week after his ordination.
6. In Ee, through an editorial oversight, this sutta is treated as a continuation of the preceding one. In Be and A-a it is correctly printed as a separate sutta.
7. "Do not be afraid of deeds of merit!" A-ṭ: "As to those meritorious deeds which monks should constantly perform, namely restraint of body and speech, attention to the monastic duties, sense restraint, mind-control through the ascetic practices, the practice of meditation, the rousing of energy—having practised these for a long time, the monks should not be afraid of them through fear that they will hinder their present, immediate happiness. These meritorious deeds will bring them the future happiness of Nibbāna; hence they should not be afraid of meritorious deeds."
8. He had developed jhānas with loving-kindness as his meditation subject and thus he did not return "to this world," to the sense-sphere world (*kāmaloka*). An aeon (*kappa)* is divided into two main phases, a phase of cosmic expansion and a phase of contraction. For seven such aeons he had dwelt in the lofty form realm. An aeon (*kappa*) is said to endure longer that the time it would take for a man to wear away a mountain of solid granite, six miles high and six miles in circumference, by stroking it once a century with a cloth of fine muslin (SN 15:5).
9. *Subhakiṇhā devā*. These are the denizens of the highest plane corresponding to the third jhāna. Though the sutta states that their lifespan is four aeons, to bring the figures into accord with the later Theravāda tradition AA explains a method by which the three lifespans actually amount to sixteen, thirty-two and sixty-four aeons. During the period of world-contraction all the realms below the devas of Streaming Radiance are destroyed and beings are generally reborn in this realm (see Text 139). When the world starts to re-emerge, the Brahma-world appears first, and the first being to be reborn there is Mahābrahmā, the overlord of the world system. The Tāvatiṃsa heaven, of which Sakka is the chief, is the second heaven of the sense-sphere realm, and thus Sakka is

far lower in cosmic stature than Mahābrahmā.

10. *Dāsī* is, literally, a female slave. Fortunately in Buddhist cultures the preceding three models of wifeship have prevailed, and we might understand the praise of the "slavelike" wife here to serve merely a rhetorical purpose.
11. The term "*bhāvanā*" (lit.: making become), usually translated "meditation," is not restricted to methodical exercises in mental concentration but comprises the entire field of mental training.
12. These seven sets make up the thirty-seven aids to enlightenment (*bodhipakkhiyā dhammā*). The four foundations of mindfulness (*satipaṭṭhāna*) are: mindful contemplation of the body, feelings, mind states and mental phenomena (see SN Ch. 47). The four right kinds of striving (*sammappadhāna*) are enumerated in Ch. V, n.10 (SN Ch. 49). The four bases of success (*iddhipāda*) are four factors—desire, energy, mind and investigation—employed in conjunction with volitional effort as vehicles for mastering concentration (SN Ch. 51). The five faculties (*indriya*) are the faculties of faith, energy, mindfulness, concentration, and wisdom (SN Ch. 48). The five powers (*bala*) are identical with the faculties, but viewed as forces overcoming opposition rather than as agents of control (SN Ch. 50). The seven factors of enlightenment (*bojjhaṅga*) are mindfulness, investigation of phenomena, energy, rapture, serenity, concentration, and equanimity (SN Ch. 46). The Noble Eightfold Path consists of the eight kinds of rightness, enumerated in Texts 29 and 99.
13. Upāli was the chief specialist in the Vinaya or monastic discipline in the Sangha.

VIII. THE CHAPTER OF THE EIGHTS

1. This is Nibbāna.
2. Nanda was the Buddha's half-brother, a son of his father Suddhodana and step-mother Mahāpajāpatī Gotamī. On the day of his wedding the Buddha led him to the monastery and had him ordained as a monk, but his mind was divided between his monastic calling and thoughts of his beautiful fiancée. Using his psychic powers, the Buddha took him to the Tāvatiṃsa heaven and showed him celestial nymphs of unsurpassed beauty, promising that he could win them by leading a good monk's life. Nanda went back to the Jetavana monastery more willing to continue his life as a monk. But when the other monks chided him for his low aim, he felt ashamed and, to vindicate himself, finally reached arahantship. Later the Buddha designated him the foremost disciple in guarding the sense faculties. See Ud 3.2, and A-a to Dhp 13, 14 (Burlingame, *Buddhist Legends,* 1:217ff.). It is

difficult to see exactly why this sutta was included among The Eights; perhaps the eight items are the four initial descriptions of Nanda in the opening paragraph, and the four aspects of Nanda's self-discipline.

3. The eightfold simile of the ocean is found, in a different setting, at Ud 5.5 and Vin II 235–40. *Naḷeru-Pucimanda*: Vin-a says that near that tree there was a shrine dedicated to the yakkha (demon) Naḷeru. The asura are titanic beings said to dwell in a region of the Tāvatiṃsa heaven; they are in constant conflict with the devas (See SN 11:1–6; 35:207). They also take delight in the ocean; see AN 8:19. The asuras had three chiefs, Vepacitti, Rāhu (AN 4:50) and Pahārāda. Rāhu is an asura king dwelling in the sky who periodically abducts the moon and the sun (see SN 2:9, 10). The myth represents the ancient Indian interpretation of the solar and lunar eclipse. A-a explains that for eleven years after the Buddha's enlightenment Pahārāda had delayed visiting the Blessed One. When, in the twelfth year, he finally came, he felt too shy to address the Buddha first, so the Buddha asked him a question about the ocean as a way to "break the ice."
4. The first three are mythical fishes of huge size. According to Ud Comy, the second can swallow the first and the third can swallow the other two. *Nāgas* are sea-serpents or dragons, dwelling beneath the ground and in the ocean, guardians of hidden treasure. *Gandhabbas* are another kind of demi-god, sometimes depicted as celestial musicians, but also said to inhabit trees and flowers. The *yojana* is a unit of length, approximately six miles.
5. *Aññā*: the knowledge of arahantship. A-a: "There is no breakthrough to final knowledge like the hop of a frog. Without having practised from the very beginning, i.e. the fulfilment of virtue, etc., there is no attainment of arahantship. Only by practising virtue, concentration and wisdom in due order can one attain arahantship."
6. According to A-ṭ, this refers to the noble disciples (*ariya-sāvaka*), i.e. the stream-enterer, etc. For them, the moral rules become unbreakable.
7. A-a: "Even if not a single being attains Nibbāna during the immeasurable aeons when no Buddhas appear, it cannot be said that Nibbāna is empty. And on the other hand, if, in the lifetime of a Buddha, during one single meeting (of instruction), innumerable beings attain to the Deathless, one cannot say that Nibbāna becomes full."
8. See Ch. VII, n.12.
9. Ugga of Vesāli was declared by the Buddha the foremost lay disciple of those who make an offering to the Sangha of what they cherish most. See AN 5:44.

10. This stock passage usually indicates the attainment of stream-entry, though in Ugga's case it signifies the attainment of the stage of non-returner, as we shall see.
11. *Brahmacariya-pañcamānī sikkhāpadāni*. In the usual enumeration of the precepts, the third precept is abstinence from sexual misconduct. Ugga took upon himself the rule of celibacy, as he had become a non-returner and eliminated sensual desire.
12. According to ancient Indian marriage ritual, water is poured over the hands of the couple by the bride's father or guardian.
13. See Ch. I, n.12. This is an indirect way of indicating that he is a non-returner (*anāgāmī*).
14. Anuruddha was a prominent prince of the Sakyan clan, Mahānāma's brother and the Buddha's cousin. He was later appointed the foremost disciple in the exercise of the divine eye.
15. "The Unworldly" = *nippapañca*; "worldliness" = *papañca*. *Papañca* "signifies the expansion, differentiation, diffuseness or manifoldness of the world; and it may also refer to the "phenomenal world' in general and the mental attitude of "worldliness'" (Nyanatiloka Thera, *Buddhist Dictionary*, (BPS), s.v. *papañca*). It is in the last-mentioned two senses that this term and its opposite, *nippapañca*, have been rendered here and in the concluding verses of this text.

    In his important book *Concept and Reality*, (BPS), Bhikkhu Ñāṇananda adds to the above-mentioned connotations the meaning "conceptual proliferation," which provides the key for understanding the term when it occurs in a psychological context, as it often does in the Suttas. However, it seems improbable that this meaning applies to our present text.
16. In ancient India fermented cow's urine (*pūtimutta*) was regarded as a remedy of great curative and invigorating efficacy. For such use, a vessel with cow's urine and myrobalan fruits was kept buried in the ground for some length of time.
17. The "cessation of the world's diffuseness" (*papañcanirodha*) is Nibbāna.
18. *Tisso vijjā*. The recollection of former births, the knowledge of the passing away and rebirth of beings, and the knowledge of the destruction of the taints.
19. Some of the "ways of giving" mentioned in this and the following text refer specifically to the gift of a meal to monks, but not exclusively so. On the subject of giving, see too AN 3:57, AN 4:57, AN 5:31, AN 5:148, and the following two texts.
20. A-a "'Aims at what is low': at the low (level of the) five sense objects. 'To what is higher': his mind has not been developed beyond that, i.e. towards the holy paths and fruits (of stream-entry, etc.)."

21. A-ṭ: "This is meant to indicate that immorality would create an impediment, and that it is not solely the meritorious act consisting of giving that leads to such a favourable rebirth."
22. Lit. "devas who delight in creating."
23. Lit. "devas who wield control over the creations of others."
24. *Free of lust* (*vītarāgassa*). A-a: "That is, one who is free of lust (A-ṭ: sensual lust) either by having eradicated it by the path of non-returning; or by having repressed it by a meditative attainment (of jhāna). For one cannot be reborn in a Brahma-world solely by giving. Giving, however, is an ennobling and supportive factor in a state of mind directed to tranquillity and insight. If one practises the *brahma-vihāra* (divine abidings) with a mind that has become gentle by giving, one will be reborn in the Brahma-world."
25. A-a: "He will be reborn in a family of low status and will be unsuccessful in life."
26. Cp. AN 4:52. Here, however, the "streams of merit" are said to arise for the ordinary lay followers, who go for refuge and observe the Five Precepts, while there they are stated for the noble disciples, who have "unwavering confidence" in the Three Jewels and "the virtues dear to the noble ones."
27. The point is that death may come so suddenly and unexpectedly that it is a sign of complacency to assume one may live long enough even to swallow four or five morsels of food.
28. A-a: "When dying as an unliberated wordling, it would be a hindrance either to a heavenly rebirth or to attaining the paths of emancipation."

IX. THE CHAPTER OF THE NINES

1. During the first twenty years of his ministry the Buddha did not have a regular attendant but would select different monks for this task, not all of whom proved satisfactory. After twenty years, when he was fifty-five, he appointed the Venerable Ānanda as his permanent attendant. Ānanda served in this post diligently for the next twenty-five years until the Master's parinibbāna.
2. See Ch. III, n.61. A-a gives a quaint explanation why these thoughts assailed him so suddenly and forcefully: "In 500 successive rebirths, Meghiya had been a king. When he went out into the royal park for sport and amusement together with dancing girls of three age groups, he used to sit down at that very spot, called "the auspicious slab'. Therefore, at the very moment when Meghiya sat down at that place, he felt as if his monkhood had left him and he was a king surrounded by beautiful dancers. And when, as a king, he was enjoying that splendour, a thought of sensuality arose in him. At that very time it happened that his great warriors brought

to him two bandits whom they had arrested, and Meghiya saw them as distinctly as if they were standing in front of him. Now when (as a king) he was ordering the execution of one bandit, a thought of ill will arose in him; and when he was ordering the manacling and imprisonment of the other, a thought of violence arose in him. So even now, as Meghiya, he became entangled in these unwholesome thoughts like a tree in a net of creepers or like a honey-gatherer in a swarm of honey bees."

3. The Buddha repeatedly emphasized the importance of noble friendship in the living of the holy life. Elsewhere he calls a noble friend the chief external support for the cultivation of the Noble Eightfold Path (proper attention being the chief internal support; SN 45:49, 55) and on several occasions he even declared the whole of the holy life to be noble friendship (SN 45:2–3).
4. This text occurs also in Ud 4.1 with an additional concluding stanza.
5. *Saṅgaha-vatthu*. These are means of propitiating others.
6. A-a explains that this monk had felt neglected by Sāriputta and, conceiving a grudge against him, he thought: "I shall put an obstacle to his journey." When leaving, Sāriputta had passed a group of monks and a whiff of wind had blown the edge of his robe against the monk's face. This was used by the monk as a pretext for the complaint. The story is also found, with some elaboration, in Dhp Comy (to v.95); see Burlingame, *Buddhist Legends*, 2:203–5.
7. According to A-a, the Buddha knew well that Sāriputta was quite incapable of hurting anyone, but to exclude the reproach of partiality he summoned him.
8. *Kāye kāyagatāsati*. See Text 8.
9. The similes of the four elements also occur at MN 62, though there they are developed somewhat differently.
10. Here *ārammaṇa* does not have its familiar meaning of "object," but its original literal meaning of "hold" or "support." A-a glosses it as condition (*paccaya*). "Name-and-form" (*nāma-rūpa*) is explained by A-a as the four mental aggregates (= "name") and the four material elements with their material derivatives (= "form"); these are the conditions for the arising of purposive thoughts.
11. An explanation derived from A-a is as follows: The elements (*dhātu*) are the six sense objects, forms, sounds, etc.; for thought about forms is one, thought about sounds another, etc. "Contact" is the contact associated with such thoughts. They converge on feeling (*vedanā-samosaraṇā*) because feeling, the affective value of an experience (as pleasant, unpleasant or neutral), holds the various aspects of a conscious moment together. Concentration is "the head" (*samādhi-pamukhā*) in the sense of playing the key role in

bringing the mind to its highest intensity. Mindfulness is said to be the "master" (*satādhipateyyā*) to emphasize its dominant role in mastery of the mind. Wisdom is "the climax" (*paññuttarā*) because it is wisdom that issues in the attainment of the supramundane path. Liberation is the "essence" or core (*vimutti-sārā*), the goal in which the path culminates; according to A-a, the essence or core is the fruition stage of emancipation (*phala-vimutti*). All these thoughts are said to "merge in the Deathless" (*amatogadha*) because they "merge with" Nibbāna by taking it as object (in the path and fruit) and because they are established upon it.

12. "Decision" (*vinicchaya*) refers to thoughts of deciding on the utilization or value of what has been acquired; whether it should be used or stored, etc. "Desire and lust" (*chanda-rāga*), according to A-a, signifies a weaker degree of desire caused by unwholesome thoughts arising from the object; this weaker desire is intensified at the next stage, "selfish tenacity" (*ajjhosāna*), the strong insistence on "I" and "mine." The nine are also mentioned in the Mahānidāna Sutta (DN 15.9–18).

X. THE CHAPTER OF THE TENS

1. This sutta partly replicates Text 96. See Ch. VI, n.16 for explanation of the technical terms.
2. A-a: "From 'the near shore' of the three realms of becoming to the 'far shore', Nibbāna."
3. A-a: "He is not percipient through perception that arises taking earth as object," The perceptions of the four elements correspond with the jhānas, which sometimes take the elements as object (see Text 139). The next four perceptions clearly refer to the formless meditations. The last two perceptions are intended to be all-inclusive, to show that he has transcended all mundane perceptions. See AN 11:10, which adds an eleventh item.
4. The word "percipient" (*saññi*) rules out the identification of this state with the cessation of perception and feeling (*saññāvedayita-nirodha*). A-a identifies this concentration with the concentration of fruition attainment (of arahantship): "If he applies his mind to the peaceful (aspect of Nibbāna), he may, while seated, continue with that thought 'peaceful' even for a full day. And so with the other (aspects of Nibbāna). All this refers to the concentration of fruition attainment (*phala-samāpatti-samādhi*)."
5. *Bhavanirodho nibbānaṃ*. The common rendering of the term *bhava* by "existence" might suggest the cessation of the objective reality, which would not be appropriate. What is meant is the cessation of re-becoming, the stopping of rebirth, in the case of an arahant.
6. See Text 47.

7. *Dasa Tathāgata-balāni.* A-a: "They are the powers of a Tathāgata only, as he does not have them in common with others." Though disciples may have them in part, only the Buddhas possess them completely, perfect in every respect. The ten Tathāgata powers also occur at MN 12, and are treated in detail at Vibh 335–44 (§§809–31) and its commentary.
8. *Brahma-cakkaṃ.* A-a: "*Brahma* has here the meaning of best, highest, superior. *Brahma-cakka* is the *dhamma-cakka*, the Wheel of Truth. And this is twofold, consisting in the knowledge of penetration (*paṭivedha-ñāṇa*) and the knowledge of teaching (*desanā-ñāṇa*). The knowledge of penetration is produced by wisdom and brought the Tathāgata to his own attainment of noble fruition (*ariyaphala*); the knowledge of teaching is produced by compassion and enables the Tathāgata to lead others to the attainment of noble fruition. The former is supramundane (*lokuttara*), the latter mundane (*lokiya*). Both kinds of knowledge, however, are not held in common with others; they are the Enlightened One's very own kinds of knowledge."
9. *Ṭhānañ ca ṭhānato aṭṭhānañ ca aṭṭhānato.* A-a: "Those phenomena, which are the cause and condition (*hetu-paccaya*) for the arising of other phenomena, are "cause' (*ṭhāna*); and those phenomena which are not cause and condition for their arising—these are "non-cause' (*aṭṭhāna*)." At Vibh 335–38 (§809), as examples of cause and non-cause, the possibilities and impossibilities mentioned at AN 1:15 (= MN 115) are given, a few of which are translated in Text 7.
10. *Ṭhānaso hetuso.* A-a explains *ṭhāna* here as those conditions (*paccaya*) which can modify results of kamma; while *hetu* (root condition) denotes kamma. At Vibh 338 (§810) it is said: "The Tathāgata comprehends thus: "There are some evil actions performed which, prevented by fortunate rebirth (*gati*) ... by fortunate body (*upadhi*) ... by fortunate time (*kāla*) ... by fortunate effort (*payoga*), do not mature; there are some evil actions performed which, because of unfortunate rebirth ... unfortunate body ... unfortunate time ... unfortunate effort, do mature." The modifications in the results of good kamma are similarly treated.
11. *Sabbatthagāmini-paṭipadā.* A-a: "Among many people who have each killed just one living being, the kammic volition of one will lead him to hell, and that of another to rebirth in the animal world. In that way, the Blessed One knows unfailingly the nature of the action, i.e. the wholesome or unwholesome volitions which arise in the same situations (but may lead to different destinies)."
12. A-a: "'Many elements', as for instance the eye element, etc., the sensuality element, etc.; "different' refers to the variegated

characteristics of those elements. The world: the world of the aggregates, sense bases, elements."

13. *Adhimutti.* Vibh 339 (§813): "There are beings with inferior dispositions and beings with superior dispositions. Those with inferior dispositions associate with, approach, and frequent beings of (likewise) inferior dispositions. Those of superior dispositions associate with, approach, and frequent beings of (likewise) superior dispositions. And so has it been in the past and will be in the future."
14. *Indriya-paropariyattaṃ.* Vibh 340 (§814): "The Tathāgata understands their inclinations (*āsaya*), underlying tendencies (*anusaya*), habits (*caritta*) and dispositions (*adhimutti*); he understands beings with little dust in their eyes and with much dust; with keen spiritual faculties (faith, etc.) and with weak faculties; of good and bad qualities; those easy or hard to instruct; capable and incapable ones."
15. *Jhāna-vimokkha-samādhi-samāpatti.* The four jhānas are at Text 33, etc.; for the eight liberations, see Nyanatiloka Thera, *Buddhist Dictionary,* s.v. *vimokkha*. The concentrations are: with thought (*vitakka*) and examination (*vicāra*), without thought but with examination, and without either. The nine meditative attainments are the four jhānas, the four formless attainments, and the cessation of perception and feeling.
    This knowledge pertains, e.g. to the progress or otherwise on the part of certain types of "jhāna-attainers" mentioned in Vibh 342–43 (§828): those who, having attained, believe that they have failed; those who, having failed, believe that they have attained, etc.; those who attain quickly or slowly, emerge quickly or slowly, both attain and emerge quickly or slowly, those who possess or lack skill either in concentrating or in maintaining the concentration, those who possess or lack skill in both.
16. A-a says "these things" are the ten Tathāgata powers (see preceding text). Doctrinal terms (*abhivuttipadāni*) are explained in A-a and A-ṭ as views (*diṭṭhi*) and concepts (*paññatti*). As concepts, these "doctrinal terms" are said to be the teachings on the aggregates, sense bases and elements, which are common to all Buddhas of the past and the future as well, since they are the main topics for a philosophical exposition of the teaching.
17. Kāsi is another name for Benares.
18. *Vipariṇāma,* that is, death (A-a).
19. *Agge virajjati;* the highest in worldly power and achievement.
20. See Ch. VII, n.9
21. "*Kasiṇa* devices" are discs or similar objects used as supports for the practice of tranquillity meditation; see Vism, Chs. IV and V.

The space *kasiṇa* and the consciousness *kasiṇa* are, respectively, the objective supports of the first and second formless meditations, the base of the infinity of space and the base of the infinity of consciousness.

22. *Abhibhāyatana*: modes of mastering the *kasiṇa* meditations. We have abridged the text here, as the intermediate stages merely describe variations in the objective forms over which the meditator achieves mastery.
23. For analysis, see AN 4:162.
24. A-a: "Limited (*paritta*) perception is that of the sense sphere, exalted (*mahaggata*) perception is that of the form sphere, measureless (*appamāṇa*) perception is supramundane perception (of the four paths and fruits), and the fourth is perception of the base of nothingness (the third immaterial jhāna)." So A-a, but it seems improbable that the Buddha would declare a mundane perception superior to supramundane perception. More likely, the "measureless" perception refers to the perception of measureless forms, or to the divine abodes (wherein loving-kindness, etc., are extended to measureless beings), or to the first two formless attainments (which take infinities as objects).
25. *No c'assaṃ no ca me siyā; na bhavissāmi, na me bhavissati.* This terse, cryptic, mantra-like saying is found in the Suttas in two forms. In the form recorded here it is expressive of the creed of the annihilationists (*uccheda-diṭṭhi*), as is explicitly confirmed by SN 22:81; the exact meaning remains a matter of conjecture. The Buddha incorporated this saying, with slight alterations in phrasing, into his own system and commended it to the monks as a theme of meditation that could lead to non-returning and even to arahantship. As adopted by the Buddha the saying reads: *No c'assa no ca me siyā; na bhavissati na me bhavissati*, which might be translated: "It might not be and it might not be mine; it will not be (and) it will not be mine." A-a explains: "If there were no defilements and kamma in the past, there would not be for me at present the five aggregates; I so determine that at present there will be no defilements and kamma, and thus in the future there will be for me no renewal of the five aggregates." At MN 106 the Buddha's version of the formula occurs as one of the reflections of a noble disciple, which, on the path of tranquillity, may lead to the base of nothingness; or, if used as a theme for insight, may culminate in arahantship. At SN 22:55, the Buddha recommends meditation on the formula as a way to cut off the five lower fetters (i.e. to reach the stage of non-returning). At AN 7:52, the formula is mentioned in connection with five types of non-returner and the attainment of arahantship.

26. *Bhave appaṭikkulyatā ... na bhavissati*: lit.: there will not be non-disgust towards existence. *Bhavanirodhe paṭikkulyatā ... na bhavissati*: lit.: there will not be disgust towards cessation of existence. As annihilationism arises from a repulsion towards existence, the annihilationist welcomes the cessation of existence, though he generally "goes too far" in misinterpreting such cessation as the annihilation of a real self, an existent person (see It 49).
27. *Paramattha-visuddhi*. A-a: This is a designation for the base of neither-perception-nor-non-perception. For the base of nothingness is highest as the foundation for insight, but the base of neither-perception-nor-non-perception is highest in terms of long lifespan.
28. *Parama-diṭṭhadhamma-nibbānaṃ*. The Brahmajāla Sutta (DN 1) mentions five varieties of this view as held by non-Buddhist ascetics: the first identifies sensual enjoyment as the supreme Nibbāna in this life, the other four identify the four jhānas with supreme Nibbāna. See *All Embracing Net of Views*, BPS
29. A-a glosses "full understanding" (*pariññā*) here with transcending (*samatikkama*). The full understanding (or transcending) of sensual pleasures comes about by the first jhāna; of forms, by the formless meditative attainments; and of feelings, by the attainment of Nibbāna, wherein all modes of feeling have been abandoned.
30. *Anupādā-parinibbānaṃ*. A-a: This is final Nibbāna which is free from any conditioning (*appaccaya*). A-a explains that the Buddha spoke this sutta to dispel the discontent of 500 bhikkhus who were feeling oppressed by the celibate life. On hearing it they overcame their discontent and attained stream-entry. On a later occasion, after developing insight further, they attained arahantship.
31. *Uyyodhikā*. This was probably an army manoeuver in which the king had actively joined one of the competing sides, which was victorious. A-a, however, perhaps influenced by the term "victorious," takes it to refer to an actual battle with King Ajātasattu. King Pasenadi performs a similar act of homage to the Buddha at MN 89, though the reasons he gives there differ from those offered in the present sutta.
32. Cp. Text 131. While in the latter the questions refer throughout to "purposive thoughts," here they are applied to "all (conditioned) things." See the explanations in Ch. IX, n.11. Some of the renderings used here are derived from Bhikkhu Ñāṇananda's translation of this text in *The Magic of the Mind*, BPS.
33. *Chandamūlakā sabbe dhammā*. The sense seems to be that the five aggregates ("all things") come to be through the craving of the previous life, which brought about the present existence.
34. *Manasikārasambhavā sabbe dhammā*. The world of objects becomes present to consciousness only through attention (*manasikāra*).

35. Since the Deathless and Nibbāna are synonymous, to justify the distinction between them here, A-a identifies "the Deathless" with the Nibbāna-element with a residue left, and "Nibbāna" with the Nibbāna-element with no residue left. See Ch.IV, n.10.
36. *Yathā-pabbajjā-paricitaṃ*: that is, in conformity with the purpose and aim of ordination, i.e. the attainment of arahantship.
37. *Bhavañ ca vibhavañ ca*: The translation follows A-a, which explains these words by *vuddhi-vināsa* (growth and decline) and *sampatti-vipatti* (success and failure).
38. This refers to the arising and dissolution of the five aggregates.
39. The perceptions of impermanence, non-self, foulness, danger, abandoning, dispassion and cessation are analysed in AN 10:60 just below.
40. Ignorance (*avijjā*) is the first link in the chain of dependent origination. By showing that ignorance is itself conditioned, our text excludes the misconception that it is a metaphysical First Cause; the same holds true of craving which, according to the second noble truth, is the origin of suffering, but likewise not an uncaused cause. Hence the same statements about ignorance are made about craving in the next paragraph. Ignorance and craving, though very powerful root conditions of *saṃsāra*, are themselves mere conditioned phenomena and therefore can be eliminated; otherwise deliverance would be impossible. See Vism XVII,36–39.
41. "Nutriment" (*āhāra*) is used here in the sense of a strong supporting condition. An example of how the five hindrances condition ignorance is found in AN 5:193, where they are said to prevent one from knowing one's own good and the good of others. In MN 9, the taints (*āsava*) are stated to be the conditioning factors for ignorance, and in Text 99 ignorance is said to be the condition for the taints. See Ch. VI, n.29.
42. Wrong conduct by way of deeds, words, and thoughts.
43. Lit.: "When association with unworthy people becomes full, it will fill up the listening to wrong teachings." So also in the following. The expression "becomes full" links up with the simile in the following paragraph.
44. The village of Nālaka was the place of the Venerable Sāriputta's birth and death. Since, after his ordination, he had visited his birthplace only once, in order to expire there, this dialogue must have taken place then.
45. These are the first three fetters, which are abandoned by the path of stream-entry.
46. Vajjiyamāhita is one of those lay disciples of whom it is said at AN 6:131: "He has come to certainty regarding the Blessed One, has seen the Deathless, and dwells having realized the Deathless."

According to A-a, this refers to the stage of a trainee (*sekha*), not an arahant, as several interpreters of that passage have assumed.

47. *Vibhajjavādī bhagavā, na so bhagavā ettha ekaṃsavādī.* In later times the Buddha's Teaching, as documented in the Pāli Tipiṭaka and handed down by the Theravāda school, was called Vibhajjavāda, i.e. a discriminative, differentiating doctrine, in contrast to a generalizing and one-sided (*ekaṃsa*) doctrine. The expression may have been derived from the present sutta.
48. The word *venayiko,* here rendered "nihilist," means literally "one who leads astray"; it seems to have been used by the brahmins to stigmatize the Buddha because he rejected the authority of the Vedas, the validity of caste distinctions and the idea of a permanent self. A-a gives, in explanation of *appaññattiko,* "not making definite declarations": "(The accusation is that) the Buddha makes declarations about an unknowable (*apaccakkha*) Nibbāna, but cannot declare anything (definite) about (the world being) self-created (or created by another), etc." See in this connection Text 149.
49. *Nīyati*: lit., "will be led out," i.e. from *saṃsāra,* the world of suffering.
50. A-a: "The Blessed One remained silent because the question was an inadmissable one, being based upon the wrong view of a self."
51. Uttiya's earlier questions about the eternity of the world, etc., as well as his later question about the salvation of the entire world, both belong to the class of questions that are "to be put aside" (*ṭhapanīya*), because they presuppose non-existent substantial entities, be it the generalized concept of "the world" or the notion of an abiding self.
52. These are the eight factors of the Noble Eightfold Path, augmented by their fruits, right knowledge and right liberation. The "Sublime Master" (*sugata*) is the Buddha. This series of suttas should dispense with the notion that traditional Buddhist tolerance means that Buddhism regards all religions as being equally viable means to deliverance. According to the Buddha, other spiritual systems might teach wholesome practices conducive to a good rebirth, but the path to final liberation—Nibbāna, release from the whole round of rebirths—is available only through his Teaching.
53. The ten items are the ten courses of unwholesome action (*akusala-kammapatha*), explained in detail in Text 152. While the present text states that these can be motivated by any of the three unwholesome roots, the commentaries align particular unwholesome actions with particular unwholesome roots, e.g. hatred with the destruction of life and harsh speech, greed with stealing and sexual misconduct, etc.

54. On the threefold ripening of kamma, see Text 20 and Ch. III, n.13. The Buddha's statement—that there is no making an end to suffering without experiencing the results of all actions performed—must be understood with the reservation (which A-a makes explicit in connection with "kamma ripening in future lives") that reference is to "kamma that is actually capable of yielding a kammic result" (*vipākāraha-kamma*). But under certain circumstances kamma can be annulled by a counteractive or destructive kamma, and the arahant, by terminating the conditions for rebirth, extinguishes the potential for ripening of all his past kamma. The statement in our text must also be understood in the light of the following sutta passage: "If one says that in whatever way a person performs a kammic action, in that very same way he will experience the result—in that case there will be no (possibility for) the holy life, and no opportunity would appear for making a complete end to suffering. But if one says that a person who performs a kammic action (with a result) that is variably experienceable, will reap its result accordingly—in that case there will be (a possibility for) the holy life, and an opportunity would appear for making a complete end to suffering" (AN 3:110).
55. The last four refer respectively to: (i) a woman protected by her co-religionists; (ii) one promised to a husband at birth or in childhood; (iii) one with whom sexual relations entail punishment by the authorities (perhaps female convicts?); and (iv) a girl whom a man has garlanded as a sign of betrothal.
56. A-a to MN 41: "For those living in this world, there is no other world (to go to after death); and for those living in another world, there is no this world (to come to after death)." Perhaps, however, the intention is that there is no rebirth either back into this world or into some other world. On either interpretation the view maintains that beings are annihilated at death.
57. *Pamāṇakataṃ kammaṃ*: A-a: = kamma belonging to the sense-sphere (*kāmāvacara-kamma*). The point is that if a person attains and masters the "liberation of the mind by loving-kindness" at the level of jhāna, the kammic potential of this jhāna attainment will take precedence over sense-sphere kamma and will generate rebirth into the form realm.
58. That is, suffering resulting from previous unwholesome kamma.
59. *Cittantaro.* A-a gives two explanations: (1) by taking *antara* in its meaning of cause, "With (kammic) consciousness as cause, one will be a deity or a hellish being"; (2) by taking *antara* in the sense of in-between, intermediate, "In immediate sequence to death-consciousness, at the second moment, i.e. the rebirth-consciousness, one will become a deity, a hell being or an animal."

60. A-a: "It will be a kamma ripening in this existence (*diṭṭha-dhamma-vedanīya-kamma*). They will not follow one along to the next existence, because the ripening in the next existence (*upapajja-vedanīya*) has been cut off through the practice of loving-kindness. This passage has to be understood as a reflection made by a stream-enterer or a once-returner."
61. "Non-returning" (*anāgāmitā*), according to A-a, refers to an attainment of non-returning based on a jhāna obtained through meditation on loving-kindness. So also in the cases of the other *brahma-vihāras.*
    A-a explains *idha-paññassa bhikkhuno* (lit. "a here-wisdom monk") as a monk with the wisdom found here, in this teaching (*imasmiṃ sāsane*), which a noble disciple possesses who is established in the noble wisdom of a life that is in conformity with the teaching but "who has not penetrated to a higher liberation," that is, to arahantship.

XI. THE CHAPTER OF THE ELEVENS

1. These benefits are explained at Vism IX, 59–76

Of related interest from the B.P.S.

UDĀNA & ITIVUTTAKA

Two small classics of the Pali Canon in one volume. The Udāna is a compilation of eighty short but deeply impressive suttas, each expressing the Buddha's joyful insight into the profound significance of apparently simple events. The Itivuttaka is a collection of 112 inspiring texts in mixed prose and verse. Both will prove to be constant friends and wellsprings of inspiration. With introductions and notes.

BP 214S, 280 pp.

THE LIFE OF THE BUDDHA

According to the Pali Canon
by Bhikkhu Ñāṇamoli.

Among the numerous lives of the Buddha that have been written, this work with its comprehensive material and original method of presentation claims a place of its own. Composed entirely from texts from the Pali Canon, the oldest and most intact authentic record, it portrays an image of the Buddha which is vivid, warm and moving. An inspiring and informative work.

BPS 101, 375 pp.

GREAT DISCIPLES OF THE BUDDHA

Their Lives, Their Works, Their Legacy
by Nyanaponika Thera and Hellmuth Hecker.

A masterly compilation of twenty-four life-stories of the closest and most eminent of the Buddha's personal disciples. The profiles, set against the colourful social and cultural background of ancient India, bring to life legendary names such as Sāriputta and Moggallāna, Ānanda and Mahākassapa, and many more, enabling us to participate in their great breakthroughs, achievements, and activities in spreading the Dharma.

BP 417, 411 pp.

The Great Discourse on Causation

The Mahanidāna Sutta and Its Commentaries

Translated by Bhikkhu Bodhi

The Mahanidāna Sutta is the Buddha's longest discourse on dependent arising, often taken to be the key to his entire teaching. The commentary treats this doctrine according to the Abhidhamma method, explained in an appendix. A penetrative introduction lays bare the sutta's structure and the philosophical significance of dependent arising.

BP 211S, 160 pp.

The Discourse on The Root of Existence

The Mūlapariyāya Sutta and Its Commentaries

Translated by Bhikkhu Bodhi

This profound and difficult discourse of the Buddha aims at exposing and eliminating the concept of the ego at its most fundamental level. The commentary offers a detailed explanation of the sutta while a long introduction investigates its meaning and its implications to philosophy and psychology.

BP 210, 90 pp.

The Path of Purification

The Visuddhimagga

Translated from the Pali by Bhikkhu Ñāṇamoli

The *Visuddhimagga* is the "great treatise" of Theravāda Buddhism, an encyclopedic manual of Buddhist doctrine and meditation written in the 5th century by the Buddhist commentator Bhadantācariya Buddhaghosa. The translation by Bhikkhu Ñāṇamoli ranks as an outstanding cultural achievement.

BP 207H, 950 pp.

A Manual of Mindfulness of Breathing

Ledi Sayādaw

Gives clear and simple instructions; a practical approach.

WH 431/432, 64 pp.

Prices according to latest catalogue
(http://www.bps.lk)

The Buddhist Publication Society

The BPS is an approved charity dedicated to making known the Teaching of the Buddha, which has a vital message for all people.

Founded in 1958, the BPS has published a wide variety of books and booklets covering a great range of topics. Its publications include accurate annotated translations of the Buddha's discourses, standard reference works, as well as original contemporary expositions of Buddhist thought and practice. These works present Buddhism as it truly is—a dynamic force which has influenced receptive minds for the past 2500 years and is still as relevant today as it was when it first arose.

For more information about the BPS and our publications, please visit our website, or write an e-mail, or a letter to the:

Administrative Secretary
Buddhist Publication Society
P.O. Box 61
54 Sangharaja Mawatha
Kandy • Sri Lanka

E-mail: bps@bps.lk
web site: http://www.bps.lk
Tel: 0094 81 223 7283 • Fax: 0094 81 222 3679